# Preserving

Ginette Mathiot

CONSERVING
SALTING
SMOKING
PICKLING

Revised and updated
by Clotilde Dusoulier

# Foreword

Ginette Mathiot was in her early forties when she published *Je sais faire les conserves* ("I Know How To Make Preserves") in 1948. This was her third opus, after the astounding success of her first two, *Je sais cuisiner* (first published in 1932 and recently translated by Phaidon as *I Know How To Cook*) and *Je sais faire la pâtisserie* (published in 1938 and translated as *The Art of French Baking*).

By then her career as a home economics teacher was well underway and even though she had originally dreamed herself a doctor, a path her stern father brushed off, she had embraced her teaching duties and would go on to climb the ladder of the French educational system to become a general inspector.

In the meantime, her publishing opportunities allowed her to reach a wider audience than just her classrooms, and in the aftermath of the war she put together this wonderful handbook of food preservation, covering every aspect of the craft, from drying herbs to making jam, from canning vegetables to butchering a pig and making your own charcuterie.

The original edition appeared at a time when food rationing was gradually disappearing (bread was the last food to be released from rationing in 1949) and economy and thrift were still very much at the forefront of every homemaker's mind. The housewife's job—Mathiot does not imagine for a second her reader might be male—was to make the most of foods while they were cheap and plentiful, and put them up for her family and guests to enjoy during the months of cold and scarcity.

Her recommendations are full of common sense and ingenuity, and she makes allowances for her readers' circumstances, whether they live in a small city apartment or in the countryside, with varying storage capacities and access to high-quality ingredients to preserve.

Delving into this volume almost seventy years after it was first published, I hear the echo of my late grandmother's voice—she was a contemporary of Mathiot's and raised four sons on a very modest food budget—and I am struck by how relevant it remains today.

Even though year-round fresh produce is more readily available now than it ever has been, and flashy convenience foods vie for our attention in every grocery store aisle, more and more cooks yearn for a simpler relationship to the contents of their plate, one that respects the ebb and flow of the seasons, and rewards foresight and patience.

The purpose of this book, revised and updated to suit the twenty-first-century kitchen, is not to imply that your every meal should be made up of things you either grew or preserved yourself.

It is rather to give you a comprehensive, helpful view of what your options are the day your neighbor drops off a crate of tiny plums from his country house, or the day you score an incredible deal on farmer's market tomatoes at closing time; to provide inspiration and guidance for whatever your vegetable garden yields this year, and if you might like to try your hand at raising a pig of your own sometime.

So whether you're a city dweller wanting to gift ruby jars of strawberry jam to lucky friends, or a country mouse needing to manage your harvest carefully, you can call upon Ginette Mathiot's no-nonsense voice and straightforward advice to guide you on your preserving journey. Months of well-earned treats await.

–Clotilde Dusoulier

According to the *Larousse Ménager*, an illustrated housewife's handbook first published in 1926, the purpose of preserving food is to "prevent the waste of perishable foodstuffs and, for those foods whose production is seasonal, spread out consumption through the year."

Ginette Mathiot published this book in 1948, an era of hardship during which the concept of nutrition, and especially of food thrift, was of tremendous importance. Being able to process garden produce at the moment it could be harvested in abundance and having it available throughout the year at little cost did indeed have considerable attractions for people who lived in the country or had a second home.

French life has of course changed considerably since the first edition of this book, thanks to the great strides made by the food industry and manufacturers of domestic appliances, with frozen products and fresh produce easily available throughout the year, and every guarantee of quality and improved logistics.

Making preserves is thus no longer a necessity, but has instead become a pleasure in an age in which quality produce has never been more greatly sought out and celebrated. For families living in the country, who have the benefit of being able to grow and harvest their own, they can nonetheless represent considerable savings.

The preserving techniques featured in this book are simple and accessible to all, and the great number of recipe suggestions will introduce both variety and pleasure into your cooking. The chapter dealing with home charcuterie will be of more particular interest to those living in the country and who keep pigs. As long as the animal was in perfect health at the time of slaughter, a number of techniques can be applied to preserve the meat for home consumption.

Food safety regulations have of course changed considerably since the first edition of this book, and the recipes have been updated to reflect the current recommended practices. But wherever possible, we have attempted to preserve—no pun intended—Ginette Mathiot's traditional techniques.

GENERAL
INFORMATION

### GENERAL ADVICE

Having a well-stocked pantry is the sign of a well-managed home, and the tighter the budget, the greater the need to plan ahead.

### THE ART OF PLANNING AHEAD

In any household it is good to keep foods on hand that can be used to prepare daily meals, but it is important to manage these stocks well to avoid waste and discarded food. It is advisable to keep a record of what you have in the pantry or larder or the particular space you are using for this purpose and, similarly, it is good to log what you take out when you need it. Items should be eaten in order of their expiration date (use-by date), and for easy access you can arrange provisions according to their purchase or storage date.

Preserving food requires an initial investment of time and money, but thrift and wisdom can reduce these expenses to the bare minimum and will provide your family and friends with more varied dishes and tempting menus.

It is important to maintain the tradition of planning ahead and preserving food when economic circumstances demand it; you will have to take the time and trouble to work out the cost price of a set of jam pots or preserving jars. Your time and efforts will be repaid when you find the results are tasty and the food you eat is cheaper than that in the stores.

### THE FOLLOWING ADVICE IS KEY

Preserve foods wisely, in other words when they are available in abundance. Those lucky enough to have a garden will know what it means to be faced with generous amounts of the same fruit, or a large vegetable harvest picked over a relatively short period of time. This is the moment to make the preserves that will come in so handy in the winter. Those living in cities should take advantage of those times when fresh fruit, vegetables, and other foods are fully ripe and at the best prices, before processing them to store for later.

Know your enemies, the ones who have an eye on your stores, and guard yourself against them by using the appropriate preparation techniques and storage methods.

Make sure you have the right tools and know how to use them.

### KITCHEN GARDEN CALENDAR

The following table indicates those fresh foods that must be processed in order to be preserved. They appear in the month in which they are abundant.

|  | MEATS | FISH | VEGETABLES | FRUITS |
|---|---|---|---|---|
| Late winter | beef |  | pumpkin | chestnuts |
|  | lamb |  |  | oranges |
|  | rabbit |  |  |  |
|  | goose / turkey |  |  |  |
|  | pork |  |  |  |
| Early spring | turkey |  |  | oranges |
|  | goose |  |  | lemons |
|  | pork |  |  | chestnuts |
| Mid spring | veal |  | cauliflower | oranges |
| Late spring | pork |  | chicory |  |
|  | veal |  | sorrel |  |
| Early summer | pigeon |  | asparagus | green walnuts |
|  | chicken |  | spinach |  |

| | | | cabbage | |
| --- | --- | --- | --- | --- |
| | | | peas | |
| | | | | |
| Mid summer | pigeon | | artichokes | early cherries |
| | chicken | | carrots | raspberries |
| | duck | | cucumbers | strawberries |
| | | | gherkins | red currants |
| | | | onions | |
| | | | green tomatoes | |
| | | | | |
| Late summer | chicken | | artichokes | apricots |
| | duck | | gherkins | black currants |
| | | | green beans | cherries |
| | | | tomatoes | strawberries |
| | | | | red currants |
| | | | | melons |
| | | | | peaches |
| | | | | |
| Early fall (autumn) | chicken | | eggplants (aubergines) | apricots |
| | turkey chicks | | green beans | cherries |
| | duck | | tomatoes | Mirabelle plums |
| | | | | blackberries |
| | | | | peaches |
| | | | | greengages |
| | | | | |
| Mid fall (autumn) | rabbit | | cauliflowers | quinces |
| | chicken | | red cabbages | Mirabelle plums |
| | game | | shelling beans | blackberries |
| | | | tomatoes | peaches |
| | | | turnips | apples |
| | | | | pears |
| | | | | plums |
| | | | | grapes |
| | | | | nuts |
| | | | | hazelnuts |
| Late fall (autumn) | beef | herrings | eggplants (aubergines) | quince |

| | | | | |
|---|---|---|---|---|
| | lamb | | tomatoes | figs |
| | pork | | celery root | apples |
| | game | | celery | pears |
| | | | | plums |
| | | | | nuts |
| Early winter | beef | herrings | artichokes | chestnuts |
| | lamb | | | |
| | pork | | | |
| | rabbit | | | |
| | goose | | | |
| Mid winter | beef | | | chestnuts |
| | lamb | | | tangerines |
| | pork | | | |
| | rabbit | | | |
| | goose | | | |
| | turkey | | | |

Nowadays, most products are available year-round, but it remains important to know in which season the greatest quantities of quality products are available so you can plan to your best advantage. The growing calendar (see pp. 18-20) will give you an idea of how things are traditionally organized.

A quick glance at this calendar reveals that fruits and vegetables are at their most varied and plentiful between early summer and late fall (autumn), and that the greatest choice of meat, poultry, and game is available between mid fall (autumn) and early spring.

Fewer pigs are slaughtered in summer than in winter: preservation is made difficult by the heat and the flies, which are extremely difficult to deter. Rabbit and chicken are less common in early spring as the young born in spring won't be slaughtered until early summer.

With a bit of planning, you can expect to be preserving for the winter months those vegetables and fruits that ripen during the spring and summer, and preserving meat (basic charcuterie) and confits during the first four months of the year.

### THE ENEMIES OF FOOD STORAGE

There are many enemies when it comes to storing food, unfortunately, and they come in all shapes and sizes.

Besides rats, which are rarely found in houses, there are other rodents such as house mice and field mice; the latter live outdoors in gardens and backyards and attack fruit and vegetables that are insufficiently protected.

Mice are on the lookout for all kinds of foodstuffs. In addition to taking active precautions (putting down poison and setting up traps) you can store all your food in glass jars with glass or metal lids, or in boxes made of food-grade plastic or stainless steel. Wood, cardboard, and paper should be avoided.

Insects such as weevils, snout beetles, silverfish, and food moths will tuck into stored legumes and pulses, grains, flour, pasta, nuts, and chocolate if these are kept in a damp, poorly ventilated space. Keep these away from moisture, light, and dust—again, glass jars with tight-fitting glass or metal lids are ideal.

And yet more foes await: the microorganisms that live in and on food, such as mold, yeasts, and bacteria, whose growth is promoted in particular by air, moisture, and low heat. In certain circumstances, these microorganisms play a useful role but in most cases they will decompose the food they live on, resulting in undesirable fermentation and rotting. Once a piece of meat or produce has reached this stage, you know what to do: you either eat it, in the case of game, or discard it without hesitation.

Some undesirable microorganisms, however, act without producing any outward sign, yet it is dangerous to consume food spoilt in this manner. And some bacteria can resist the precautions you take against them and produce spores that are extremely hard to kill and may disrupt preservation. For this reason, it is vital to take the utmost care and food safety precautions when preserving food in the home. But if you're organized, use proper techniques and hygiene, and exercise caution, you can avoid these potential hazards.

The microorganisms that present a danger to food preservation can be fought in a number of ways:

- By freezing;
- By refrigerating;
- By drying;
- By using bacteriostatic agents such as salt, sugar, or vinegar, or by curing;
- By shielding the food from the air, such as with fat (confits).

Prevent microbial growth using the method of heat-processing.

### STORING FOOD

#### THE REFRIGERATOR

The refrigerator is the most commonly used appliance to keep food for several days in complete safety, at a temperature between 37.4 and 40°F/3 and 4°C). Food should be carefully wrapped or placed in airtight plastic boxes to prevent smells from spreading. Refrigerated food should not be kept for too long before being eaten; follow expiration dates (use-by dates) when provided.

#### THE FREEZER

The freezer allows you to keep frozen products at a temperature that should be kept below 0°F /-18°C). An expiration date (use-by date) will be indicated on store-bought frozen products.

When freezing your own foods (meat, fish, vegetables, fruits, cooked dishes), they should be in perfect condition and divided into small portions. The portions should be sealed in plastic freezer bags with the air removed, or airtight plastic tubs. They should be packed evenly so as to be quickly and completely frozen through.

NOTE: Refrigerating or freezing will not improve foods that are not in perfect condition: cold slows the growth of bacteria but it does not kill them. As soon as a food that hasn't been previously cooked or sterilized is removed from the refrigerator or freezer, it will suddenly find itself at a favorable temperature for microorganisms to multiply. These foods should be cooked as soon as possible to avoid potentially serious consequences.

### THE PANTRY

The pantry (store cupboard). A well-stocked pantry should include products such as cocoa, chocolate, various grains, pasta, oil, nuts, dried fruit, and vinegar. However, these won't keep indefinitely, and it is essential to follow these general rules:

- Keep them safe from rodents and insects (SEE p.21).
- Keep them away from light, heat, and damp.
- Keep an eye on the expiration dates (use-by dates) and the best-before dates.
- Opt for food-grade plastic tubs, stainless-steel or glass jars with tight-fitting lids over any other packaging.
- Keep the pantry or cupboard well ventilated.

### TRADITIONAL TECHNIQUES

Plenty of fruits and vegetables can be kept for two or three months before being eaten. In large cities where living space is at a premium, it is difficult to dedicate a special room to storing food, and the cellar, which is often too humid or too hot (because of the boiler for the central heating) is also unsuitable. Here are several techniques that can be used to best preserve the food set aside for the winter.

### FRUIT

Fruit can be kept in rows on a fruit rack in a cool place, covered with a thick sheet of paper to protect them from dust. Apples should be stored stalk-down, and pears stalk-up. They must not touch each other during storage.

You can also use cardboard boxes arranged on top of one another like shelves, with the fruit placed in rows so that you can check easily for damage, which you should do every couple of days.

If you have a larder room, you can make slatted shelves upon which to place the fruit. The slatted shelves are made from slats of wood or food-grade plastic, 1¼ –1½ inches/34 cm in width. The shelves should be of a size that allows you to reach the fruit at the back easily: 23 inches/60 cm would be a maximum, unless they are staggered shelves (FIG. 1). Each shelf would then be 4 inches /10 cm deep and if you make seven, the entire shelving would be 27 inches/70 cm deep.

Fig. 1

Stand-alone fruit cabinets (FIGS. 2 and 3) are also very practical. Some models can be folded or disassembled, for convenient storage when all the fruit has been eaten. The racks may be rimmed, with handles, or flat, but you should be able to clean them easily from one season to the next.

Fig. 2, 3

A larder room for keeping fruit should be dry, and exposed to the minimum possible amount of sunlight. The temperature should be constant and not exceed 42.8°F/6°C. It can vary between 32 and 42.8°F/0 and 6°C as long as this variation is gentle.

Ventilation should be monitored with care—any excess humidity will be a danger to effective preservation. This can be dealt with by placing calcium chloride, which is hydrophilic, in the room.

A final option is to keep apples in a silo (FIG. 4).

Fig.4

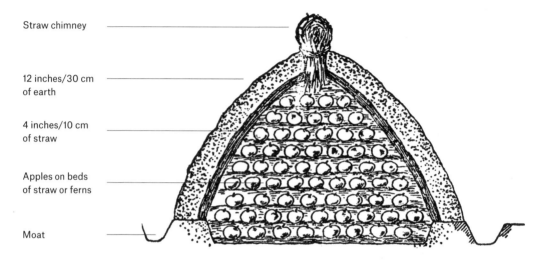

Straw chimney

12 inches/30 cm of earth

4 inches/10 cm of straw

Apples on beds of straw or ferns

Moat

Commercial pickers keep fruit in large refrigerated containers in which the air has been replaced with an inert gas to stop biochemical reactions.

For specific details on how to keep different varieties of fresh fruit for a few days or a few months, please refer to the section on each fruit in chapter 8.

### VEGETABLES

Vegetables are most often kept in the bottom of the refrigerator. You can, however, store them in the cellar if it is cool and dark. To keep them separate and allow for air circulation, place them on racks or crates, slightly raised from the ground using bricks.

Beets (beetroots), carrots, celery, cabbages, cauliflowers, chicory, turnips, leeks, potatoes, and salsify can most successfully be kept fresh throughout the winter, though they will lose moisture through respiration and evaporation. For more details, please refer to the section on each vegetable in chapter 7.

Vegetables such as carrots, beets (beetroots), and potatoes may also be kept in silos (SEE opposite).

### PRESERVING TECHNIQUES

In order to preserve food, the causes of microbial growth must be suppressed or entirely blocked.

### TEMPERATURE

The most favorable temperature for microbial growth is kitchen room temperature, and the "danger zone" is more specifically 40–140°F/4–60°C. No perishable food should be stored in this temperature range.

The potential for microbial activity is greatly reduced at 40–32°F/4–0°C. At 149°F/65°C in a damp heat most microorganisms are destroyed, but some bacteria, yeasts, and molds are extremely resistant and will only succumb at higher temperatures.

You can therefore preserve food by exposing it to either:

- Great cold (freezing or deep-freezing);
- A temperature between 32–40°F/0–4°C (refrigeration);
- A high temperature, of 212–248°F/100–120°C (heat-processing), for the appropriate duration.

### HUMIDITY

Microorganisms have more trouble spreading in a dry atmosphere, so for certain foods the goal will be to remove as much moisture as possible. Drying techniques may then be used, either by exposing those foods to air and sun, or by placing them in a warm oven or dehydrator. In the absence of water, most bacteria are partially dried and unable to pursue an active life, but yeasts and molds can remain unaffected. Some foods, however, can't be subjected to drying as they contain too much water to lose it without damage.

### AIR

Some microorganisms require air to live and are known as aerobic; to prevent their growth, you must deprive them of air.

Others are anaerobic, in other words they survive perfectly well without air, and some bacteria are both aerobic and anaerobic, which just shows how complex the problem is, as all these types coexist in and on food.

Simply protecting food from air is not enough to guarantee its preservation, and this technique is generally used in combination with another (boiling followed by coating in a protective substance, drying followed by airtight storage, boiling followed by storing in jars…).

Another way to go about preserving food is to use an offensive approach and introduce chemical substances that will halt the growth of undesirable microorganisms, or kill them. Such antiseptics must of course be edible. The products used, applied at the appropriate dosage, are intended to be poisonous to the microbes but not to the eater. You can use:

### SEA SALT

Salt has two properties of interest here. First, it attracts water. When placed in contact with food that contains water, the water is drawn out from the food, thereby removing some of the moisture that would otherwise encourage microbial growth. It is also antiseptic when used in great concentration (at least 15–20 percent).

### SUGAR

Sugar, like salt, has antiseptic properties, but only when used in the right proportions; there must be a proportion of 65 percent when the preservation process is finished, such as in jam. In lesser concentrations, the preserve will not have the proper texture and may present small sugar crystals. The sugar must be cooked along with the food to be preserved in order to achieve the right concentration (p.36).

### ALCOHOL

Alcohol is an antiseptic at a minimum strength of 18 percent. If a food containing water is placed in such a spirit, the strength of the alcohol is quickly attenuated and once lowered, it is no longer antiseptic. Alcohol with a strength of 40–45 percent should be used instead; once the water-containing foods have been added, the strength should only drop to 25–30 percent, which is still antiseptic.

### ACETIC ACID OR VINEGAR

An acidic environment stops microbial growth as long as it is acidic enough and the food has shed as much of its moisture as possible. Good vinegar is excellent for preserving.

We'll describe the most used techniques now.

### DRYING

This process consists of removing the majority of the water content in a food, in order to suppress microbial growth. Bacterial life is considerably hindered when moisture content falls below 25 percent but, as a rule, a level of 14 percent should be reached for the process to work satisfactorily.

Drying may be carried out in three different ways—using the sun's heat, artificial heat, or both.

### SOLAR HEAT

This technique is used in regions with a very hot climate. The process should be carried out relatively quickly, over the course of 4–5 days, to minimize contact with insects. Dust should also be avoided.

Traditionally, wooden racks with wicker slats are raised slightly from the ground and placed in direct sunlight. These are sometimes put in boxes with glass lids, and positioned to receive the sun's rays at a perpendicular angle.

The fruit should be flipped every day and should not be left out overnight.

### ARTIFICIAL HEAT

You can simply use the heat from a warm oven set to 122–140°F/50–60°C/lowest possible Gas Mark (meat should be dried at a higher temperature of 158°F/70°C/Gas Mark ¼), leaving the oven door slightly open to allow the moisture to escape.

Electric food dehydrators are now widely available for home use, either with stackable trays or tray "drawers" in a rigid box. A heating element warms the food gently to draw the moisture out, while a fan blows the humid air out of the appliance.

## SOLAR HEAT COMBINED WITH ARTIFICIAL HEAT

This technique is used in regions where the heat from the sun isn't very strong. Produce is blanched (SEE below), then set out on racks to dry in the sun. The process is finished in a warm oven (traditionally, this was done in the residual heat of a bread baker's oven) or dehydrator.

## PRECAUTIONS TO TAKE BEFORE DRYING FOODS

Select fruits and vegetables in perfect condition, and just ripe.

Use produce of a single variety and similar size for each batch, to ensure drying time is the same for all pieces.

Before drying, dip peeled apple and pear quarters into cold water salted to 1 percent (¼ oz/10 g salt per 4¼ cups/34 fl oz/1 liter water). This will prevent the flesh from turning brown.

To speed up the drying process, blanch the food first. This means bringing a pan of water to a boil, then adding the food, and blanching it briefly, 1–2 minutes in the boiling water until tender, then draining.

Some fruits, such as plums or grapes, are covered with bloom, a natural waxy coating that can slow or hamper the drying process. This coating should be removed by immersing the fruit in sodium carbonate water: add ¾ oz (20 g) sodium carbonate per 4¼ cups (34 fl oz/1 liter) of water and leave for 24 hours to dissolve. Pour the clear liquid into a pan and bring to a boil, then immerse the fruit for 15–20 seconds at a rolling boil. Plunge immediately into a bowl of ice-cold water for 1 minute, then drain.

## PRECAUTIONS TO TAKE WHILE FOODS ARE DRYING

The temperature must be stable throughout the process and drying should begin at a gentle heat.

Peeled fruit and vegetables should begin drying at a higher temperature than unpeeled.

The heat should be equally distributed between the racks. You may have to switch the racks around regularly to expose them to the heat source equally.

When drying fruit, alternate periods of heating (10–12 hours) with periods of cooling (10–12 hours).

### FRUIT AND VEGETABLES SUITABLE FOR DRYING

Fruit: apricots, cherries, pears, apples, plums.
Vegetables: carrots, celery root (celeriac), leaf celery, cabbage (in strips), beans, leeks (sliced), peas, onions (sliced), mushrooms.
Aromatic herbs: parsley, tarragon, lovage, savory, marjoram, basil, rosemary, etc.

### DRYING GUIDELINES

| PRODUCT | TEMPERATURE | | DRYING | YIELDS |
|---|---|---|---|---|
| | initial | final | time (in hours) | average |
| Apricots | 104°F (40°C) | 158°F (70°C) | 10–12 | 18% |
| Cherries | 104°F (40°C) | 158°F (70°C) | 10–12 | 18% |
| Pears (sliced) | 104°F (40°C) | 158°F (70°C) | 20–30 | 18–20% |
| Apples (sliced) | 104°F (40°C) | 158°F (70°C) | 12–18 | 12% |
| Plums | 104°F (40°C) | 158°F (70°C) | 16–20 | 20% |
| Grapes | 104°F (40°C) | 158°F (70°C) | 20–24 | 20% |
| Carrots | 104°F (40°C) | 158°F (70°C) | 4–6 | 8% |
| Celery | 104°F (40°C) | 158°F (70°C) | 3–6 | 10% |
| Cabbage (strips) | 104°F (40°C) | 158°F (70°C) | 4–6 | 10% |
| Green beans | 104°F (40°C) | 158°F (70°C) | 6–8 | 14% |
| Leeks (strips) | 104°F (40°C) | 158°F (70°C) | 2–3 | 8% |
| Petits pois | 104°F (40°C) | 158°F (70°C) | 6–8 | 18% |
| Onions (sliced) | 104°F (40°C) | 158°F (70°C) | 4–5 | 10% |
| Mushrooms | 104°F (40°C) | 158°F (70°C) | 4–6 | 8–14% |
| Aromatic herbs | 104°F (40°C) | 158°F (70°C) | | 8% |

Dried fruits and vegetables should be stored in airtight containers in a dark, dry place. Check your stocks periodically for parasites or mold.

### USING DRIED PRODUCE

Dried fruit can be eaten or added to baked goods as they are. If you wish to rehydrate dried fruits and vegetables, soak them in one and a half times to twice their volume of cold drinking water. (Do not use lukewarm or hot water as this promotes bacterial growth and will start to cook the produce.) The soaking water can be saved and used in cooking.

### PRESERVING WITH SALT

Salt is an extremely useful antiseptic agent for preserving food such as vegetables, meats, and fish. It must be perfectly clean and used in appropriate quantities.

### SALT QUALITY

You should use very dry (and thus old) salt. If the salt has not been properly protected from dust, however, it can contain bacteria or spores and the salt should then be sterilized by heating it in a dry pan, stirring constantly with a wooden spoon. Keep it on the heat for about 10 minutes and cool completely before using. This ensures that whatever moisture it still contained has evaporated and it will kill most microorganisms.

### DRY CURING

Salt can be used dry for a technique known as dry curing. Allow 4½ lb–5 lb (2 kg–2.2 kg) of salt for every 22 lb (10 kg) of meat. Rub the salt into the meat all over, concentrating in particular on the area around the bones to make sure the salt penetrates deeply. Lay the pieces in a salting tub, sprinkling a layer of salt between each layer of meat, along with some bay leaves, thyme, juniper berries, and black peppercorns, and keep in a dry atmosphere at 41°F/5°C.

After several days, the salt (which is hydrophilic, SEE p.26) will have drawn out the water to the surface of the meat. After six weeks, the meat will have lost about 25 percent of its water and the liquid covering the meat will discourage bacterial growth.

When food is in contact with salt, it can foster the development of beneficial microorganisms, such as those involved in lacto-fermentation (as with sauerkraut), which produce lactic acid. This acid provides protection from potential harmful fermentation.

Lacto-fermentation also occurs during dry salting of meat, which contributes to its preservation. Other microorganisms lend the meat a pink tinge and give salted pork belly its particular taste.

### BRINING

This technique involves immersing food in a water bath with enough salt to have an antiseptic effect; about ¾–scant 1 cup (7–9 oz/200–250 g) of salt should be added per 4¼ cups (34 fl oz/ 1 liter) of water. You can use this technique to preserve vegetables (beans, tomatoes, olives, gherkins) or meat. Always make sure the salt is clean, and use boiled water. The brine can also be flavored with thyme and bay leaves.

### USING SALTED FOODS

These should always be soaked in fresh water to remove some of the salt with which they are saturated. You will need to use several changes of water, and no salt should be added when cooking the food.

### PRESERVING WITH SUGAR

Adding sugar to a food—most often fruit—for preserving should be done while heating the food, as it will need to lose some of its water content by evaporation. Boiling serves the double purpose of ensuring the preserve is sterilized, while increasing the concentration of the sugar.

The combined actions of heat and sugar can lead to different formulations that will all be perfectly preserved.

- Liquid sugar-based preserves: syrups.
- Sugar-based preserves with a set or softer, runnier texture: jellies and jams.
- Thick sugar-based preserves: fruit pastes (pâte de fruits).
- Fruit preserved whole and coated with sugar: candied (crystallized or glacé) fruit.

### MAKING SUGAR SYRUP FOR FRUIT SYRUPS

You should use white sugar for preserves. Unrefined or less-refined sugars (such as raw brown/Demerara) may change the taste of the preserve and induce fermentation.

To make a sugar syrup to use for the recipes in this book, either vary the amount of sugar you put in the water, or alter the cooking time of the mixture to achieve the desired concentration.

A hydrometer is used to measure this concentration, traditionally expressed in degrees Baumé (from 0 to 45°) or, in more recent usage, in density (from 1000 to 1400 g/L). Since some readers may still be using the old scale, degrees Baumé are indicated in this book as a reminder, along with degrees Fahrenheit and degrees Celsius.

To make a sugar syrup, pour water into a large pan and add the quantity of sugar indicated in the table (SEE p. 36). Bring to a boil, leave the pan at a boil for 2–3 seconds, then remove from the heat. The syrup may be used cold or lukewarm.

It is very important to dissolve the sugar completely before the water boils. Some cooks stir the mix to help the sugar dissolve more quickly, others just shake the pan but, once it has dissolved and the syrup comes to the boil, you mustn't stir any more or crystals will form. Similary, if you don't completely dissolve the sugar before boiling, you'll never get rid of the remaining crystals.

The best way to test if the sugar has completely dissolved is to run the syrup off the back of a spoon to show it is completely clear.

| For 4¼ cups (34 fl oz/1 liter) of water | Cups (lb /g) of sugar | Density (g/L) |
|---|---|---|
| | 2¾ cups (1¼ lb/550 g) | 1.142 |
| | 3½ cups (1½ lb/700 g) | 1.160 |
| | 4¼ cups (1 lb 14 oz/850 g) | 1.210 |
| | 4¾ cups (2 lb/950 g) | 1.230 |
| | 7 cups (3 lb/1400 g) | 1.262 |

For preserving fruit syrups successfully, the concentration required is 1.285. To achieve this density you will have to use 4¼ cups (1 lb 4 oz/850 g) sugar for every 2¼ cups (18 fl oz/500 ml) fruit juice. Place all the ingredients in a pan and bring to a boil. Boil for 15–20 seconds and then strain through a very fine strainer without pressing. Cool before bottling.

### MAKING SUGAR SYRUP FOR JAMS AND CANDIED FRUIT

When sugar is mixed with a certain amount of water (1–1¼ cups [9–10 fl oz/250–300 ml] water per 5 cups [2¼ lb/1 kg] sugar) and heated, it begins to dissolve. When exposed to constant and even heat, the water will slowly evaporate and the syrup will change consistency, passing through the different stages below. It is recommended to use a hydrometer to assess these different stages, but we are also giving a visual test to gauge the stages. It is recommended that you drop a teaspoon of the syrup into a glass of cold water and look for the visual guides suggested below. When testing each stage, remove the pan from the heat so that it stops cooking the syrup and possibly going to the next stage.

### COATED (NAPPE)

221°F/105°C (28° Baumé—density 1.2047): small bubbles form at the surface of the syrup, which thinly coats the back of a skimmer dipped into the syrup.

### SMALL THREAD OR SMALL GLOSS

224.6°F/107°C (29° Baumé—density 1.2515): the syrup thickens and the bubbles grow larger. When a teaspoon of the syrup is dropped into a glass it should form thin threads that cannot be rolled into small balls when lifted out.

### LARGE THREAD OR LARGE GLOSS

228.2–230°F/109–110°C (30° Baumé—density 1.2624): forms firmer threads when dropped into water, about ¾–1¼ inches/ 2–3 cm long.

### SMALL PEARL

231.8°F/111°C (33° Baumé—density 1.2964): tiny round beads form at the surface of the syrup. When dropped into water, it forms a wider thread of about 11/2–2 inches/4–5 cm in length.

### LARGE PEARL OR SOUFFLÉ

237.2°F/114°C (35° Baumé—density 1.3199): small beads form on the surface of the syrup. If you blow on a skimmer coated with syrup, bubbles form at the edges.

### SMALL BALL

239–242.6°F/115–117°C (37° Baumé—density 1.344): if you blow on the skimmer, the bubbles will blow off.

### BALL

248°F/120°C: when a small amount of syrup is dropped into a bowl of cold water, it forms a soft ball the size of a pea.

### LARGE OR HARD BALL

257–266°F/125–130°C (39° Baumé—density 1.357): in the water, the syrup forms a hard ball the size of a hazelnut.

### SMALL OR SOFT CRACK

275–284°F/135–140°C (39° Baumé—density 1.369): the small ball of sugar is hard and will crack under pressure.

### HARD CRACK

293–302°F/145–150°C (40° Baumé—density 1.383): Drop 1 teaspoon of the syrup into cold water and it will form thin threads that when removed should not bend, will be hard, and crack easily.

### LIGHT CARAMEL

311–329°F/155–165°C and brown or dark caramel, 330.8–347°F/166–175°C: the sugar has lost all its water and is beginning to color and caramelize.

### SUGAR-BASED FRUIT PRESERVES

Fruit can be preserved in sugar in the following ways.

### JAMS

Whole or quartered pieces of fruit are cooked and preserved in a sugar syrup at 231.8°F/111°C/33° Baumé (small pearl stage).

### MARMALADES

Whole pieces of fruit are left to macerate in plain sugar for 12 hours before cooking. The fruit breaks down during cooking, combining with the sugar, and the marmalade is cooked when the syrup is fairly thick.

### JELLIES

The juice of the fruit is cooked with sugar. The consistency of the jelly arises from the sugar concentration and from the pectin, which the fruit contains in varying quantities: when exposed to heat and acidity, pectin tends to jell.

Fruits that are rich in pectin (apples, quinces, red currants) are easy to preserve as jelly. But if a fruit is not acidic enough, it will have difficulty forming a jelly even if it is rich in pectin. Lemon juice can be added then, such as for apple jelly.

To fruit that is low in pectin, such as cherries, you can add apple juice or commercially produced pectin, which can be purchased in liquid or powdered form. In season, red currant juice can be added instead.

### EQUIPMENT

You will find the following tools useful in your fruit preserving.

### PRESERVING PAN

This container has a large flat base, wide mouth, two handles, and a capacity of between 10½–16 quarts (17.5–26 UK pints/10–15 liters). The pan should have a diameter of around 14–16 inches/36–40 cm and it should be made of copper or stainless steel.

### SKIMMER

This should also be stainless steel. Skimmers for jam usually have an elongated shape.

### HYDROMETER

To use, lower the hydrometer gently into the syrup, let it find its natural floating point, and take a reading at surface level.

### JUICER OR FRUIT PRESS

This can be electric or manual, and will allow you to extract the juice or pulp from fruit.

### ELECTRIC OR MANUAL PIT-REMOVER

Use for cherries and Mirabelle plums.

### STRAINER

Choose a fine-mesh stainless-steel strainer with a diameter of 11–16 inches/28–40 cm.

### PRESERVING JARS

These should be made of thick glass to resist the heat from the jam, which is boiling when poured in.

The closure should be airtight. Good options include self-sealing lids consisting of a flat lid and metal screw band, as well as glass lids with round rubber rings, held in place with spring clamps.

Calculate in advance how many jars you will need: this can be worked out based on the weight of fruit and sugar. Err on the side of too many.

The jars and lids must be sterilized just before using: boil for 10 minutes in a large amount of water. Drain and keep in the oven at 225°F/110°C/Gas Mark ¼ until ready to fill.

Jars may be reused, after carefully checking for chipping or hairline cracks. Self-sealing lids and rubber rings should be replaced after each use.

For jam, we recommend a maximum capacity of 1 lb 2 oz (500 g). Choose jars that stack perfectly on top of one another to save space during storage.

### JELLY FUNNEL

This is used to fill the jars, avoiding any spills on and around the containers.

### WOODEN SPOON

A vital tool!

### JAM-MAKING TECHNIQUE

Making jam is a delicate operation. You need to get familiar with the process first, and be very careful when you attempt it. Try to set aside some free time: you will need a few hours to complete the task without being interrupted.

Selecting your fruit is vital: it should be in perfect condition and fully ripe. The equipment used to prepare the jam must be scrupulously clean. Cooking is done on a constant, high heat so you will need to watch the pot closely and stir regularly.

### SKIMMING

Skim off any scum as it appears during cooking; this removes any impurities that shouldn't be left in the jam, and ensures that it is clear.

### TESTING FOR A SET

Put several small saucers in the freezer before you start making your jam. To test for a set, take the pan off the heat and spoon a little jam onto one of the cold saucers, leave it for a few seconds to cool, then push with your finger. The surface should wrinkle. As jam firms up as it cools, it shouldn't be too solid beforehand.

### PUTTING IN JARS

Once the jam is cooked, it should be ladled into jars as soon as possible, while it is still hot.

Place each jar on a plate and pour the jam in through a funnel, leaving ¼ inch/5 mm of headspace. The volume will decrease when the mixture has cooled.

When all the pots have been filled, clean the rims meticulously with a clean, damp cloth: the tiniest grain of sugar or drop of liquid can harm the seal, which will no longer be airtight.

Put the two-piece lid or glass lid and rubber ring in place, securing them according to the manufacturer's directions.

Although the high sugar content of jams and jellies makes them rather inhospitable to microorganisms, it is recommended that you process the jars for 5 minutes in a boiling-water canner according to the directions on p. 48.

Traditional methods of sealing the jars with wax (greaseproof) paper, paraffin wax, cellophane, or paper soaked in egg white can no longer be recommended as safe.

### STORING

When the jam is cold, place a label on each jar with the name of the fruit and the date of production. Store in a cool, dry place.

### TROUBLESHOOTING

If you take all the precautions described above, your jams will turn out fine and keep perfectly. On your first attempt, follow the instructions given in the recipe to the letter.

If the jam is moldy, it has likely not been cooked long enough and the sugar level is too low. It was suggested in the past to remove the surface mold, tip the remaining contents of the jars into the preserving pan and boil again until the required sugar concentration is reached, before pouring the jam into clean jars. But it is now recommended to discard any home-canned product that shows signs of mold.

If the jam hasn't set and stays liquid, it is because it contains too much water or the fruit has too little pectin. If you suspect the first case, you should boil it again for a while until it thickens. In the second case, you should cook it again with a gelling agent.

If the jam has crystallized, the fruit likely did not contain enough acid. In such cases you should boil the mixture again, adding lemon juice, tartaric acid, or citric acid as you see fit.

Crystallization may also occur if the jam has been overcooked or over-sugared. Here, you might pour a little hot water on the crystallized surface of the jam when you are about to use it. Once it has dissolved, stir the jam and serve within a few hours.

### PRESERVING WITH ALCOHOL

Alcohol is a perfect antiseptic—it is used in medicine and surgery—that works by killing undesirable microorganisms while it dries out the product on which they live.

You can use this property to preserve fruit, but it will not retain all of its characteristics; the sweet and aromatic elements will be dissolved in the alcohol and the mixture can only be eaten with the addition of sugar.

Alcohol has antiseptic properties at concentrations above 25 percent. As reactions take place between the fruit and alcohol while the preserve is macerating for several months, this concentration drops considerably. You should therefore use alcohol with a strength of 45 percent so the final concentration will be 25–30 percent, which is enough for a liqueur.

NOTE:    Remember that such preserves are high in alcohol and should be consumed responsibly.

## CHOOSING YOUR ALCOHOL

You should use white, unflavored eau-de-vie. It is best to avoid calvados or marc brandy—such spirits have a particular flavor that will affect that of your fruit. You can also use 90 percent alcohol and halve its strength by adding the same amount of distilled or boiled water.

## CHOOSING YOUR CONTAINERS

Use glass containers with a large opening, to make it easy to remove the contents. These will not be subjected to high temperatures, so any type of glass quality is suitable.

The containers must be carefully and thoroughly sealed. The top will probably be opened numerous times, so you will need a sturdy lid—a cork stopper with the same dimensions as the container opening is quite practical. Traditionally, this was also wrapped in one or two layers of fine cloth to create an airtight seal, and covered with another layer of cloth.

You can also use a preserving jar with a glass lid and a rubber seal; once the lid is securely clamped, the seal will be airtight.

## TECHNIQUE FOR ALCOHOL-BASED FRUIT PRESERVES

Choose fruit of good quality and in perfect condition. Let it macerate for four to five months. Keep adding sugar syrup in the amounts indicated.

Some fruit preserved in alcohol, such as cherries, red currants, black currants, Mirabelle plums, and grapes, can be used in confectionery. Once steamed, they are covered with white or colored fondant sugar.

Vinegar was once considered an excellent antiseptic due to its acetic acid content, but acidophilic microorganisms flourish in acidic environments, so the appearance of microbes can never be ruled out completely. Bear in mind also that vegetables have a high water content: placing them in vinegar will dilute it and reduce its strength. Eliminating as much water as possible from the food you plan to preserve is key. Coarse salt is used for this purpose, as it is hydrophilic: if the ingredients are left in contact with the salt overnight, it will cause them to give up most of their water content. They are then wiped dry before preserving.

### METHOD

Use quality vinegar with an 8 percent alcohol content. Salt the food to be preserved or blanched, i.e. cook for 2–3 seconds in boiling water to remove most of its water content. As an extra precaution, you can boil the vinegar in which you've started the maceration; do this two or three times, 24 hours apart, and water will evaporate. Gherkins made with hot vinegar will also stay green and firm.

Food preserved in vinegar is stored in airtight jars with a large opening so fruit and vegetables can be easily removed. It should be stored in a cold, dark environment while unopened.

NOTE:    Do not use a silver implement to remove fruit and vegetables preserved in vinegar: use wooden tongs, or a wooden or stainless-steel fork. Never put your fingers in the preserving vinegar as this will introduce germs and the preserve will spoil quickly.

### MAKING VINEGAR AT HOME

Vinegar results from the transformation of an alcoholic drink (wine or hard cider) through acetic fermentation.

Cooks would often notice that leftover wine had turned into vinegar in the bottle. Three conditions are required for this change to take place—sometimes by accident:

- the presence of a ferment;
- the circulation of air;
- a temperature between 77 and 86°F/25 and 30°C.

You can use a small wooden or ceramic barrel, with an opening at the top (1½–2 inches/4–5 cm in diameter) through which air can pass. This opening should be stoppered with a wad of hydrophilic cotton, for example, to keep out insects, especially fruit flies.

A wooden tap at the bottom of the cask will allow you to pour out vinegar when you need it.

In this container you will place hard cider or leftover wine that is on the turn or has already gone sour. If you can get hold of a "mother of vinegar" starter culture, which looks like a gelatinous film or skin, place it carefully on the surface of the alcoholic liquid. You should keep the barrel in a spot where the temperature is not too low, such as the kitchen. After two weeks, you can carefully add 4¼–8½ cups (35–70 fl oz/1–2 liters) of wine or hard cider, taking care not to push the mother of vinegar down below the surface. You will be able to tap off the first 4¼ cups (34 fl oz/1 liter) of vinegar after about a month.

NOTE:  Refrain from stirring the mixture as this will disturb the acidification process, and you risk sinking the "mother."

NOTE:  The vinegar barrel must never be kept in a cellar where there is a wine barrel; fruit flies may transfer the acidifying ferment to the wine, which will rapidly turn into vinegar.

With your homemade vinegar you can make the following flavored vinegars:

### TARRAGON VINEGAR

Pick or purchase a dozen sprigs of tarragon about 4 inches/10 cm long, and dry in the shade for a week. Tap off 4¼ cups (34 fl oz/1 liter) of the vinegar, pour it in a bottle, and add the tarragon. Steep for two months.

### SHALLOT VINEGAR

Peel 4–5 shallot bulbs and place them in 4¼ cups (34 fl oz/1 liter) of vinegar. Steep for two months.

### SEASONED VINEGAR

Into 4¼ cups (34 fl oz/1 liter) of vinegar add your choice of aromatic herbs, such as parsley, chervil, tarragon (all dried in advance as above), a few cloves, and as much garlic and shallot as you like. Steep for two months.

NOTE:  For preserving, it is best to use spirit vinegar, which is stronger than wine vinegar (8° versus 6°–7°). This will ensure that the food is properly preserved.

### STERILIZING WITH HEAT

The advantage of heat-processing food is that the product is neither too salty nor too sweet, and can be consumed straight out of the jar with no further processing. Two conditions must be satisfied, however:

The bacteria, yeasts, and molds present in the food must be eliminated by exposing them to a temperature of 212°F/100°C (sufficient for acid foods) or more (required for low-acid foods) for a period of time that will vary on the nature of the food;

After it's been exposed to these high temperatures, the food should not come into contact with air again.

| Acid foods | Low-acid foods |
| --- | --- |
| Fruits | Meats |
| Most tomatoes | Seafood |
| Sauerkraut | All fresh vegetables |

### EQUIPMENT

Home-canned foods must be processed in a dedicated appliance called a canner, either a boiling-water canner or a pressure canner.

Bacteria are generally killed when exposed to a wet heat between 176 and 212°F/80 and 100°C for an extended period, but spores, such as the ones causing botulism, are extremely tenacious.

Therefore the higher temperatures (at least 240.8°F/116°C) achieved by a pressure canner are required for low-acid foods. Acid foods may be processed in either type of canner, but the boiling-water canner is generally deemed a better option because the process is faster and more economical.

### BOILING-WATER CANNER

This is a heavy pot with a fitted lid. Inside is a removable rack used to keep glass containers in place, and preventing them from touching the bottom of the pot. The pot should be deep enough to allow 1¼–2 inches/3–5 cm of briskly boiling water to circulate over the tops of the jars.

You should take care to wedge your jars in place, leaving them just a little room for movement. If they are not held securely enough, they may be knocked out of place or tipped over as the water comes to a boil.

### PRESSURE CANNER

This is most often a metal pot with a lock-on lid, a removable rack to place the jars, a steam vent, a safety fuse, and a gauge that indicates and regulates the pressure. It is important to make yourself familiar with the model you own by reading the manual carefully. A nonspecialized pressure cooker can be used for the same purpose.

### PRESERVING JARS

You should use tempered-glass home-canning jars with special closures. There are several kinds, each with their individual features, but they are all manufactured on the same principle.

The opening has to be wide so the jar can be cleaned easily, and the glass should be quite thick to withstand the heat and boiling time.

The closure should be airtight. Good options include self-sealing lids consisting of a flat lid and metal screw band, as well as glass lids with round rubber rings, held in place with spring clamps. The rubber rings should be submerged in boiling water for 3 minutes, then kept in water until just before using.

Jars may be reused, after carefully checking for chipping or hairline cracks. Self-sealing lids and rubber rings should be replaced after each use.

Before using, jars and lids should be washed thoroughly in hot soapy water, and rinsed. This is sufficient if the recipe calls for boiling the jars for 10 minutes or more. If the recipe involves a shorter boiling time, or if you are reusing jars that have borne signs of mold, the jars and lids must be sterilized by boiling in water for 10 minutes before filling.

### SMALL WOODEN SPATULA

This will allow you to tamp down the contents of the jar without touching them with your fingers, and remove air from the filled jars.

### JAR LIFTER

This is a special tong-like tool that clamps around the neck of jars and is very useful for picking them up hot from the canner.

### CANNING TECHNIQUE

The various procedures for home canning must be carried out with the utmost care and cleanliness. Pick a moment when you won't be disturbed so you can concentrate on the various stages in the process without being distracted. Certain parts of the job, such as washing and peeling ingredients, can be entrusted to others, including children.

### CHOOSING INGREDIENTS

You must use fruit and vegetables that are fully ripe and in perfect condition. Ideally, you would be using produce picked in the garden that morning before the sun gets too hot, or perfectly fresh produce bought during peak season (SEE pp.18–20).

### PEELING AND REMOVAL OF PITS (STONES)

Most vegetables are peeled before processing. Some fruits, such as cherries and Mirabelle plums, are not pitted as their flavor is better preserved when left whole, and kiwis, pineapple, and peaches for example, will need to be peeled.

### WASHING

Wash fruit before pitting and wash vegetables after peeling.

### BLANCHING

Fruits and vegetables are blanched (cooked briefly in boiling water, then drained) before canning for the following reasons:

- It kick-starts the cooking process;
- It helps eliminate or weaken bacteria, yeasts, and molds;
- It removes impurities that may be present on the produce to be canned;

- It fixes the color by destroying the oxidases that cause discoloring.

Use a reasonably large pan for blanching. Do not put in too much fruit or vegetables at once; the temperature of the water, which will be 212°F/100°C when you start proceedings, would drop considerably and you would have to wait for it to return to 212°F/100°C. Likewise, make sure there is enough boiling water that it won't come off a boil when you add your ingredients.

One convenient method for blanching delicate vegetables such as asparagus is to place them in a clean cloth that is then immersed in boiling water with the corners hanging over the edge of the pan. You can remove them afterward by pulling the cloth up by the four corners.

You can use a metal colander for small-size fruit or vegetables; plunge it in, and lift it out after blanching.

Do not keep or reuse blanching water.

### REFRESHING
This process involves rapid chilling of fruit and vegetables that have been placed in boiling water, in order to firm them up. Have a bowl of ice-cold water ready to refresh your produce straightaway.

### STRAINING
Place the fruit and vegetables in a colander, or on clean, dry cloths, to remove any water remaining on their surface.

### FIRST COOKING
Fruit can be canned without preliminary cooking, but cooking is necessary for vegetables and vital for all meats, which should be cooked thoroughly, as if they were to be eaten straightaway.

Set out the clean jars for filling on a table covered with a clean cloth. Carefully place the fruit or vegetables in the jars, packing them as tightly as you can and avoiding any spills. Push down with a wooden spatula.

If you are filling the jars with a liquid such as a syrup or savory jus, do not fill right to the top; the top of the liquid should be about ½ inch/1 cm below the lid, so the rubber seal or lid are never in contact with the juice or syrup. Run the spatula gently around the insides of the jar to remove any air bubbles.

Clean the rim of each jar meticulously with a clean, damp cloth: the tiniest grain of sugar or drop of liquid can harm the seal, which will no longer be airtight.

Put the two-piece lid or glass lid and rubber ring in place, securing them according to the manufacturer's directions.

Keep the jars upright at all times.

### HEAT-PROCESSING USING A BOILING-WATER CANNER

Pour water in the canner to about half the depth of the pot, and heat to 140°F/60°C if you're canning uncooked ingredients, 176°F/80°C if you're canning hot ingredients.

Lower the jars in carefully with the jar lifter and check the water level: it should cover the tops of the jars by ¾–1¼ inches/2–3 cm; add more boiling water as needed. Cover, heat, and boil.

The canning time given in recipes is always from the moment the water comes to a boil, and you should take care to maintain a brisk boil throughout. (If the water stops boiling at any time, bring it back to a brisk boil and start timing the canning from the beginning to ensure proper processing.)

Do not leave the jars in the canner while the water is cooling; this would cause the food to overcook and soften.

Remove the jars with a jar lifter. Place the jars upright on a rack or a table lined with a towel, and cool at room temperature, away from drafts, for 12–24 hours.

### HEAT-PROCESSING USING A PRESSURE CANNER

Place the rack in the pot and pour water in so it is 2–3¼ inches/ 5–8 cm deep, unless the recipe states a different amount of water to use. Heat to 140°F/60°C if you're canning uncooked ingredients, 176°F/80°C if you're canning hot ingredients.

Lower the jars in carefully with the jar lifter.

To ensure proper processing, the pressure canner must be vented before pressurizing: with the lid in place but the steam vent open, heat the canner to reach a boil, and allow a continuous stream of steam to escape from the vent for a full 10 minutes before closing the steam vent and pressurizing the canner.

The canning time given in recipes is always from the moment the canner is pressurized, and you should take care to maintain this steady pressure throughout. (If the pressure falls below that point at any time, bring it back up and start timing the canning from the beginning to ensure proper processing.)

Remove the canner from the heat and let cool naturally until fully depressurized. Remove the steam vent carefully, wait for 10 minutes, and unlock the lid, taking care not to burn yourself with the steam that will escape from the canner.

Remove the jars with a jar lifter. Place the jars upright on a rack or a table lined with a towel, and cool at room temperature, away from drafts, for 12–24 hours.

### CHECK THE SEALS

You must verify that a vacuum has been formed in the jar to ensure the canned food will keep well. Remove the clamps or screw bands carefully. For glass lids with rubber rings, check that each lid sticks strongly to the jar. For self-sealing lids, check that the lid does not spring back when you press the middle with your finger.

If the test fails, check the rim of the jar to see if a small crack is responsible to preventing the seal, and replace it as needed. Use a new rubber ring or self-sealing lid, close securely, and start the heat-processing from the beginning. This second run should only be done if there are several jars to reseal; it would not be economical to start the boiling process for just one or two jars.

If you have just one jar that has not sealed properly, you can eat the contents immediately, unless water has gotten into it.

### STORING YOUR JARS

Wipe the jars and lids clean to remove any trace of food, then label and date. The jars should be kept in a dry and dark place—meat preserves are especially sensitive to light—at a temperature between 50 and 68°F/10 and 20°C. Use within a year.

### USING HOME-CANNED FOODS

Before opening any jar, check the seal again as above. If you find the seal has been broken, do not consume the food to avoid potentially serious health consequences.

Conversely, you may find the jar tricky to open if the vacuum is perfect and the lid sticks too well to the rim. If such is the case, place the jar in a pan of cold water and heat slowly. After 10–15 minutes of heating, you will find it easy to open the jar by pulling on the tab of the rubber seal, or lifting the metal lid with the back edge of a knife, or you can by a tool specifically for the purpose.

NOTE:   Canned meat and vegetables should be eaten in one go after opening; do not keep leftovers.

**TROUBLESHOOTING**

If you have taken all the precautions listed above, your canning will be successful and your food will keep perfectly. However, if your concentration was broken and this caused you to make a mistake, the consequences may only become apparent later on. Never serve canned foods about which you have doubts as this could lead to serious illness. Discard any jar of food that does not look right, presents air bubbles or mold, or has an odd smell.

NOTE:   This book includes processing times for canning food at sea level. If you live at an altitude of more than 984 feet/300 meters above sea level, you will need to adjust the boiling time or canner pressure to compensate for the lower boiling temperature and ensure safe canning. As a rule of thumb, for every 984 feet above sea level, increase the boiling time by 1 minute if the boiling time is under 20 minutes. If it is over 20 minutes, increase the boiling time by 2 minutes for every 984 feet above the sea level.

AROMATIC
HERBS

Aromatic herbs are now easily available in stores throughout the year in different forms, fresh, frozen, or dried. But if you grow them in your garden or backyard you will have an interest in preserving them when they are plentiful.

## PARSLEY

Pick parsley when the weather is warm
and dry.

—

Tie up in small bunches and hang up by the
stalks, in the shade, in a well-ventilated place.

Pick long stalks as the stalks have plenty
of flavor.

## BAY LEAVES

Pick long branches with plenty of leaves; tie
up in a bunch and hang up to dry in the shade.

—

Keep in a jar in a dry place.

## CHERVIL

Pick chervil when the weather is warm
and dry.

—

Tie up in small bunches and hang up by the
stalks, in the shade, in a well-ventilated place.

—

Keep in a metal tin or in a paper bag.
Unfortunately, chervil loses much of its flavor
when dried.

## THYME

Pick thyme in warm, dry weather. Keep it
in bunches and use the stems in bouquet garni
(SEE p. 273).

—

Once the leaves are dried, strip them from the
stems onto a piece of paper and save them.
You can then use the leaves in cooking, placing
them in a cheesecloth (muslin) bag first if
you want the flavor but not the leaves in the
finished dish.

## ROSEMARY

Pick rosemary when the weather is warm
and dry.

—

Tie up in small bunches and hang up by the
stalks, in the shade, in a well-ventilated place.

## TARRAGON

Pick tarragon when the weather is warm
and dry.

—

Tie up in small bunches and hang up by the
stalks, in the shade, in a well-ventilated place.

# MARJORAM

Can be dried like parsley.

# SAGE

Can be dried like parsley.

# SAVORY

Can be dried like parsley.

# BASIL

Can be dried like thyme.

# MIXED HERBS & SPICE POWDER

**Preparation time 5 minutes, plus drying time**
**Makes 5 oz (150 g)**

1¼ oz (30 g) bay leaves
¾ oz (20 g) savory leaves
1¼ oz (30 g) sprigs thyme
¾ oz (20 g) sage leaves
¾ oz (20 g) marjoram leaves
3 tablespoons ground cloves
2½ tablespoons chili powder
4 teaspoons ground cinnamon

This mix can be used to season a wide variety of meats, pâtés, and terrines.

Preheat the oven to the lowest temperature.

—

Spread the herbs out on a baking sheet, then place in the oven until they are brittle to the touch. Strip the thyme leaves from the stems, keeping the leaves and discarding the stems.

—

Using a mortar and pestle, pound the herbs to a fine powder.

—

Mix in the cloves, chili powder, and cinnamon.

—

Store in an airtight jar.

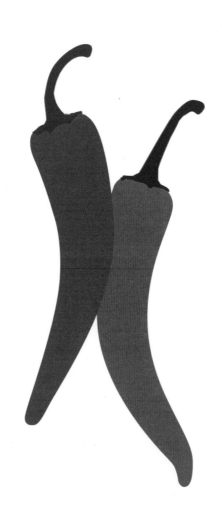

# CONDIMENTS

# GARLIC

Garlic, white or pink, is harvested in late summer and early fall (autumn).

—

Braid the stalks together to make garlands, about 23 inches/60 cm long, and hang in a dry place.

# CAPERS

Capers are berries from a perennial shrub that grows in hot and dry climates. They can be purchased in grocery stores, preserved in vinegar. Nasturtium berries can be preserved in the same way.

# PICKLED NASTURTIUM BERRIES

**Preparation time 20 minutes**
**Cooking time 10 minutes**
**Pickling time 48 hours, plus 2 months**
**Makes 9 oz (250 g)**

2 cups (17 fl oz/475 ml) distilled vinegar, plus
    extra for covering
9 oz (250 g) nasturtium berries, picked and
    wiped clean
tarragon sprigs, to taste

Bring the vinegar to a boil in a pan, then remove from the heat. Place the nasturtium berries in a large nonmetallic bowl, pour in the boiling vinegar, cover with plastic wrap (clingfilm), and steep for 24 hours.

—

Strain the vinegar into a pan and bring to a boil again. Add the berries and remove from the heat before it comes back to a boil. Cover and steep for another 24 hours. Strain.

—

Place the berries in small, sterilized bottles (SEE p. 40), and add a tarragon sprig to each. Help them to settle by tapping the bottles lightly on a counter (work surface). Cover with vinegar and seal the bottles tightly.

—

Pickle for two months before eating.

# GHERKINS

## GHERKINS, HOT-VINEGAR METHOD

Preparation time 25 minutes, plus cooling
Cooking time 20 minutes
Pickling time 48 hours, plus 2 months
Makes 1 large jar, 3 lb (1.4 kg)

2¼ lb (1 kg) gherkins, about 2½–2¾ inches/
  6–7 cm, picked at the end of July, stalks
  removed
2 cups (16 oz/300 g) coarse salt
3 cups (26 fl oz/750 ml) distilled vinegar
3½ oz (100 g) pearl (baby) onions
1 shallot, sliced
10 cloves garlic
10 sprigs tarragon, or to taste

Place the gherkins in a coarse cloth with
a handful of the salt. Tie the cloth into a
bundle and shake vigorously. Wipe each
gherkin individually and place in a ceramic
or nonmetallic bowl. Sprinkle with the
remaining salt, then cover and steep for
24 hours.

—

Drain the gherkins and brush off as much of
the salt as you can, then return the gherkins
to the cleaned terrine or bowl. Pour half the
vinegar into a pan, bring to a boil, and boil for
5 minutes, then pour over the gherkins. Cover
and steep for another 24 hours.

—

Strain the vinegar into a pan and bring to a
boil again. Remove from the heat and cool
completely.

—

Arrange the gherkins in a large sterilized glass
jar or ceramic pot (SEE p. 40), layering them
with the onions, shallot, garlic, and tarragon.
Pour over the cooled vinegar, then top off
with the remaining vinegar. Seal tightly with
a sterilized lid. Pickle for two months before
eating. Always use clean wooden tongs to
remove the gherkins from the jar.

## GHERKINS, COLD-VINEGAR METHOD

Preparation time 25 minutes
Pickling time 24 hours, plus 10 weeks
Makes 1 large jar, 3 lb (1.4 kg)

2¼ lb (1 kg) gherkins, about 2½–2¾
  inches/6–7 cm, picked at the end of July,
  stalks removed
2 cups (11 oz/300 g) coarse salt
3½ oz (100 g) pearl (baby) onions
1 shallot, sliced
10 cloves garlic
10 sprigs tarragon, or to taste
6¼ cups (53 fl oz/1.5 liters) cold distilled
  vinegar

This method uses a larger amount of vinegar
and is a little more time-consuming, but it will
produce greener and firmer gherkins.

—

Place the gherkins in a coarse cloth with
a handful of the salt. Tie the cloth into a
bundle and shake vigorously. Wipe each
gherkin individually and place in a ceramic or
nonmetallic bowl. Sprinkle with the remaining
salt, then cover and steep for 24 hours.

—

Drain the gherkins, wipe them individually
with paper towels, and pack them tightly into
a large sterilized jar (SEE p. 40), alternating with
the onions, shallot, garlic, and tarragon. Pour
in cold (not boiled) vinegar to cover. Seal tightly
with a sterilized lid and steep for three weeks.

—

Drain the vinegar from the jar and cover again
with fresh vinegar. Cover and steep for another
three weeks.

—

Drain the vinegar from the jar one more time,
and cover again with fresh vinegar. Seal tightly
with a sterilized lid.

—

Pickle for one month before eating. Always use
clean wooden tongs to remove the gherkins
from the jar.

## SALTED LARGE GHERKINS

Preparation time 10 minutes
Cooking time 15 minutes
Brining time 10 days
Makes 1 jar, 3 lb (1.4 kg)

5 oz (150 g) grape (vine) leaves
12-15 cucumbers, about 4-5 inches /
    10-2 cm long
10 sprigs thyme
8 bay leaves
2 teaspoons black peppercorns
6 cloves
⅔ cup (3½ oz/100 g) coarse salt

Place a layer of grape (vine) leaves in a wide,
sterilized ceramic pot or glass jar (SEE p. 40)
and arrange the cucumbers with alternating
layers of the herbs, peppercorns, cloves, and
more grape (vine) leaves, packing them in well,
until the pot is full.

—

Make a brine using ⅔ cup (3½ oz/100 g) coarse
salt per 4¼ cups (35 fl oz/1 liter) water. Boil for
10 minutes, then remove from the heat, cool,
and pour over the cucumbers.

—

Push down using a small wooden plate (like the
ones used for sauerkraut), place a weight on it,
and cover with a clean cloth.

—

Pickle for 10 days before eating. Salted
gherkins keep well in the refrigerator. Simply
rinse before serving.

# SHALLOTS

Shallots keep well simply hung up in bunches;
never braid or knot the stalks.

## SHALLOTS IN VINEGAR

Preparation time 10 minutes
Cooking time 10 minutes
Pickling time 2 months
Makes 1 jar, 2½ lb (1.2 kg)

2¼ lb (1 kg) small round shallots
3-4 small red chiles
4 sprigs tarragon
1 teaspoon black peppercorns
3 cups (26 fl oz/750 ml) distilled vinegar

Place the shallots in a sterilized jar (SEE p.40)
with the chiles, tarragon, and peppercorns.

—

Bring the vinegar to a boil in a pan and boil for
5 minutes, then remove from the heat and pour
over the shallots to cover. Seal tightly with a
sterilized lid.

—

Pickle for two months before eating.

# ONIONS

For drying, pick onions in fall (autumn) when the leaves are dry, arranging them in garlands and hanging them up in a dry place. Check on them from time to time and remove any that show signs of rotting or start to germinate.

## PEARL ONIONS IN VINEGAR

Preparation time 10 minutes
Cooking time 10 minutes
Pickling time 2 months
Makes 2 lb (900 g)

2¼ lb (1 kg) pearl (baby) onions
2 teaspoons black peppercorns
3-4 red chiles
6 sprigs tarragon
3 cups (26 fl oz/750 ml) distilled vinegar
salt

Pearl (baby) onions should be planted in summer and harvested in the fall (autumn).

—

Bring a large pan of salted water to a boil over high heat. Carefully add the onions and blanch for 2 minutes, or until tender, then drain and peel.

—

Arrange the onions in sterilized jars (SEE p. 40), alternating with the peppercorns, chiles, and tarragon.

—

Bring the vinegar to a boil in a pan and boil for 5 minutes, then remove from the heat and pour over the onions to cover. Seal tightly with sterilized lids.

—

Pickle for two months before eating.

# OLIVES

## BLACK OLIVES IN OIL

Preparation time 20 minutes
Pickling time 20–30 days
Makes 1 jar, 2 lb (900 g)

2¼ lb (1 kg) very ripe olives, stalks removed
1 tablespoon black peppercorns
6 bay leaves
6 cloves
1¼ cups (10 fl oz/300 ml) good-quality olive oil
salt

Prick each olive with a pin, then place in a ceramic terrine or glass bowl, cover with salt, and steep for 10–15 days to let the salt draw out the moisture. Drain the water daily, stirring the olives each time to coat well with the salt. When no more water is drawn out, rinse the olives thoroughly, drain, and wipe dry with paper towels.

—

Place the olives in a sterilized jar (SEE p. 40) with the peppercorns, bay leaves, and cloves. Pour in enough olive oil to cover, seal tightly with a sterilized lid, and steep for another 10–15 days.

# PICKLED VEGETABLES

Preparation time 10 minutes
Cooking time 15 minutes
Pickling time 24 hours, plus 2 weeks
Makes 1 tall ceramic pot, 3 ¼ lb (1.5 kg)

1 small cauliflower, cut into small florets
3 tablespoons nasturtium berries
12 oz (350 g) thin haricot beans, trimmed and
    chopped into small pieces
7 oz (200 g) pearl (baby) onions, chopped into
    small pieces
5 oz (150 g) small green tomatoes, chopped into
    small pieces
8 oz (225 g) small new-season carrots, chopped
    into small pieces
7 oz (200 g) asparagus tips, chopped into small
    pieces
6 cloves garlic, chopped into small pieces
2½ cups (19 fl oz/550ml) distilled vinegar
2 tablespoons black peppercorns
6 cloves
1 teaspoon mustard powder
4 red chiles
1 tablespoon juniper berries
6 sprigs tarragon
salt
cold meats, to serve

Bring a large pan of salted water to a boil over
high heat. Carefully add the vegetables
and blanch for 5 minutes, or until tender, then
drain. Run cold water over them.

Arrange the vegetables in a tall, sterilized
ceramic pot or small sterilized jars (SEE p. 00).

Bring the vinegar to a boil in another pan then
pour over the vegetables to cover. Let steep for
24 hours.

Strain the vinegar into a pan, bring back to a
boil, and carefully pour back into the pot or
jars, adding the peppercorns, cloves, mustard
powder, chiles, juniper berries, and tarragon.
Seal tightly with a sterilized lid.

Pickle for two weeks before eating. Serve with
cold meats.

# CHILES

Use red chiles that are not too hot.

## SHALLOTS IN VINEGAR

Preparation time 10 minutes
Cooking time 5 minutes
Makes 1 jar, 1 lb (450 g)

8 oz (225 g) red chiles, stalks removed
1 cup (9 fl oz/250 ml) distilled vinegar
8 cloves garlic
2 shallots, sliced
5 oz (150 g) pearl (baby) onions
salt

Bring a large pan of salted water to a boil over
high heat. Carefully add the chiles and blanch
for 2 minutes, or until tender, then drain
and rinse in ice-cold water to keep them firm.

Pat the chiles dry on a clean cloth then place in
a sterilized jar (SEE p. 40).

Pour in enough cold vinegar to cover,
alternating with the garlic, shallots, and pearl
(baby) onions. Seal tightly with a sterilized lid.

Pickle for two months before eating.

# MILK

# MILK

## BOILED MILK

Preparation time 5 minutes
Cooking time 10 minutes

raw milk

To preserve raw milk for the day for home use, pour the milk into a pan, bring to a boil, and boil for 10 minutes. As the milk heats up break the skin that forms on the surface to prevent it boiling over: milk that simply rises up has not boiled, which means any undesirable microorganisms have not been destroyed.

—

Small enamel or glass disks, known as milk watchers, milk guards, or pot minders, are extremely practical to boil milk over low heat without accidents.

## MILK CURDS

Preparation time 5 minutes
Standing time 15 minutes
Makes 2 cups (17 fl oz/475 ml)

4¼ cups (34 fl oz/1 liter) milk
1-2 drops liquid rennet
sugar or salt, to taste (optional)

Pour the milk into a bowl, add the liquid rennet, and leave for 15 minutes in a fairly warm place until it has separated into solid curds and liquid whey. In cold weather, heat the milk gently in a pan over low heat for about 5 minutes, or until it is lukewarm before adding the rennet. Eat the curds plain, or add sugar or salt to taste.

—

NOTE: Some plants can also be used to curdle milk: split the end of a clean fig branch and stir into the lukewarm milk. You can also use the flowers of *Galium verum* (commonly known as Lady's Bedstraw in English, and *caille-lait* or "milk curdler" in French), immersing them in the lukewarm milk. At higher heats, milk will curdle spontaneously because of the lactic ferments it contains.

## FROMAGE BLANC

Preparation time 10 minutes
Standing time 12 hours
Makes 1 lb (450 g)

4¼ cups (34 fl oz/1 liter) milk
1-2 drops liquid rennet
sugar or salt, to taste (optional)
chopped herbs, cayenne pepper, or fresh
    cream, for serving (optional)

Pour the milk into a bowl, add the liquid
rennet, and leave for 15 minutes in a fairly
warm place until it has separated into solid
curds and liquid whey. In cold weather,
heat the milk gently in a pan over low heat
for about 5 minutes, or until it is lukewarm
before adding the rennet.

—

Scoop the milk curds into three layers of
cheesecloth (muslin) and tie the four corners
together tightly. Hang up over a bowl to catch
the whey. After 12 hours, the cheese will have
drained enough to eat. Eat it plain, or with
salt or sugar, to taste, or topped with chopped
herbs, cayenne pepper, or fresh cream.

## YOGURT

Preparation time 10 minutes
Setting time 4-6 hours
Makes 2¼ lb (1 kg)

3 oz (75 g) special ferment, such as fresh yogurt
7¼ cups (60 fl oz/1.7 liters) milk
2 oz (50 g) skim milk powder (optional)

To make yogurt, a special ferment is diluted
in a little warm milk to serve as a starter
culture for a larger amount of warmed milk.
Fresh yogurt may also be used as the starter.
You can increase the milk's casein content
and achieve a more set texture by adding skim
milk powder.

—

The milk mixture then needs to be kept at a
temperature around 113°F/45°C for 4–6 hours
to set. To achieve this, different containers
can serve as incubators: a heavy pot wrapped
in towels and placed in a preheated oven,
a slow cooker, a preheated thermos flask,
a cooler, or an electric yogurt maker specially
designed for that purpose.

—

Once set, store the yogurt in the refrigerator.
The flavors will develop over time.

## MILK KEFIR

Preparation time 10 minutes
Fermenting time 24–48 hours
Makes 1 cup (9 fl oz/250 ml)

1 cup (9 fl oz/250 ml) milk
1 teaspoon kefir grains

This was traditionally made with goat milk but cow's milk can also be used. It requires the use of kefir grains, a starter culture of beneficial bacteria and yeasts that thicken the milk and give it a pleasant aroma.

—

The kefir grains are added to the milk in a wide-mouth glass jar sealed tightly with a thin layer of cloth, and left to ferment for 24–48 hours in a warm place.

—

The grains may be reused again and again.

## GOAT CHEESE

Preparation time 5 minutes
Standing time 15 minutes
Makes 8 oz (225 g)

4¼ cups (34 fl oz/1 liter) goat milk
1-2 drops liquid rennet
salt

Pour the milk into a bowl, add the liquid rennet, and leave for 15 minutes in a fairly warm place until it has separated into solid curds and liquid whey. In cold weather, heat the milk gently in a pan over low heat for about 5 minutes, or until it is lukewarm before adding the rennet.

—

Strain the milk curds, then pour into small ceramic containers with holes in the bottom of them to drain. When the cheese is thoroughly drained, remove from the containers, sprinkle salt on both sides, and place on a clean straw mat to dry. The cheese can be eaten fresh.

—

If you wish to age the cheese, place the straw mat in a cool and well-ventilated place, such as a cellar or, more commonly these days, the refrigerator. Placing the cheeses in a cabinet with a mesh door and mesh walls (also called a meat safe) is ideal as it keeps them safe from insects. Flip the cheeses every so often.

—

NOTE: You can add cow's milk to goat milk in the proportion of 1 part cow's milk to 4 parts goat milk, or up to 1 part cow's milk to 2 parts goat milk.

# FISH

Although fish is now readily available, fresh or frozen, those readers who live near the sea or on a river particularly rich in fish may be suddenly confronted with a large quantity of fresh fish. The following methods will prove useful. Fish is a delicate product, and successful preserving requires the following precautions:

- Choose extremely fresh fish;
- Be extremely careful and keep your environment and tools perfectly clean as you work;
- When the fish requires cooking in the recipe, the fish needs to be thoroughly cooked, all the way through to the center, before preserving;
- When in doubt, err on the side of overcooking. You can always use it in a fish gratin or a fish loaf;
- Favor those cooking environments that are least favorable to bacterial growth: acidic (white wine, vinegar, lemon juice) or oil-rich (with as much water as possible removed);
- The canning times are indicated for jars no larger than 1 lb 2 oz (500 g) in capacity; the canning time must be increased if using larger jars.

Here we highlight those fish you are most likely to have in large quantities because they swim in schools.

# ANCHOVY

## MARINATED ANCHOVY

Preparation time 15 minutes, plus cooling
Marinating time 2 weeks, plus 5–6 days
Makes 1 large jar, 1 lb (500 g)

1 lb 2 oz (500 g) whole anchovies
⅔ cup (3½ oz/100 g) coarse salt
4 cloves
4 bay leaves
4 sprigs tarragon
1 tablespoon black peppercorns
2½ cups (21 fl oz/600 ml) good-quality distilled
  vinegar

Keep the anchovies whole. There is no need to clean them or remove their heads.

—

Place the anchovies in a nonreactive container.

—

Make a brine using ⅔ cup (3½ oz/100 g) coarse salt per 4¼ cups (34 fl oz/1 liter) water. Bring the water and salt to a boil in a pan and stir until the salt has dissolved. Remove from the heat and let the brine cool to room temperature.

—

Pour the brine over the fish, cover with plastic wrap (clingfilm), and marinate in the refrigerator for two weeks.

—

Meanwhile, steep the cloves, bay leaves, tarragon, and peppercorns in the vinegar.

—

Drain the anchovies from the brine, return the fish to the cleaned container, and pour in the flavored vinegar. Cover again and marinate for 5–6 days.

—

Transfer the fish to a sterilized jar (SEE p. 40), alternating with the black peppercorns and bay leaves, and top off with the vinegar used for marinating the fish. Seal tightly with a sterilized lid. Use a clean wooden fork to remove the anchovies as required.

# HERRING

## HERRING MARINATED IN WHITE WINE

Preparation time 30 minutes, plus cooling
Cooking time 30 minutes
Serves 8

24 small herrings with roe sacks, scaled,
  cleaned, washed, and patted dry
6 sprigs thyme
6 sprigs parsley
4 bay leaves
2 tablespoons salt
2 tablespoons black peppercorns
6 cloves
4 shallots, minced
1 lemon, sliced
4¼ cups (34 fl oz/1 liter) dry white wine or half
  and half mix of distilled vinegar and water

Lay the herring top to tail in a fish kettle (SEE below), making two or three layers and separating the layers with the herbs, bay leaves, salt, peppercorns, cloves, shallots, and lemon slices. Pour in the wine or vinegar and water mixture to ensure that the fish is not dry.

—

Bring the herring to a boil over high heat, then reduce the heat, and simmer for 15 minutes. Remove the fish kettle from the heat and cool.

—

Place the herring top to tail and belly up in an oval or rectangular dish. Strain the cooking broth (stock) through a strainer into a clean pitcher (jug) and pour over the fish, adding the bay leaves and peppercorns.

—

Cover with plastic wrap (clingfilm) and store in the refrigerator for up to two weeks.

—

NOTE: A fish kettle is a cooking pot with a grid at the bottom that allows for easy lifting of the cooked fish, without breaking it. If you don't have one, arrange a clean cloth at the bottom of a large pot, and lift it up by the corners to remove the cooked fish from the liquid.

## ROLLMOPS (PICKLED HERRING FILLETS)

Preparation time 20 minutes
Cooking time 5 minutes
Marinating time 8 days
Serves 8

3 cups (26 fl oz/750 ml) distilled vinegar
8 herrings, scaled, cleaned, filleted, and all
    bones removed
1 bouquet garni (SEE p. 273)
12 black peppercorns
2 large onions, thinly sliced
2 large carrots, thinly liced
toothpicks (cocktail sticks)

Measure ½ cup (4 fl oz/125 ml) vinegar in a large pan for every 2 herring fillets. Add the fish, bouquet garni, and peppercorns and bring to a boil.

—

Remove the fish from the pan and drain. Set the vinegar aside. Top each fish fillet with a few slices of onion and carrot. Roll up and secure with a small wooden toothpick pushed right through the roll.

—

Arrange the rollmops in a large sterilized jar (SEE p. 40), top off with the hot vinegar, and seal tightly with a sterilized lid.

—

Marinate in the refrigerator for eight days, and eat within three weeks.

# MACKEREL

## MACKEREL MARINATED IN WHITE WINE

Preparation time 30 minutes, plus cooling
Cooking time 30 minutes
Serves 12

24 small mackerel, cleaned, washed, and
    patted dry
8 sprigs thyme
8 sprigs parsley
8 bay leaves
2 tablespoons salt
2 tablespoons black peppercorns
8 cloves
4 shallots, minced
2 lemons, sliced
4¼ cups (34 fl oz/1 liter) dry white wine or half
    and half mix of distilled vinegar and water

Lay the mackerel top to tail in a fish kettle (SEE below), making two or three layers and separating the layers with the herbs, bay leaves, salt, peppercorns, cloves, shallots, and lemon slices. Pour in the wine or vinegar and water mixture to ensure that the fish is not dry.

—

Bring the mackerel to a boil over high heat, then reduce the heat, and simmer for 15 minutes. Remove the fish kettle from the heat and cool.

—

Place the mackerel top to tail and belly up in an oval or rectangular dish. Strain the cooking broth (stock) through a strainer into a clean pitcher (jug) and pour over the fish, adding the bay leaves and peppercorns.

—

Cover with plastic wrap (clingfilm) and store in the refrigerator for up to two weeks.

—

NOTE: A fish kettle is a cooking pot with a grid at the bottom that allows for easy lifting of the cooked fish, without breaking it. If you don't have one, arrange a clean cloth at the bottom of a large pot, and lift it up by the corners to remove the cooked fish from the liquid.

# SARDINES

## SARDINES IN OIL

Preparation time 20 minutes, plus cooling
Marinating time 2 hours
Cooking time 5 minutes
Draining time 3-4 hours
Canning time 1 hour 40 minutes
Serves 8

24 sardines, heads removed, rinsed,
  and drained
⅔ cup (3½ oz/100 g) coarse salt
oil, for frying

---

Use extremely fresh, medium-size sardines.
—
Make a brine using ⅔ cup (3½ oz/100 g) coarse
salt per 4¼ cups (34 fl oz/1 liter) water. Bring
the water and salt to a boil in a pan and stir
until the salt has dissolved. Remove the pan
from the heat and let the brine cool to room
temperature.
—
Pour the brine into a dish, add the sardines,
cover with plastic wrap (clingfilm),
and marinate for 2 hours in the refrigerator.
—
Rinse the fish and drain on clean dishtowels
(tea towels). Heat a shallow pool of oil in a large
deep pan or deep-fryer over high heat until
hot but not smoking. Place the sardines in the
pan or frying basket and cook for 5 minutes.
Remove the fish from the hot oil and drain on
dishtowels for 3-4 hours. Set the oil aside.
—
Arrange the sardines, packing them neatly,
ideally top to tail, in sterilized jars (SEE p. 40).
Top off each jar with the hot oil and seal
tightly with sterilized lids.
—
Process in a pressure canner (SEE p. 53 and
follow the manufacturer's instructions) for
1 hour 40 minutes.

# TROUT

## POACHED TROUT

Preparation time 20 minutes, plus cooling
Cooking time 1 hour 10 minutes
Canning time 1 hour 40 minutes
Serves 4

4 whole trout, cleaned
1¼ cups (10 fl oz/300 ml) dry white wine
2 carrots, thinly sliced
2 onions, thinly sliced
1 bouquet garni (SEE p. 273)

---

Choose small trout.
—
Pour the wine into a large pan and add the
same amount of water. Add the carrots,
onions, and bouquet garni and simmer over
low heat for 1 hour.
—
Add the trout to the pan and poach at a gentle
simmer for 5 minutes, then remove the pan
from the heat and let the fish cool in the broth
(stock).
—
Drain and arrange the trout in clean sterilized
jars (SEE p. 40), packing them tightly. Strain the
broth and pour into the jars to cover the fish.
—
Seal with sterilized lids and process in
a pressure canner (SEE p.53 and follow the
manufacturer's instructions) for 1 hour
40 minutes.

POULTRY

Farmyard fowl raised for their meat are known as poultry, and in France the equivalent term *volaille* also includes the domestic rabbit. The following preservation methods will be of particular interest to those who keep poultry.

For safe preserving, keep in mind the following recommendations:

- Only use the freshest meat;
- Cut meat in small pieces to ensure the heat processing reaches through to the center;
- Always cook meat before canning: this serves as a first sterilization;
- Take care to keep a perfectly clean environment and work quickly so the meat isn't unnecessarily exposed to air;
- Sterilize the jars before using (SEE p. 40);
  The canning times are indicated for jars no larger than 1 lb 2 oz (500 g) in capacity; the canning time must be increased if using larger jars;
- Canned meat products should not be kept for more than six months, and once open, they should be eaten within 24 hours;
- When opening, if you have any doubt on the contents of the can, discard without hesitation, even if the smell seems normal.

# DUCK

## DUCK CONFIT

**Preparation time 40 minutes,**
**plus cooling overnight**
**Marinating time 48 hours**
**Cooking time 2-4 hours**
**Canning time 1½ hours (optional)**
**Serves 4**

1 tablespoon black peppercorns
4 bay leaves
6 sprigs thyme
4 cloves
1 whole duck, about 4-5 lb (1.8-2.2 kg), cleaned
    and cut into pieces
9 oz (250 g) duck fat or rendered pork fat, such
    as bacon fat (optional)
2 oz (50 g) lard
salt

For this recipe the duck's head, neck, carcass, heart, and liver are not needed, so use them in the Stuffed Duck Neck, p. 90.

—

Line the bottom of a ceramic bowl or terrine with salt, the peppercorns, bay leaves, thyme, and cloves. Pack the duck pieces into the bowl and cover generously with salt. Place a board or small plate on top and add a weight to compress the meat.

—

Marinate in the refrigerator for 48 hours.

—

Wipe the meat carefully. Trim the fat from the meat, then slice the fat thinly, and melt it in a pan over low heat. If there isn't much fat, add extra duck fat or rendered fat. Strain.

—

Melt a little of the fat in a pan over medium heat and brown the duck pieces for 10 minutes, or until golden brown. Add the remaining hot fat, reduce the heat to low, and cook, covered, for 2-4 hours, depending on the amount of meat, until it is tender enough to pierce with a straw. Avoid cooking for too long as the meat will dry out and may become tough.

—

Remove the meat with a fork or skimmer and arrange in a sterilized jar (SEE p. 40). Top off with the hot fat, which should cover the pieces by ¾ inch/2 cm. Cool until the next day in the refrigerator.

—

Melt the lard in a pan over low heat, then pour it into the jar, and seal tightly with a sterilized lid. Store covered in the refrigerator.
The confit will keep for six months as long as you remember to cover the leftovers with fat each time you remove a piece.

—

Duck confit may be eaten cold (scrape off the fat that covers the meat), or briefly reheat in the oven or on the stove.

—

NOTE: For longer storage, process in a pressure canner (SEE p. 53) and follow the manufacturer's instructions) for 1½ hours.

## STUFFED DUCK NECK

Preparation time 40 minutes
Cooking time 2 hours
Serves 4

1 duck neck
1 duck carcass
1 duck liver
1 duck heart
4 oz (125 g) lard
4 oz (125 g) pork sausage meat
1 tablespoon ground spices, such as cloves and
    nutmeg
9 oz (250 g) duck fat
salt and freshly ground black pepper

First, make sure the neck has been thoroughly
singed, then remove the skin to get a tube like
a sausage casing. Trim all the scraps of meat
from the carcass. Remove the bile from the
liver and process in a meat grinder with the
heart and lard. Mix well with the duck meat
scraps and the sausage meat, and season
with the spices, salt, and pepper.

Wash the neck skin thoroughly and stitch up
one end to close it completely. Fill this tube
with the mixture, and tie off at the other end.
The neck should be generously filled.

—

Melt the duck fat in a pan over very low heat,
add the stuffed neck, and cook, covered,
for 2 hours along with the duck pieces for the
confit (SEE p. 91). Hang up, cool, then store
in the refrigerator for up to two weeks.

## DUCK TERRINE

Preparation time 1 hour, plus cooling
Cooking time 8½–9½ hours
Serves 10–12

1 whole duck, about 1¾ lb (800 g), boned and
    meat cut into strips
7 oz (200 g) veal meat
7 oz (200 g) lean (streaky) bacon
1 egg per 2¼ lb (1 kg) meat, plus 1 egg white
scant ¼ cup (1¾ fl oz/50 ml) liqueur, such as
    brandy or cognac
7 oz (200 g) bacon strips
1⅔ cups (7 oz/200 g) all-purpose (plain) flour
salt and freshly ground black pepper

    For the aspic
1½ calves' feet, deboned
1 lb 2 oz (500 g) veal bones
3¼ lb (1.5 kg) poultry carcass, giblets, and feet
1 lb 2 oz (500 g) beef shin
2¼ lb (1 kg) veal shank
2 carrots, sliced
3 small onions, sliced
1 bouquet garni (SEE p. 273)
2 teaspoons salt

The aspic must be made the day before.

—

To make the aspic, preheat the oven to
350°F/180°C/Gas Mark 4.

—

Bring a large pan of salted water to a boil
over high heat. Carefully add the calves' feet
and blanch for 2 minutes, or until tender,
then drain.

—

Place the bones, carcass, beef, and veal in
an ovenproof dish and roast in the oven
for 30 minutes.

—

Place the carrots and onions in a large, heavy-
bottomed pan and cover with the calves' feet,

browned bones and meat, and bouquet garni. Cover with a lid and cook over medium heat for 10 minutes.

—

Add scant ½ cup (3½ fl oz/100 ml) water and cook for another 10 minutes. Pour in scant 4 quarts (8 UK pints/4.5 liters) water and the salt, and bring to a boil. Skim, reduce the heat, and simmer for 6–7 hours. Strain through cheesecloth (muslin) into a bowl and cool.

—

Skim off the fat that has formed on the surface. When the jelly is completely cooled, any impurities remaining will have sunk to the bottom. For a clear jelly, pour slowly when using, taking care to leave the impurities behind.

---

The next day, preheat the oven to 350°F/180°C/Gas Mark 4.

—

For the terrine, weigh the duck meat, and measure a quarter of this weight in veal meat, and a quarter in lean (streaky) bacon.

—

Process the duck heart, liver, and lungs in a meat grinder, then grind the veal and bacon. Add the eggs and liqueur and mix well.

—

Line the inside of a lidded terrine with some of the bacon strips. Arrange alternating layers of duck meat and stuffing until both are used up, finishing off with a layer of stuffing. Top with a final layer of bacon strips. Leave about ¾ inch/2 cm of headspace between this last layer and the rim of the terrine.

—

Melt 1¼ cups (10 fl oz/300 ml) aspic in a pan over low heat, then pour a little onto the pâté.

For the sealing dough, mix the flour and about scant ½ cup (3½ fl oz/100 ml) cold water together in a bowl until it is a soft consistency, a little sticky but not too wet. Roll the dough into a rough log and press onto the rim of the terrine, making sure it is covered all around. Place the lid on the terrine and press to seal. Cook in the oven for 1½ hours then cool.

—

The terrine will keep for a week, covered, in the refrigerator. For slightly longer storage, pour ½-inch/1-cm layer of melted lard onto the surface of the meat, cover, and refrigerate.

—

NOTE: If the aspic is not as firm as you need it, you can add gelatin: ½ teaspoon gelatin per 4¼ cups (34 fl oz/1 liter) of jelly, softened in cold water for 30 minutes. After skimming the jelly of fat, return to the clean pan, add the drained gelatin, and bring just to a simmer, stirring frequently. You can flavor the jelly with Madeira, which will also give it a good color, if desired.

# TURKEY

## DUCK RILLETTES

Preparation time 20 minutes, plus cooling
Cooking time 5½–6½ hours, plus 20 minutes

pork back fat (same weight as the duck meat,
    plus extra for covering)
duck meat on the bone, cut into pieces
salt and freshly ground black pepper

Process the pork fat finely in a food processor,
then place in a pan and melt slowly over low
heat. Set aside.
—

Place the duck meat in a large heavy-bottomed
pan, add scant ½ cup (3½ fl oz/100 ml) water
per 2¼ lb (1 kg) meat, cover, and cook over low
heat for 5–6 hours, or until the meat is falling
off the bone.
—

Remove the bones. Shred the meat finely, add
the pork fat, season, and mix well. Return to
the pan and cook for another 20 minutes.
—

Place the mixture in sterilized jars (SEE p. 40)
and cool completely.
—

Re-melt pork fat in a pan over low heat, then
pour on the top of the mixture. Seal tightly
with sterilized lids.
—

Rillettes will keep for months in a cool,
dry place, as long as the top layer of fat is
undisturbed.

## TURKEY RILLETTES

Preparation time 20 minutes, plus cooling
Cooking time 6½–8½ hours, plus 20 minutes

pork back fat (same weight as the turkey meat),
    plus extra for covering
turkey meat on the bone, cut into pieces
salt and freshly ground black pepper

Process the pork fat finely in a food processor,
then place in a pan and melt slowly over low
heat. Set aside.
—

Place the turkey meat in a large heavy-
bottomed pan, add scant ½ cup (3½ fl oz/100
ml) water per 2¼ lb (1 kg) meat, cover, and
cook over low heat for 6–8 hours, or until the
meat is falling off the bone.
—

Remove the bones. Shred the meat finely,
add the pork fat, season, and mix well.
Return to the pan and cook for another 20
minutes.
—

Place the mixture in sterilized jars (SEE p. 40)
and cool completely.
—

Re-melt pork fat in a pan over low heat, then
pour on the top of the mixture. Seal tightly
with sterilized lids.
—

Rillettes will keep for months in a cool,
dry place, as long as the top layer of fat is
undisturbed.

# GOOSE

## STUFFED GOOSE NECK

Preparation time 40 minutes
Cooking time 2 hours
Serves 4

1 goose neck
1 goose carcass
1 goose liver
1 goose heart
4 oz (125 g) lard
4 oz (125 g) pork sausage meat
2 teaspoons ground spices, such as cloves and
    nutmeg
12 oz (350 g) goose fat
salt and freshly ground black pepper

First, make sure the neck has been thoroughly singed. Remove the skin to get a tube like a sausage casing. Trim all the scraps of meat from the carcass. Remove the bile from the liver and process in a meat grinder with the heart and lard. Mix well with the goose meat scraps and the sausage meat, and season with the spices, salt, and pepper.

—

Wash the neck skin thoroughly and stitch up one end to close it completely. Fill this tube with the mixture, and tie off at the other end. The neck should be generously filled.

—

Cook for 2 hours in goose fat along with the goose pieces for the confit (SEE p. 96). Hang up, cool, then store in the refrigerator for up to two weeks.

## TRUFFLED GOOSE LIVER

Preparation time 30 minutes, plus 12 hours
    chilling
Cooking time 20 minutes
Canning time 2 hours
Makes 1 large jar

1 goose liver, about 1 lb 5 oz (600 g) (white and
    firm), deveined, rinsed, and patted dry
milk, for poaching
1 small black truffle
2 oz (50 g) pork back fat
2 oz (50 g) goose fat
salt and freshly ground black pepper

Wrap the liver in cloth and refrigerate for 12 hours.

—

Fill a large saucepan with three parts water to one part milk. Bring to a simmer and poach the liver until firm; this will take 15–18 minutes per 2¼ lb (1 kg) of liver. Remove the pan from the heat and cool.

—

Drain the liver. Cut the truffle into thin slivers and place between the lobes of the liver before placing it in a sterilized jar (SEE p. 40). Press down well so the top of the liver will have about 1¼ inches/3 cm of headspace in the jar.

—

Melt the pork and goose fats in a pan over low heat, then pour over the liver to fill the jar up to ¾ inch/2 cm from the rim. Seal tightly with a sterilized lid.

—

Process in a pressure canner (SEE p. 53) and follow the manufacturer's instructions) for 2 hours.

—

Store in the refrigerator before opening and eating.

## GOOSE CONFIT

Preparation time 40 minutes, plus cooling
   overnight
Marinating time 48 hours
Cooking time 2-4 hours
Canning time 1½ hours (optional)
Makes 1-2 jars, serves 6

1 tablespoon black peppercorns
6 bay leaves
8 sprigs thyme
6 cloves
1 goose, about 10 lb (4.5 kg), cleaned and cut
   into pieces
1 lb 5 oz (600 g) goose fat or rendered pork fat
3½ oz (100 g) lard
salt

Line the bottom of a ceramic bowl or terrine
with salt, the peppercorns, bay leaves, thyme,
and cloves. Pack the goose pieces into the
bowl and cover generously with salt. Place
a board or small plate on top and add a
weight to compress the meat. Marinate in the
refrigerator for 48 hours.

—

Wipe the meat carefully. Trim the fat from the
meat, then slice the fat thinly, and melt it in a
pan over low heat. If there isn't much fat, add
extra goose fat or rendered fat. Strain.

—

Melt a little of the fat in a pan over medium
heat and brown the goose pieces for 8–10
minutes until golden brown. Add the
remaining hot fat, reduce the heat to low, and
cook for 2–4 hours, depending on the amount
of meat, until it is tender enough to pierce with
a straw. Avoid cooking for too long as the
meat will dry out and may become tough.

—

Remove the meat with a fork or skimmer and
arrange in sterilized jars (SEE p. 40).

Top off with the hot fat, which should cover
the pieces by ¾ inch/2 cm. Cool in the
refrigerator until the next day.

—

Melt the lard in a pan over low heat, then pour
it into the jar, and seal tightly with sterilized
lids. Store in the refrigerator.

—

The confit will keep for six months as long as
you remember to cover the leftovers with fat
each time you remove a piece.

—

Goose confit may be eaten cold (scrape off the
fat that covers the meat), or briefly reheated in
the oven or on the stove.

—

For longer storage, process in a pressure
canner (SEE p. 53 and follow the manufacturer's
instructions) for 1½ hours.

## CASSOULET

Preparation time 30 minutes, plus soaking
overnight
Cooking time 5-5½ hours
Canning time 1½ hours
Makes 2 large jars, serves 6-8

2¾ cups (1 lb 2 oz/500 g) dried white beans
2¼ oz (60 g) fat
1 lb 10 oz (750 g) goose meat, cut into pieces
1 lb 2 oz (500 g) lamb meat, cut into pieces
scant ½ cup (2 oz/50 g) all-purpose (plain) flour
3 cups (25 fl oz/700 ml) hot stock
3½ oz (100 g) tomato concentrate
salt and freshly ground black pepper

Soak the beans in a bowl of cold water
overnight. The next day, drain, place in a large
pan, pour in enough fresh water to cover,
and bring to a boil. Boil for 10 minutes, then
reduce the heat and simmer for 1–1½ hours, or
until tender but still keeping their shape.
Drain and set aside.

—

Melt the fat in a large pan over medium heat.
Add the goose and lamb pieces and cook for
10 minutes, or until browned, then remove
them from the pan.

—

Remove the pan from the heat, add the flour
to the fat still in the pan, and stir well with a
whisk. Return the pan to medium heat and
cook for 2–3 minutes, stirring frequently,
until the roux has thickened slightly, but not
colored. Stir in the hot stock, add the tomato
concentrate, and season. Return the meat
to the pan, stir, and cook over low heat for
3½ hours.

—

Place the pieces of meat in sterilized jars
(SEE p. 40), alternating with the cooked beans
and sauce. Seal tightly with sterilized lids.

—

Process in a pressure canner (SEE p. 53 and
follow the manufacturer's instructions) for 1½
hours.

—

When serving the cassoulet, add thinly sliced
dried sausage and browned Toulouse sausages,
and cook for 20 minutes before serving.

## GOOSE TERRINE

**Preparation time 1 hour, plus cooling**
**Cooking time 9 hours**
**Serves 12–14**

1 whole goose, about 11 lb (5 kg), boned and
    meat cut into strips
7 oz (200 g) veal meat
7 oz (200 g) lean (streaky) bacon
11 oz (300 g) bacon strips
2 eggs, plus 1 egg white
scant ¼ cup (1¾ fl oz/50 ml) liqueur, such as
    brandy or cognac
1⅔ cups (7 oz/200 g) all-purpose (plain) flour
salt and freshly ground black pepper

    For the aspic
1½ calves' feet, deboned
1 lb 2 oz (500 g) veal bones
3¼ lb (1.5 kg) poultry carcass, giblets, and feet
1 lb 2 oz (500 g) beef shin
2¼ lb (1 kg) veal shank
2 carrots, sliced
3 small onions, sliced
1 bouquet garni (SEE p. 273)
2 teaspoons salt

The aspic must be made the day before.
—
To make the aspic, preheat the oven to
350°F/180°C/Gas Mark 4.
—
Bring a large pan of salted water to a boil over
high heat. Carefully add the calves' feet and
blanch for 2 minutes, or until tender, then
drain.
—
Place the bones, carcass, beef, and veal meat in
an ovenproof dish and roast in the oven for
30 minutes.
—
Place the carrots and onions in a large, heavy-
bottomed pan and cover with the calves' feet,

browned bones and meat, and bouquet garni.
Cover with a lid and cook over medium heat
for 10 minutes.
—
Add scant ½ cup (3½ fl oz/100 ml) water and
cook for another 10 minutes. Pour in scant 3½
quarts (6¾ UK pints/3.9 liters) water and the
salt, and bring to a boil. Skim, reduce the heat,
and simmer for 6–7 hours. Strain through
cheesecloth (muslin) into a bowl and cool.
—
Skim off the fat that has formed on the surface.
When the jelly is completely cooled, any
impurities remaining will have sunk to the
bottom. For a clear jelly, pour slowly when
using, taking care to leave the impurities
behind.

The next day, preheat the oven to
350°F/180°C/Gas Mark 4.
—
For the terrine, weigh the goose meat, and
measure a quarter of this weight in veal meat,
and a quarter in lean (streaky) bacon.
—
Process the goose heart, liver, and lungs in a
meat grinder, then grind the veal and bacon.
Add the eggs and liqueur and mix well.
—
Line the inside of a lidded terrine with some of
the bacon strips. Arrange alternating layers of
goose meat and stuffing until both are used up,
finishing off with a layer of stuffing. Top with
a final layer of bacon strips. Leave about
¾ inch/2 cm of headspace between this last
layer and the rim of the terrine.
—
Melt 1¼ cups (10 fl oz/300 ml) aspic in a large
pan over low heat, then pour a little onto the
pâté.

For the sealing dough, mix the flour and about scant ½ cup (3½ fl oz/100 ml) cold water together in a bowl until it is a soft consistency, a little sticky but not too wet. Roll the dough into a rough log and press onto the rim of the terrine, making sure it is covered all around. Place the lid on the terrine and press to seal. Cook in the oven for 1½ hours, then cool.

——

The terrine will keep for a week, covered, in the refrigerator. For longer storage, pour ½-inch/1-cm layer of melted lard onto the surface of the terrine, cover, and refrigerate.

——

NOTE: If the aspic is not as firm as you need it, you can add gelatin: ½ teaspoon gelatin per 4¼ cups (34 fl oz/1 liter) of jelly, softened in cold water for 30 minutes. After skimming the jelly of fat, return to the clean pot, add the drained gelatin, and bring close to a simmer, stirring frequently. You can flavor the jelly with Madeira, which will also give it a good color.

# CHICKEN

## CHICKEN IN ASPIC

Preparation time 20 minutes
Cooking time 2 hours 10 minutes
Canning time 1½ hours
Makes 2 medium jars, serves 4

3 oz (75 g) butter
1 whole chicken, about 4 lb (1.8 kg), cut into
    8 pieces
1¼ cups (10 fl oz/300 ml) white wine
1 calf's foot, halved
salt and freshly ground black pepper

Melt the butter in a large pan over medium heat, add the chicken pieces and cook for 8–10 minutes, until golden brown all over. Pour in enough boiling water to almost cover the meat and top off with the wine to cover completely. Season and add the calf's foot, then reduce the heat to low and simmer for 2 hours.

—

Arrange the chicken pieces in sterilized jars (SEE p. 40), pressing down to pack. Strain the cooking juices and pour over the meat, leaving ¾ inch/2 cm headspace; the juices will turn to jelly after cooling. Seal with sterilized lids.

—

Process in a pressure canner (SEE p. 53 and follow the manufacturer's instructions) for 1½ hours.

## CHICKEN TERRINE

Preparation time 1 hour, plus cooling
Cooking time 9-10 hours
Serves 8

¼ cup (2¼ oz/60 g) butter
1 whole chicken, about 2½ lb (1.2 kg), cut into
    small pieces and bones removed
7 oz (200 g) ham
9 oz (250 g) fresh pork
9 oz (250 g) veal meat
2 eggs
scant ¼ cup (1¾ fl oz/50 ml) brandy or cognac
12 oz (350 g) bacon strips
1 small black truffle (optional)
2 teaspoons ground spices, such as nutmeg
    and cloves
1⅔ cups (7 oz/200 g) all-purpose (plain) flour
2 oz/50 g clarified butter, melted for covering
    (optional)
salt and freshly ground black pepper

    For the aspic
1½ calves' feet, deboned
1 lb 2 oz (500 g) veal bones
3¼ lb (1.5 kg) poultry carcass, giblets, and feet
1 lb 2 oz (500 g) beef shin
2¼ lb (1 kg) veal shank
2 carrots, sliced
3 small onions, sliced
1 bouquet garni (SEE p. 273)
2 teaspoons salt

The aspic must be made the day before.

—

To make the aspic, preheat the oven to 350°F/180°C/Gas Mark 4.

—

Bring a large pan of salted water to a boil over high heat. Carefully add the calves' feet and blanch for 2 minutes, or until tender, then drain.

—

Place the bones, carcass, beef, and veal meat in

an ovenproof dish and roast in the oven for 30 minutes.

Place the carrots and onions in a large, heavy-bottomed pan and cover with the calves' feet, browned bones and meat, and bouquet garni. Cover with a lid and cook over medium heat for 10 minutes.

—

Add scant ½ cup (3½ fl oz/100 ml) water and cook for another 10 minutes. Pour in scant 3½ quarts (6¾ UK pints/3.9 liters) water and the salt, and bring to a boil. Skim, reduce the heat, and simmer for 6–7 hours. Strain through cheesecloth (muslin) into a bowl and cool.

—

Skim off the fat that has formed on the surface. When the jelly is completely cooled, any impurities remaining will have sunk to the bottom. For a clear jelly, pour slowly when using, taking care to leave the impurities behind.

The next day, preheat the oven to 350°F/180°C/Gas Mark 4.

—

For the terrine, melt the butter in a large pan over medium heat, add the chicken, and cook briefly for 5–8 minutes until firm and whitened but without coloring.

—

Process the ham, pork, and veal in a meat grinder. Add the eggs and brandy, and season with the spices, salt, and pepper.

—

Place a layer of bacon strips at the bottom of a lidded oval terrine. Add a layer of stuffing, followed by a layer of chicken, and a layer of truffles, if using, adding some of the melted aspic after each layer so it's not dry. Repeat until you have used all the ingredients, finishing with a layer of bacon strips.

—

For the sealing dough, mix the flour and about scant ½ cup (3½ fl oz/100 ml) cold water together in a bowl until it is a soft consistency, a little sticky but not too wet. Roll the dough into a rough log and press onto the rim of the terrine, making sure it is covered all around. Cook in the oven for 2 hours.

—

Let the terrine rest in the refrigerator until the next day before eating. It can be kept in the refrigerator for up to 12 days as long as the lid is kept on.

—

For longer storage, remove the lid as soon as the terrine is cooked, press down on the meat to pack, and place a board on top with a weight pressing down on it. Once cool, pour melted lard on the surface to cover completely, and keep for up to four months in the refrigerator.

—

NOTE: If the aspic is not as firm as you need it, you can add gelatin: ½ teaspoon gelatin per 4¼ cups (34 fl oz/1 liter) of jelly, softened in cold water for 30 minutes. After skimming the jelly of fat, return to the clean pot, add the drained gelatin, and bring just to a simmer, stirring frequently. You can flavor the jelly with Madeira, which will also give it a good color.

# RABBIT

## RABBIT RILLETTES

Preparation time 20 minutes, plus cooling
Cooking time 4 hours, plus 20 minutes

pork fat (same weight as the rabbit meat), plus
extra for covering
rabbit meat on the bone, cut into pieces
salt and freshly ground black pepper

---

Process the pork fat finely in a food processor,
then place in a pan and melt slowly over low
heat. Set aside.

—

Place the rabbit meat in a heavy-bottomed
pan, add scant ½ cup (3½ fl oz/100 ml) water
per 2¼ lb (1 kg) meat, cover, and cook over low
heat for 4 hours, or until the meat is falling off
the bone.

—

Remove the bones. Shred the meat finely, add
the pork fat, season, and mix well. Return to
the pan and cook for another 20 minutes.

—

Place the mixture in sterilized jars (SEE p. 40)
and cool completely.

—

Re-melt pork fat in a pan over low heat, then
pour on the top of the mixture. Seal tightly
with sterilized lids.

—

Rillettes will keep for months in a cool,
dry place, as long as the top layer of fat is
undisturbed.

## RABBIT BALLOTTINE

Preparation time 1 hour, plus cooling
Cooking time 8–9½ hours
Canning time 1½ hours
Makes 2 medium jars

1 whole rabbit, about 3 lb (1.4 kg), cut into
pieces, bones removed
3 oz (75 g) butter
11 oz (300 g) bacon strips
chicken stock, in equal quantity to wine, to
reach halfway up the pan while cooking
white wine
3 oz (75g) pork fat
salt and freshly ground black pepper

For the aspic
1½ calves' feet, deboned
1 lb 2 oz (500 g) rabbit bones
3¼ lb (1.5 kg) poultry carcass, giblets, and feet
1 lb 2 oz (500 g) beef shin
2¼ lb (1 kg) veal shank
2 carrots, sliced
3 small onions, sliced
1 bouquet garni (SEE p. 273)
2 teaspoons salt

---

The front and back legs and the saddle of the
rabbit are only needed for this dish. Save the
front quarters, ribs, and head for a stew and use
the rabbit bones to make the aspic. Make the
aspic the day before.

—

To make the aspic, preheat the oven to
350°F/180°C/Gas Mark 4.

—

Bring a large pan of salted water to a boil over
high heat. Add the calves' feet, blanch for
2 minutes, or until tender, then drain.

—

Place the bones, carcass, beef, and veal shank
in an ovenproof dish and roast in the oven for
30 minutes.

Place the carrots and onions in a large, heavy-bottomed pan and cover with the calves' feet, browned bones and meat, and bouquet garni. Cover with a lid and cook over medium heat for 10 minutes.

—

Add scant ½ cup (3½ fl oz/100 ml) water and cook for another 10 minutes. Pour in scant 4 quarts (6¾ UK pints/3.9 liters) water and the salt, and bring to a boil. Skim, reduce the heat, and simmer for 6–7 hours. Strain through cheesecloth (muslin) into a bowl and cool.

—

Skim off the fat that has formed on the surface. When the jelly is completely cooled, any impurities remaining will have sunk to the bottom. For a clear jelly, pour slowly when using, taking care to leave the impurities behind.

The next day, melt the butter in a pan over medium heat and cook the rabbit pieces for 8–10 minutes until browned all over. Season, add stock and wine in equal parts to reach halfway up the pan, reduce the heat to low, and simmer for 1–1½ hours. The rabbit should be cooked but still firm.

—

Melt the aspic in a pan over low heat. Use sterilized ballottine jars (SEE p. 40), which are round and fairly narrow, preferably, and line the bottom and sides with bacon strips. Pack the rabbit pieces inside and fill the gaps with the melted aspic. Seal with sterilized lids.

—

Process in a pressure canner (SEE p. 53 and follow the manufacturer's instructions) for 1½ hours.

—

Melt pork fat in a pan over low heat, then pour

on the top of the mixture. Seal tightly with sterilized lids. Rabbit ballottine is best eaten well chilled and cooled completely.

—

Rillettes will keep for months in a cool, dry place, as long as the top layer of fat is undisturbed.

# RABBIT

## RABBIT CONFIT

Preparation time 40 minutes, plus cooling
Marinating time 24 hours
Cooking time 2 hours
Makes 1-2 jars

1-2 large rabbits, each weighing 4½-5½ lb
  (2-2.5 kg) after skinning and cleaning, cut
  into pieces
scant ¼ cup (1½ oz/40 g) salt per 2¼ lb (1 kg)
  rabbit
2 teaspoons ground spices, such as nutmeg or
  cloves
6 sprigs thyme
3 bay leaves
1 lb 2 oz (500 g) pork fat per 2¼ lb (1 kg) rabbit,
  finely chopped, plus extra for covering

Place the rabbit pieces in a ceramic bowl, add
the salt, spices, thyme, and bay leaves, and
mix to coat the rabbit. Cover with plastic wrap
(clingfilm) and marinate in the refrigerator for
24 hours.
—
Wipe the pieces of rabbit dry. Remove any
fat from the rabbit meat and chop finely. Set a
small portion of the pork fat aside to top the
jars at the end, and melt the rest with the rabbit
fat in a large pan over low heat. Add the rabbit
pieces and cook for 2 hours; the meat is ready
when you can push a knitting needle through
easily.
—
Arrange the rabbit pieces in sterilized jars
(SEE p. 40), packing them well. Tamp them
down and pour over the cooking fat to cover by
¾ inch/2 cm. If there isn't enough, melt and
add more fat as needed. Cool. When the fat has
completely set, pour a thin layer of melted pork
fat on top to make sure the seal is perfect.
Seal with sterilized lids.

## RABBIT TERRINE

Preparation time 40 minutes
Cooking time 2 hours
Serves 8

7 oz (200 g) bacon strips
1 rabbit, about 4½-5½ lb (2-2.5 kg), jointed into
  pieces, bones removed, and meat cut into
  pieces
7 oz (200 g) fresh lean pork, cut into strips
4 oz (125 g) lean (streaky) bacon
4 shallots, finely sliced
scant ¼ cup (1¾ fl oz/50 ml) brandy or cognac
2 teaspoons ground spices, such as nutmeg
  and cloves
1 bay leaf
1⅔ cups (7 oz/200 g) all-purpose (plain) flour
salt

Preheat the oven to 350°F/180°C/Gas Mark 4.
—
Line the bottom of a terrine dish with some of
the bacon strips. Arrange layers of rabbit meat
in the terrine, alternating with layers of fresh
pork, bacon, and shallots. Season with salt
and ground spices as you go, pouring in a little
of the brandy as well, and repeat until all the
ingredients are used up. Place the bay leaf on
top and finish with a layer of bacon strips.
—
For the sealing dough, mix the flour and about
scant ½ cup (3½ fl oz/100 ml) cold water
together in a bowl until it is a soft consistency,
a little sticky but not too wet. Roll the dough
into a rough log and press onto the rim of
the terrine, making sure it is covered all
around. Cook in the oven for 2 hours until
cooked through.
—
This terrine will keep in the refrigerator,
unopened, for 4–5 days. Once opened, eat
immediately.

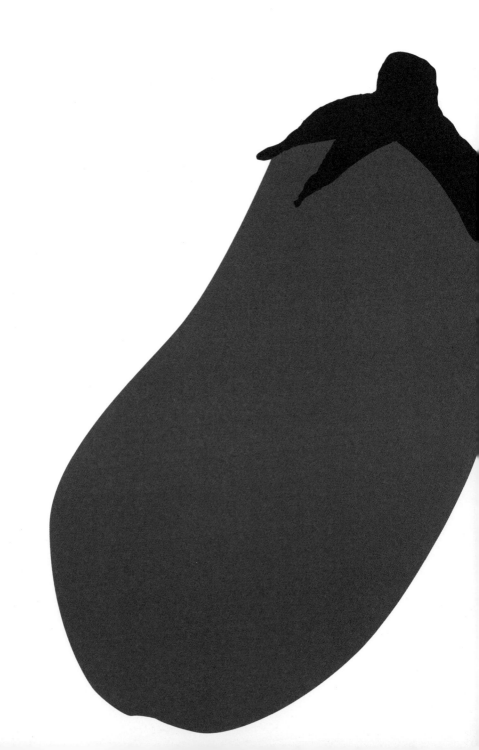

VEGETABLES

A quick glance at the kitchen garden calendar (SEE pp. 18–20) shows that in any cycle of twelve months, there are times in the year during which certain vegetables are scarce or unavailable.

In spring and summer, however, there is such a glut that people naturally tend to preserve produce for the colder season. Children are also on vacation for some of this time, and can help with the peeling, sorting, and other small tasks.

It's worth making an effort to set aside some little corner in your home to stash away a few jars for the winter, as they will brighten up dishes that might otherwise be a little boring without some condiment or garnish.

Those lucky enough to own a backyard or garden and grow their own food will be missing out if they don't take the opportunity to store up some goodies for the winter. There are so many options for making preserves in the countryside that it is little wonder the practice has survived.

### SOME GENERAL NOTES

Sort your vegetables with extreme care, choosing only those that are in perfect condition with no blemishes.

Wash them as many times as it takes to remove all the dirt, and do this just before they are to be preserved, not hours ahead.
Blanch all your vegetables in salted boiling water, then cook for another 4–5 minutes before canning; this completes the cleaning process and kills certain kinds of yeasts that could affect the preserve; the blanching water should not be kept or reused.

Vegetables that are very tender are then immediately plunged in ice-cold water, which will help them retain their color, before being transferred to sterilized jars.

Jars containing vegetables that have been cut into pieces and immersed in brine need a shorter canning time than those containing a puree.

Because of the low acidity of vegetables, they require the use of a pressure canner for safe preserving. Full instructions are given on pp. 53–4.

The canning times are indicated for jars no larger than 1 lb 2 oz (500 g) in capacity; canning time must be increased if using larger jars.

Some vegetables, such as carrots, sweet potatoes, and pumpkins, lend themselves well to jam making, too, and for these recipes you will need to refer to the full instructions given in the General Advice chapter.

Where salt is used for salting or brining, it should be dry-heated in a cooking pot or skillet or frying pan for 12–15 minutes; when making a brine, use boiled water.

Some vegetables can be preserved in their fresh state with some precautions to keep them away from cold and light. These vegetables should never be washed before being stored, but should be left out for a while so they'll lose any trace of surface moisture.

# ARTICHOKES

## WHOLE ARTICHOKES AU NATUREL

Preparation time 20 minutes
Cooking time 15 minutes
Canning time 35 minutes
Makes 2¼ lb (1 kg)

2¼ lb (1 kg) small artichokes
2 lemons, cut into wedges
salt

Trim the artichoke bases with a knife to make them cone-shaped. Use scissors to trim the ends of the leaves. Wash well and rub the bases with lemon wedges to stop them discoloring.

—

Have ready a large bowl filled halfway with ice cubes and enough cold water to cover the ice. Bring a large pan of salted water to a boil. Add the artichokes and cook for 15 minutes, or until the bases are tender. Remove the artichokes with a slotted spoon and plunge into the ice-cold water. Leave for 1 minute, then drain.

—

Transfer the artichokes to sterilized jars (see p. 40). Bring enough salted water to a boil (1 teaspoon salt per 4¼ cups/34 fl oz/1 liter water) in a pan and use to top off the jars. Seal with sterilized lids.

—

Process in a pressure canner (see p. 53 and follow the manufacturer's instructions) for 35 minutes.

## ARTICHOKE HEARTS AU NATUREL

Preparation time 20 minutes
Preparation time 20 minutes
Cooking time 10 minutes
Canning time 25 minutes
Makes 1 lb 2 oz (500 g)

2¼ lb (1 kg) small artichokes
2 lemons, cut into wedges
bottled lemon juice or citric acid,
    for the jars
salt

Remove the leaves and choke from the artichokes.

—

Rub the artichoke hearts with lemon wedges to prevent their color from turning.

—

Have ready a large bowl filled halfway with ice cubes and enough cold water to cover the ice. Bring a large pan of salted water to a boil. Add the artichokes and cook for 10 minutes. Remove the artichokes with a slotted spoon and plunge into the ice-cold water. Leave for 1 minute, then drain and dry carefully with a clean cloth.

—

Arrange the artichoke hearts in layers in sterilized jars (see p. 40). Bring enough salted water to a boil (1 teaspoon salt per 4¼ cups/ 34 fl oz/1 liter water) in a pan. In a large pitcher (jug), combine enough lemon juice or citric acid with water (2 tablespoons bottled lemon juice or a little under ⅓ teaspoon/1.5 g citric acid per 4¼ cups/34 fl oz/1 liter water) and use both types of water to top off the jars. Seal with sterilized lids.

—

Process in a pressure canner (see p. 53 and follow the manufacturer's instructions) for 25 minutes.

# ASPARAGUS

## WHOLE ASPARAGUS AU NATUREL

**Preparation time 20 minutes**
**Cooking time 3 minutes**
**Canning time 40 minutes**
**Makes 3 lb (1.4 kg)**

36 asparagus spears
salt

Rinse the asparagus in two or three changes of water to remove any dirt or sand. Trim the stems to even up the sizes, and make sure they will fit easily into the jars when standing up. Peel any rough spots off the stems.

Bring a large pan of salted water to a boil. Make little bunches of a dozen asparagus spears, tying them up with kitchen string. As the tips are the most delicate part, arrange the bundles vertically in a reasonably tall pan, ideally in a basket or wrapped in a cloth that you can pick up by its four corners. Carefully add the boiling salted water, filling the pan about halfway up the stems and boil for 2 minutes.

Now add enough boiling water to cover the tips and boil for another 1 minute. Have ready a large bowl filled halfway with ice cubes and enough cold water to cover the ice. Remove the bundles with a slotted spoon and plunge into the ice-cold water. Leave for 1 minute, then drain. Place the bundles flat on a cloth to dry and undo the strings.

Arrange the asparagus tip down in sterilized jars (SEE p. 40): when pulling them out of the jar for eating it will be easier to get hold of the stem as the tip is very fragile. Bring enough salted water to a boil (1 teaspoon salt per

4¼ cups/34 fl oz/1 liter water) in a pan and use to top off the jars. Seal with sterilized lids.

Process in a pressure canner (SEE p. 53 and follow the manufacturer's instructions) for 40 minutes.

When it is time to eat the asparagus, reheat them in their preserving liquid and strain before serving.

## ASPARAGUS TIPS

Preparation time 15 minutes
Cooking time 2 minutes
Canning time 40 minutes
Makes 1–2 x 2 lb (900 g) jars

36 asparagus spears
salt

Trim off the asparagus tips to make pieces 2½–2¾ inches/6–7 cm in length. Set the stems aside for another use: they can be peeled, cooked in boiling salted water, cut into slices, and eaten with your choice of sauce.

—

Have ready a large bowl filled halfway with ice cubes and enough cold water to cover the ice. Bring a large pan of salted water to a boil over high heat. Carefully add the asparagus tips and blanch for 2 minutes, or until tender. Remove the asparagus with a slotted spoon and plunge into the ice-cold water. Leave for 1 minute, then drain.

—

Arrange the tips in sterilized jars (SEE p. 40), packing them well. Bring enough salted water to a boil (1 teaspoon salt per 4¼ cups/34 fl oz/ 1 liter water) in a pan and use to top off the jars. Seal with sterilized lids.

—

Process in a pressure canner (SEE p. 53 and follow the manufacturer's instructions) for 40 minutes.

# EGGPLANT

## EGGPLANTS AU NATUREL

Preparation time 10 minutes
Standing time 1 hour
Cooking time 5 minutes
Canning time 40 minutes
Makes 2 lb (900 g)

2¼ lb (1 kg) eggplants (aubergines), peeled, stalks removed, and cut into crosswise slices or small cubes
coarse salt

Place the eggplants (aubergines) in a large bowl, sprinkle ¼ with coarse salt, and stand for 1 hour. Drain and wipe the pieces dry carefully with paper towels.

—

Bring a large pan of salted water to a boil over high heat. Carefully add the eggplants (aubergines) and blanch for 5 minutes, or until tender, then drain.

—

Arrange the eggplants (aubergines) in sterilized jars (SEE p. 40), packing them well. Bring enough salted water to a boil (1 teaspoon salt per 4¼ cups/34 fl oz/1 liter water) in a pan and use to top off the jars. Seal with sterilized lids.

—

Process in a pressure canner (SEE p. 53 and follow the manufacturer's instructions) for 40 minutes.

—

When it is time to eat the eggplants (aubergines), reheat them in their preserving liquid and strain before serving.

## RATATOUILLE

Preparation time 30 minutes
Cooking time 40 minutes
Canning time 30 minutes
Makes 3¼ lb (1.5 kg)

2¼ lb (1 kg) eggplants (aubergines), peeled and
   cut into circles (rounds)
6 tablespoons olive oil
1 large onion, sliced
1 lb 2 oz (500 g) tomatoes, cored and sliced
4 large cloves garlic, finely chopped
2 teaspoons salt
1 bouquet garni (SEE p. 273)

Have ready a large bowl filled halfway with
ice cubes and enough cold water to cover the
ice. Bring a large pan of salted water to a boil
over high heat. Carefully add the eggplants
(aubergines) and blanch for 5 minutes, or until
tender. Remove the eggplants (aubergines)
with a slotted spoon and plunge into the ice-
cold water. Leave for 1 minute, then drain.

—

Heat the oil in a large pan over medium heat.
Add the onion and tomatoes and cook for
5 minutes, or until the juices start to simmer.
Add the garlic, salt, the eggplants (aubergines),
and the bouquet garni, and simmer for
30 minutes.

—

Remove the bouquet garni and transfer the
mixture to sterilized jars (SEE p. 40). Seal with
sterilized lids.

—

Process in a pressure canner (SEE p. 53 and
follow the manufacturer's instructions) for
30 minutes.

—

To serve, transfer the mixture in a pan and
bring to a simmer, adding more chopped
garlic to taste.

# BEETS

## RED BEETS, STORED FRESH IN THE CELLAR

Beets (beetroots) are quite resistant to cold.
Remove the leaves from the beets (beetroots)
and make an even pile of the roots in the
cellar. Cover with dry leaves, sawdust, or dry
sand. If the cellar is damp, don't leave the
beets (beetroots) in contact with the ground,
especially if it is cement; make a little raised
bed with bricks.

## SALTED BEETS

Preparation time 10 minutes, plus cooling
Brining time 10 days
Cooking time 10 minutes
Makes 2¼ lb (1 kg)

2¼ lb (1 kg) raw beets (beetroots), unpeeled and
    cut into slices ⅝–¾ inch/1.5–2 cm thick
3 oz (75 g) grape (vine) leaves
6 sprigs thyme
6 bay leaves
1 tablespoon black peppercorns
4 cloves
⅔ cup (3½ oz/100 g) coarse salt

The beets (beetroot) don't need to be peeled.
After rinsing, just carefully brush the skin with
a scrubbing brush.

—

Place a layer of grape (vine) leaves in a wide,
sterilized ceramic pot or glass jar (SEE p. 40) and
arrange the beets (beetroots) with alternating
layers of the herbs, peppercorns, cloves, and
more grape (vine) leaves, packing them in well,
until the pot is full.

—

Make a brine using ⅔ cup (3½ oz/100 g) coarse
salt per 4½ cups (34 fl oz/1 liter) water. Boil for
10 minutes, then remove from the heat, cool,
and pour over the beets (beetroots).

—

Push down using a small wooden plate (like the
ones used for sauerkraut), place a weight on it,
and cover with a clean cloth.

—

Pickle for 10 days in a cool place.

These salted beets (beetroots) can be used in
salads. When you are ready to eat them, rinse
and cook in a large pan of boiling water for
15 minutes until tender.

# CARDOONS

## CARDOONS (THISTLES) AU NATUREL

Preparation time 20 minutes
Cooking time 20 minutes
Canning time 25 minutes
Makes 2¼ lb (1 kg)

24 cardoons (thistles)
bottled lemon juice or citric acid, for the jars
salt

Select the most tender part of each stem and
cut into pieces 4 inches/10 cm long, trimming
them to fit into your jars. If the variety you
are dealing with has thorns, remove them
carefully.

—

Have ready a large bowl filled halfway with ice
cubes and enough cold water to cover the ice.
Bring a large pan of salted water to a boil. Add
the cardoon pieces and cook for 10 minutes.
Remove the cardoons with a slotted spoon and
plunge into the ice-cold water. Leave for
1 minute, then drain. Peel; this will be much
easier now the cardoons are poached.

—

Arrange the cardoon pieces in sterilized jars
(SEE p. 40). Bring enough salted water to a
boil (1 teaspoon salt per 4¼ cups/34 fl oz/
1 liter water) in a pan. In a large pitcher (jug),
combine enough lemon juice or citric acid
with water (2 tablespoons bottled lemon juice
or a little under ⅓ teaspoon/1.5 g citric acid
per 4¼ cups/34 fl oz/1 liter water) and use both
types of water to top off the jars. Seal with
sterilized lids.

—

Process in a pressure canner (SEE p. 53 and
follow the manufacturer's instructions) for
25 minutes.

# CARROTS

## CARROTS, STORED FRESH IN THE CELLAR

Wait for a spell of dry weather in late fall (autumn) to pick ripe carrots. Do not wash them. Leave them out to dry in a sheltered spot, such as a shed. The dirt will fall off as it dries and any external moisture will disappear.

Trim off the leafy tops, leaving ½ inch/1 cm attached to the end of each carrot. Arrange in a neat pile in the cellar and cover with sawdust or fine sand.

## CARROTS AU NATUREL

**Preparation time 10 minutes**
**Cooking time 15 minutes**
**Canning time 30 minutes**
**Makes 2¼ lb (1 kg)**

**2¼ lb (1 kg) short (small) carrots**
**salt**

Choose the short, early-harvest carrots that are ready to harvest in late early summer. Wash them very carefully; the skin is thin enough that you won't have to scrub them.

Have ready a large bowl filled halfway with ice cubes and enough cold water to cover the ice. Place the carrots in a large pan of salted water. Bring to a boil, reduce the heat, and simmer for 10 minutes. Remove the carrots with a slotted spoon and plunge into the ice-cold water. Leave for 1 minute, then drain.

Arrange the carrots in sterilized jars (SEE p. 40). Bring enough salted water to a boil (1 teaspoon salt per 4¼ cups/34 fl oz/1 liter water) in a pan and use to top off the jars. Seal with sterilized lids.

Process in a pressure canner (SEE p. 53 and follow the manufacturer's instructions) for 30 minutes.

Carrots preserved like this will make a wonderful side dish to winter dishes. Before serving, place the carrots with the canning liquid in a large pan and bring to a simmer over medium heat. Simmer for 10 minutes.

## CARROT AND LEMON JAM

Preparation time 20 minutes
Cooking time 4 hours
Canning time 5 minutes
Makes 2-3 x 1 lb 8½ oz(700 g) jars

1 lb 2 oz (500 g) carrots, cut into thin circles
    (rounds)
finely grated zest and juice of 3 lemons
scant 2 cups (13 oz/375 g) sugar

Arrange layers of carrot, lemon zest, and sugar
in a large preserving pan. Add the lemon juice
and just enough water to cover the contents of
the pan. Cook over low heat for 4 hours. The
finished jam is a golden puree with a flavor
that's surprisingly different from that
of carrots.

—

Pour into sterilized jars (SEE p. 40) and seal with
sterilized lids.

—

Process in a boiling-water canner (SEE p. 48)
and follow the manufacturer's instructions) for
5 minutes.

## DRIED CARROTS

Preparation time 5 minutes
Drying time 4-6 hours

carrots, cut into circles (rounds) ⅟₁₆-⅛ inch/
    2-3 mm thick

Dry using one of the techniques described on
pp. 30–32. The drying heat should be regular
and gentle, so the carrots will lose all their
moisture without becoming hard as wood.

—

Keep in a bag of cheesecloth (muslin) or plastic-
backed paper in a dry place. Dried carrots
may be added to soups; soak in water overnight
before using.

# CELERY

## CELERY AU NATUREL

**Preparation time 20 minutes**
**Cooking time 20 minutes**
**Canning time 25 minutes**
**Makes 2–4 x4 lb (1.8 kg) jars**

**4 bunches of celery**
**bottled lemon juice or citric acid, for the jars**
**salt**

Trim the celery bunches to a length of
4 inches/10 cm from the base. Do not separate
the sticks; leave them attached. Rinse.

—

Have ready a large bowl filled halfway with ice
cubes and enough cold water to cover the ice.
Bring a large pan of salted water to a boil. Add
the celery and cook for 10 minutes. Remove the
celery with a slotted spoon and plunge into the
ice-cold water. Leave for 1 minute, then drain.

—

Arrange the celery in sterilized jars (SEE p. 40).
Bring enough salted water to a boil (1 teaspoon
salt per 4¼ cups/34 fl oz/1 liter water) in a pan.
In a large pitcher (jug), combine enough lemon
juice or citric acid with water (2 tablespoons
bottled lemon juice or a little under ⅓
teaspoon/1.5 g citric acid per 4¼ cups/34 fl
oz/1 liter water) and use both types of water to
top off the jars. Seal with sterilized lids.

—

Process in a pressure canner (SEE p. 53 and
follow the manufacturer's instructions) for
25 minutes.

## CELERIAC, STORED FRESH IN THE CELLAR

Trim off the leaves from each head, retaining
about four from the heart.

—

Celeriac are quite resistant to cold. Remove
most of the leaves from the celeriac and
make an even pile of the roots in the cellar.
Cover with dry leaves, sawdust, or dry sand.
If the cellar is damp, don't leave the celeriac
in contact with the ground, especially if it is
cement; make a little raised bed with bricks.

—

Alternatively, place in crates filled with
12 inches/30 cm of sand or damp earth,
pushing the celeriac down so the heads are
halfway buried.

## CELERIAC AU NATUREL

Preparation time 20 minutes
Cooking time 10 minutes
Canning time 25 minutes
Makes 3 lb (1.4 kg)

2 large celeriac, peeled and cut into pieces
    ¾ inch/2 cm thick and of a diameter that
    will fit into your jars
1 lemon, cut into wedges
bottled lemon juice or citric acid, for the jars
salt

Keeping celeriac fresh in the cellar is our preferred method of preserving, and it is fairly easy to find in winter, but if you wish to can it, you'll be able to use it instead of artichoke hearts.

—

Rub the celeriac pieces with lemon wedges to prevent their color from turning.

—

Have ready a large bowl filled halfway with ice cubes and enough cold water to cover the ice. Bring a large pan of salted water to a boil. Add the celeriac and cook for 10 minutes. Remove the celeriac with a slotted spoon and plunge into the ice-cold water. Leave for 1 minute, then drain and dry carefully with a clean cloth.

—

Arrange the celeriac in layers in sterilized jars (SEE p. 40). Bring enough salted water to a boil (1 teaspoon salt per 4¼ cups/34 fl oz/1 liter water) in a pan. In a large pitcher (jug), combine enough lemon juice or citric acid with water (2 tablespoons bottled lemon juice or a little under ⅓ teaspoon/1.5 g citric acid per 4¼ cups/34 fl oz/1 liter water) and use both types of water to top off the jars. Seal with sterilized lids.

—

Process in a pressure canner (SEE p. 53 and follow the manufacturer's instructions) for 25 minutes.

# MUSHROOM

## GENERAL NOTES ON MUSHROOMS

Preserving mushrooms is only appropriate for people who live in the countryside. Mushrooms are most plentiful when there is a warm spell punctuated by a few downpours, as happens at the beginning of summer and in fall (autumn).

—

The most recommended varieties for preserving are field (or meadow) mushrooms (*Agaricus campestris*), Scotch bonnets (*Marasmius oreades*), ceps or porcini (*Boletus edulis*), chanterelles (*Cantharellus cibarius*), horns of plenty (*Craterellus cornucopioides*), and morels (*Morchella deliciosa*).

—

These are some of the best-known mushrooms, easiest to identify and most guaranteed to be safe. If you have any doubt whatsoever about a mushroom when out picking, leave it alone.

—

The following advice should be heeded for successful mushroom preservation:
• Pick your mushrooms in dry weather.
• Choose smaller mushrooms for preference.
• Discard any that have opened out too much or have worm damage.
• Preserve the mushrooms as soon as possible after collecting them.

## MUSHROOMS AU NATUREL

**Preparation time 15 minutes**
**Cooking time 15 minutes**
**Canning time 45 minutes**
**Makes 1 lb 2 oz (500 g)**

2¼ lb (1 kg) mushrooms, stalks trimmed
2 tablespoons vinegar or lemon juice,
    for rinsing
bottled lemon juice or citric acid, for the jars
salt

For mushrooms au naturel, use field
mushrooms, brown (cultivated) mushrooms,
small ceps, or chanterelles. If you have a large
quantity of mushrooms, work in smaller
batches, pound by pound.

—

Fill a large bowl with fresh water and add the
vinegar or lemon juice. Bring a large pan of
salted water to a boil.

—

Rinse the mushrooms in the acidulated water,
changing the water as many times as needed
and working delicately to avoid damaging the
mushrooms. Keep small mushrooms whole
and cut larger ones into even-size pieces.

—

Have ready a large bowl filled halfway with
ice cubes and enough cold water to cover
the ice. As soon as possible after cutting (the
mushrooms will turn black if they are left
to wait), carefully add them to the boiling
water and blanch for 10 minutes, then remove
the mushrooms with a slotted spoon and
plunge into the ice-cold water. Leave for 1
minute, then drain.

—

Transfer the mushrooms to sterilized jars (SEE
p. 40) with a skimmer, which will help drain
them further. Bring enough salted water to a
boil (1 teaspoon salt per 4¼ cups/34 fl oz/
1 liter water) in a pan. In a large pitcher (jug),
combine enough lemon juice or citric acid with
water (2 tablespoons bottled lemon juice or
a little under ⅓ teaspoon/1.5 g citric acid per
4¼ cups/34 fl oz/1 liter water) and use both
types of water to top off the jars. Seal with
sterilized lids.

—

Process in a pressure canner (SEE p. 53 and
follow the manufacturer's instructions) for
45 minutes.

## DRIED MUSHROOMS

You can use ceps, Scotch bonnet, chanterelles, horns of plenty, or morels.

—

Trim the stalks, keep only the caps of Scotch bonnets.

—

Thread the mushrooms together into garlands using a large needle and thin string or strong thread.

—

Hang in the sun for 5–6 days, then hang up in a dry place, such as the attic, for another 5–6 days. If the mushrooms are not completely dried after this time, finish drying in a low oven or a dehydrator, but never start the drying process in the oven.

—

Keep in airtight boxes.

—

To use, soak the dried mushrooms in cold water for 12 hours, changing the water several times. You can then cook the mushrooms in the same way as fresh ones.

## MUSHROOMS IN VINEGAR

Preparation time 15 minutes, plus draining
Cooking time 5 minutes
Pickling time 1 month
Makes 1 x 2¼ lb (1 kg) jar

2¼ lb (1 kg) mushrooms, stalks trimmed
2 tablespoons vinegar or lemon juice, for rinsing
4 cloves garlic, thinly sliced
2 shallots, thinly sliced
8 pearl (baby) onions, thinly sliced
4¼ cups (34 fl oz/1 liter) distilled vinegar, cold

Use brown mushrooms (cultivated), field mushrooms, or small chanterelles.

—

Fill a large bowl with fresh water and add the vinegar or lemon juice. Bring a large pan of salted water to a boil.

—

Rinse the mushrooms in the acidulated water, changing the water as many times as needed and working delicately to avoid damaging the mushrooms. Keep small mushrooms whole and cut larger ones into even-size pieces.

—

Have ready a large bowl filled halfway with ice cubes and enough cold water to cover the ice. As soon as possible after cutting (the mushrooms will turn black if they are left to wait), carefully add them to the boiling water and blanch for 5 minutes, then remove the mushrooms with a slotted spoon and plunge into the ice-cold water. Leave for 1 minute, then drain for several hours on kitchen paper.

—

Transfer the mushrooms to a large sterilized jar (SEE p. 40), in alternating layers of thinly sliced garlic, shallots and sliced pearl onions. Top off with cold vinegar. Seal with a sterilized lid.

## CEPS (PORCINI) IN OLIVE OIL

**Preparation time 15 minutes**
**Cooking time 25 minutes**
**Canning time 1 hour**
**Makes 2 x 2¼ lb (1 kg) jars**

2¼ lb (1 kg) ceps (porcini)
1¼ cups (12 fl oz/350 ml) olive oil
4 cloves garlic, chopped
1 bay leaf
4 sprigs thyme
1 tablespoon black peppercorns

Preheat the oven to 300°F/150°C/Gas Mark 2.

Separate the tops from the stems of the ceps
(porcini) and clean very carefully; worms can
often be found in larger ceps. Wipe dry with
paper towels. Cut the stems and caps into even-
size pieces.

Place the mushroom pieces on a baking sheet
in the oven for 10–15 minutes to remove some
of their moisture and wipe dry again with
paper towels.

Heat a scant ½ cup (3½ fl oz/100 ml) of the
oil in a skillet or frying pan over low heat.
Add the mushrooms and garlic and cook
over low heat for 10 minutes. Don't let the
mushrooms brown.

Transfer the mushrooms and garlic to
sterilized jars (SEE p. 40), alternating with the
bay leaf, thyme and peppercorns. Top off with
hot olive oil and seal with sterilized lids.

Process in a pressure canner (SEE p. 53 and
follow the manufacturer's instructions) for
1 hour.

# LENTILS

Dig up the lentil plants just before they come
to full maturity, otherwise the seeds will drop
to the ground. Tie them in bundles and hang
them up to dry in the attic or in a cool and well-
ventilated place.

To collect the seeds, place the lentil plants in
a cloth bag, tie it off with a string, and hit with
a stick. The pods will open and the lentils will
fall into the bag. Sort the lentils from the pods
and stems, and place them in a large-mesh
strainer to rid them of chaff.

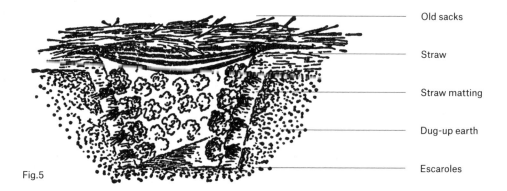

Old sacks

Straw

Straw matting

Dug-up earth

Fig.5     Escaroles

## ENDIVE (CURLY OR ESCAROLE), STORED FRESH IN THE GROUND

Curly endive (chicory) and escarole endive (broad-leaved) are two sturdy leaf vegetables that can be left in the ground through a mild winter, provided they are covered with straw matting or dry leaves. Uncover them very now and then, on a sunny day.

———

If the winter temperatures are harsher, dig a trench 2–2½ feet/60–80 cm deep, and about 3 feet/1 m wide at the top and 2 feet/60 cm wide at the bottom (FIG. 5).

———

Using a spade, dig up each head of endive and the ball of earth surrounding the root and replant in the sides of the trench. Cover with old sacks and straw (which you can keep in place with small wooden slats) or better, with straw matting. Uncover every now and then, on a sunny day.

# CABBAGE

## CABBAGE, STORED FRESH IN THE GROUND

Angle the cabbages when they are still in the ground, leaning their heads north to temper the effects of an abrupt thaw.

## IN THE OPEN AIR

Dig a shallow trench along a wall, and line the cabbages at the bottom with their heads pointing north. Cover with straw or straw matting.

## IN THE CELLAR

You can keep cabbages in stacks. Alternatively, fill crates with sand or slightly damp earth, about 12 inches/30 cm deep. Bury the stalk in the sand, leaving about 1¼ inches/3 cm between the surface and the cabbage itself.

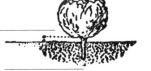

1¼ inches (3 cm)

Sand or damp earth

Fig.6

## IN THE ATTIC (PROVIDED IT WON'T FREEZE)

Tie the cabbages together in pairs by the stalks, and hang them across a beam or a piece of wood you have put up especially for this purpose, suspending it about 20 inches/50 cm from the ceiling (FIG. 7).

Fig.7

## SAUERKRAUT

**Preparation time 20 minutes**
**Pickling time 1 month at least**
**Makes 2 x 1.1 litre (2 UK pints) jars (or use**
**a small sauerkraut barrel)**

3⅓ lb (1.5 kg) green cabbage, outer leaves
    removed
2 tablespoons coarse salt
1 tablespoon black peppercorns
11 tablespoon juniper berries
salt

Line the bottom of a small sauerkraut barrel or jars with the outer green leaves.

Slice the rest of the cabbage into thin ribbons, place in a large bowl and sprinkle with the salt, rubbing the salt into the cabbage ribbons with your hands. Do this for about 5–10 minutes or until the cabbage has become watery and limp.

Add the peppercorns and juniper berries. Put the cabbage ribbons into the barrel or jars, pushing it down every so often with your fist so it is tightly packed and until the barrel or jars are about three-quarters full. Pour in any juices left in the bowl.

Cover the barrel with a piece of scrupulously clean, heavy cloth. Place the wooden lid of the barrel on top and weigh it down with a heavy weight. If using jars put a smaller jar with a weight inside on top of the cabbage to press it down and keep it submerged. Cover with a heavy cloth, fixed in place with a rubber band.

Leave in a cool place. After a couple of days the brine level will rise above the lid. Drain off some of this but make sure the cabbage is always submerged.
Let the sauerkraut pickle for at least one month; it will taste better after two months.

Every time you remove a serving of sauerkraut to eat, replace the wet cloth with a clean one and wash the lid.

Rinse the sauerkraut in several changes of water before cooking to remove the excess salt.

# CAULIFLOWER

## CAULIFLOWER, STORED FRESH IN THE CELLAR

Fill a crate with 12–16 inches/30–40 cm of damp earth, and bury the cauliflowers up to the leaves. Make sure the earth remains moist at all times.

## IN THE ATTIC (PROVIDED IT WON'T FREEZE)

When you harvest the cauliflowers, keep at least 6 inches/15 cm of the stem, and trim most of the leaves so only the first layer remains. Tie the heads together in pairs and hang astride a beam or piece of wood you have put up especially for this purpose, suspending it about 20 inches/50 cm from the ceiling.

—

The heads of cauliflower will keep this way for about two months. You will find the heads have shriveled up in the absence of water.

—

Before using, trim off a small section of the stem and make a cross-shaped cut through the base, about 1¼ inches/3 cm deep. Place the stem in water for 24 hours; the head will plump back up.

## CAULIFLOWER AU NATUREL

**Preparation time 20 minutes**
**Cooking time 3 minutes**
**Canning time 45 minutes**
**Makes 1¾ lb (800 g)**

2 tablespoons vinegar, for rinsing
2 cauliflowers, leaves removed and cut into
    even-size florets
distilled vinegar, for the jars
salt

Use summer-harvest cauliflowers for this.

—

Fill a large bowl with fresh water and add the vinegar. Bring a large pan of salted water to a boil.

—

Have ready a large bowl filled halfway with ice cubes and enough cold water to cover the ice. Rinse the cauliflower florets carefully in the vinegar water, then carefully add them to the pan of boiling water and cook for 3 minutes. Remove the cauliflower with a slotted spoon and plunge into the ice-cold water. Leave for 1 minute, then drain.

—

Arrange the florets in sterilized jars (SEE p. 40). Bring enough salted water to a boil (1 teaspoon salt per 4¼ cups/34 fl oz/1 liter water) in a pan. In a large pitcher (jug), combine enough vinegar with water (1 tablespoon distilled vinegar per 8½ cups/70 fl oz/2 liters water) and use both types of water to top off the jars. Seal with sterilized lids.

—

Process in a pressure canner (SEE p. 53 and follow the manufacturer's instructions) for 45 minutes.

## CAULIFLOWER IN VINEGAR

Preparation time 20 minutes
Cooking time 3 minutes
Pickling time 35 minutes
Makes 1lb 12 oz (800 g)

8 tablespoons vinegar, for rinsing
2 cauliflowers, 14 oz (400 g), leaves removed
    and cut into even-size florets
distilled vinegar, for the jars
salt

For sauerkraut, choose a late-harvest green cabbage variety that grows to large, dense heads with a white interior.

—

Fill a large bowl with fresh water and add a little vinegar. Bring a large pan of water a little vinegar added (1 tablespoon per 4¼ cups/ 34 fl oz/1 liter water) to a boil.

—

Have ready a large bowl filled halfway with ice cubes and enough cold water to cover the ice. Rinse the cauliflower florets carefully in the vinegar water, then carefully add them to the pan of boiling water and cook for 3 minutes. Remove the cauliflower with a slotted spoon and plunge into the ice-cold water. Leave for 1 minute, then drain thoroughly.

—

Arrange the cauliflower florets in a sterilized jar (SEE p. 00). Top off with cold vinegar until the cauliflower is completely covered. Seal with a sterilized lid (SEE p. 40).

—

Pickle for one month before eating.

# KOHLRABI

Kohlrabi is harvested in August and September, and should be small in size to ensure it is tender. It is quite resistant to cold. Remove the leaves from the kohlrabi and make an even pile of the roots in the cellar. Cover with dry leaves, sawdust, or dry sand. If the cellar is damp, don't leave the kohlrabi in contact with the ground, especially if it is cement; make a little raised bed with bricks.

—

Alternatively, place in crates filled with 12 inches (30 cm) of sand or damp earth, pushing the kohlrabi down so the heads are halfway buried.

# RED CABBAGE

## RED CABBAGE, STORED FRESH

Red cabbage can be stored in the cellar, their stalks pushed into crates of sand, leaving about 1¼ inches/3 cm between the surface and the cabbage itself.

Alternatively, they can be stored in a frost-free attic. Tie the cabbages together in pairs by the stalk, and hang them across a beam or a piece of wood you have put up especially for this purpose, suspending it about 20 inches/50 cm from the ceiling (FIG. 7, page 123).

# BELGIAN ENDIVE

## BELGIAN ENDIVES AU NATUREL

Preparation time 20 minutes
Cooking time 5 minutes
Canning time 1 hour 45 minutes
Makes 2¼ lb (1 kg)

2¼ lb (1 kg) Belgian endives, outer leaves
    removed and wiped clean
distilled vinegar, for the jars
salt

The Belgian endive is a variety of chicory with a large root. It can be grown from chicory roots, replanted in soil in a cellar at a mild temperature. This is both a way of preserving and growing the plant. Choose endives that are nicely rounded and all the same size.

—

Arrange a cloth at the bottom of a large pan (so the endives are easy to remove), then bring enough water to a boil. Carefully add the endives and blanch for 5 minutes. Pull the cloth out cautiously by four corners to drain the endives without damaging them, then refresh.

—

Arrange them neatly in sterilized jars (SEE p. 40). Bring enough salted and acidulated water to a boil (1 teaspoon salt and 1 teaspoon vinegar per 4¼ cups/34 fl oz/1 liter water) in a pan and use to top off the jars. Seal with sterilized lids.

—

Process in a pressure canner (SEE p. 53 and follow the manufacturer's instructions) for 1 hour 45 minutes.

# SPINACH

## SPINACH AU NATUREL

Preparation time 20 minutes
Cooking time 8 minutes
Canning time 90 minutes
Makes 2¼ lb (1 kg)

5 lb (2.2 kg) spinach, tough stalks removed and
    thoroughly rinsed
salt

You will have no trouble finding fresh spinach in winter, so the only benefit of preserving it is that all the preparatory work has been done and you can have a dish ready in no time. Spinach should be canned in the spring, when the leaves are tender.

—

Have ready a large bowl filled halfway with ice cubes and enough cold water to cover the ice. Bring a large pan of salted water to a boil. Carefully add the spinach in small batches and blanch for 3 minutes. Remove the spinach with a slotted spoon and plunge into the ice-cold water. Leave for 1 minute, then drain carefully.

—

Pack the spinach into sterilized jars (SEE p. 40), filling them by three-quarters. Bring enough salted water to a boil (1 teaspoon salt per 4¼ cups/34 fl oz/1 liter water) in a pan and use to top off the jars. Seal with sterilized lids.

—

Process in a pressure canner (SEE p. 53 and follow the manufacturer's instructions) for 90 minutes.

# GREEN BEANS

## GREEN BEANS AU NATUREL

**Preparation time** 20 minutes
**Cooking time** 8 minutes
**Canning time** 25 minutes
**Makes** 2¼ lb (1 kg)

2¼ lb (1 kg) green beans, trimmed
salt

Have ready a large bowl filled halfway with ice cubes and enough cold water to cover the ice. Bring a large pan of water to a boil. Carefully add the beans in small batches and blanch for 5 minutes, placing the beans in a wire basket to make them easier to remove from the pan. Remove the beans and plunge into the ice-cold water. Leave for 1 minute, then drain
—
Arrange the beans in sterilized jars (SEE p. 40), standing them up if they are too long to be laid down horizontally; you will find it easiest to lay the jar down on the table and then pile the beans up on top of one another.
—
Bring enough salted water to a boil (1 teaspoon salt per 4¼ cups/34 fl oz/1 liter water) in a pan and use to top off the jars. Seal with sterilized lids.
—
Process in a pressure canner (SEE p. 53 and follow the manufacturer's instructions) for 25 minutes.

## SALTED GREEN BEANS

**Preparation time** 20 minutes
**Soaking time** 12 hours
**Cooking time** 6 minutes
**Makes** 2¼ lb (1 kg)

2¼ lb (1 kg) green beans, rinsed well and patted
    dry with a cloth
salt
baking soda (bicarbonate of soda), for cooking

Use freshly picked beans.
—
Arrange the beans in a sterilized ceramic pot or jar (SEE p. 40), alternating a layer of salt with each layer of beans.
—
When the pot is full, place a very clean board on top and place a heavy weight on top. Cover with a cloth and store in a cool place. Leave for a minimum of three days.
—
To use the salted beans, put them in a large bowl, cover with fresh water, and soak for 12 hours to remove the salt.
—
Have ready a large bowl filled halfway with ice cubes and enough cold water to cover the ice. Bring a large pan of water to a boil. Carefully add half of the beans and blanch for 3 minutes, then remove the beans with a slotted spoon and plunge into the ice-cold water. Leave for 1 minute, then drain. Repeat with the remaining beans using fresh water.
—
Trim the beans. Cook the beans as if they were fresh, taking care to add a little baking soda (bicarbonate of soda) to the water.

## GREEN BEANS IN VINEGAR

### DRIED SHELLING BEANS

Preparation time 15 minutes
Cooking time 5 minutes
Pickling time 1 month
Makes 2½ lb (1.2 kg)

2¼ lb (1 kg) green beans, trimmed
2 cloves garlic, thinly sliced
4 shallots, thinly sliced
3½ oz (100 g) pearl (baby) onions, thinly sliced
1½ cups (12 fl oz/350 ml) distilled vinegar, cold
salt

These can be used in the same way as gherkins.

—

Bring a large pan of salted water to a boil and
have ready a large bowl filled halfway with ice
cubes and enough cold water to cover the ice.
Carefully add the beans to the boiling water
and blanch for 5 minutes, then remove them
with a slotted spoon and plunge into the ice-
cold water. Leave for 1 minute, then drain.

—

Transfer the beans to a large sterilized jar (SEE
p. 40), in alternating layers of thinly sliced
garlic, shallots and sliced pearl onions. Top off
with cold vinegar. Seal with a sterilized lid.

—

Pickle for one month before eating.

Let the pods dry and turn yellow on the plant,
and harvest at the beginning of fall (autumn).
Make sure you harvest them before the end of
the dry season.

—

Tie the beans in bunches and hang them in a
cool and well-ventilated place to finish drying.

—

To shell, place the beans in a cloth bag, tie it
off with a string, and hit with a stick. The pods
will open and the beans will fall into the bag.
Sort the beans from the pods and stems, and
place them in a large-mesh strainer to rid them
of chaff.

—

Store the beans in bags or crates, exposing
them to air regularly.

—

Dried beans should not be kept for more than
two years, or they will take too long to cook
and will remain tough.

—

To use dried beans, put them in a large bowl,
cover with fresh water, and soak for 12–20
hours. Drain.

—

To cook, put the beans in a large pan of cold
water (for older beans, add 1 teaspoon of
baking soda/bicarbonate of soda) and bring
to a boil. Reduce the heat and cook at a gentle
simmer, adding salt only when the beans are
nearly ready.

# LETTUCE

## WHOLE LETTUCES AU NATUREL

Preparation time 20 minutes
Cooking time 5 minutes
Canning time 90 minutes
Makes 2¼ lb (1 kg)

2 tablespoons vinegar
2 crisp lettuces, such as iceberg, outer leaves
    removed and core trimmed
salt

---

Fill a large bowl with fresh water and add the vinegar. Bring a large pan of salted water to a boil.

—

Have ready a large bowl filled halfway with ice cubes and enough cold water to cover the ice. Rinse the lettuce in the acidulated water, changing the water as many times as needed to remove any worms and dirt, then carefully add them to the boiling water and blanch for 5 minutes. Remove the lettuce with a slotted spoon and plunge into the ice-cold water. Leave for 1 minute, then drain.

—

Transfer the lettuce to sterilized jars (SEE p. 40), packing them well. Bring enough salted water to a boil (1 teaspoon salt per 4¼ cups/34 fl oz/1 liter water) in a pan and use to top off the jars. Seal with sterilized lids.

—

Process in a pressure canner (SEE p. 53 and follow the manufacturer's instructions) for 90 minutes.

# SORREL

## STEWED SORREL

Preparation time 20 minutes, plus overnight
    cooling
Cooking time 3 minutes
Makes 1 lb 2 oz (500 g)

4½ lb (2 kg) sorrel leaves, trimmed, stalks and
    large ribs removed
fat, such as beef, veal, or pork using 1½ oz
    (40 g) per 2¼ lb (1 kg) of sorrel
3 oz (75 g) lard

---

Sorrel is best picked in spring or early fall (autumn); it is more acidic and often turns yellow during the summer.

—

Heat the fat in a large nonreactive pan over medium heat. Add the sorrel and cook, stirring frequently for 3 minutes, or until wilted. The sorrel will reduce in volume and turn very soft.

—

Drain, transfer to a sterilized jar (SEE p. 40), and cool overnight. There should be no water on the surface in the morning. If there is, repeat the cooking and cooling process until you get a puree with no excess moisture.

—

Melt the lard in a skillet or frying pan over low heat. Drizzle the melted lard over the surface of the sorrel until it is ¾ inch/2 cm deep. Seal with a sterilized lid. This will keep in the refrigerator for a few weeks; once the fat seal is broken, eat within 4–5 days.

## SORREL AU NATUREL

Preparation time 20 minutes
Cooking time 5 minutes
Canning time 90 minutes
Makes 1 lb 2 oz (500 g)

4½ lb (2 kg) sorrel leaves, trimmed, stalks
    and large ribs removed
salt and freshly ground black pepper

Cook the sorrel in a large nonreactive pan over medium heat, stirring frequently for 5 minutes, or until wilted. Season with salt and pepper.
—
Transfer the sorrel to sterilized jars (SEE p. 40). Bring enough salted water to a boil (1 teaspoon salt per 4¼ cups/34 fl oz/1 liter water) in a pan and use to top off the jars. Seal with sterilized lids.
—
Process in a pressure canner (SEE p. 53 and follow the manufacturer's instructions) for 90 minutes.

# SWEET POTATOES

## SWEET POTATOES, STORED FRESH

The tubers are very fragile and should not be bruised or scratched. They will keep well buried in dry earth, but at a warm temperature (64–60°F/18–20°C), ideally in a heated cellar or a greenhouse.

## SWEET POTATO JAM

Preparation time 20 minutes
Cooking time 40-65 minutes
Canning time 5 minutes
Makes 2¼ lb (1 kg)

2 lb (900 g) sweet potatoes, unpeeled
2 lb (900 g) sugar
1 vanilla bean (pod) or ¼ teaspoon vanilla
    powder (optional)

Preheat the oven to 400°F/200°C/Gas Mark 6. Pierce the sweet potatoes several times with a fork, place on a nonstick baking sheet, and roast in the oven for 45 minutes, or until tender. Leave until cool enough to handle, then peel. Alternatively, steam the sweet potatoes for 20 minutes, or until tender, then peel off the skins. Put the sweet potatoes in a large bowl and mash to a puree.
—
Weigh the puree, and transfer to a large preserving pan with the same weight of sugar, and 1¼ cups (10 fl oz/300 ml) water per 2¼ lb (1 kg) of puree. Add some vanilla if desired and cook over low heat for 20 minutes. The mixture will resemble sweet chestnut puree when it is finished cooking.
—
Transfer the puree to a sterilized jar (SEE p. 40) and seal with a sterilized lid.
—
Process in a boiling-water canner (SEE pp. 52–3 and follow the manufacturer's instructions) for 5 minutes.

# PEAS

## PETITS POIS AU NATUREL

> Preparation time 30 minutes
> Cooking time 2 minutes
> Canning time 40 minutes
> Makes 2¼ lb (1 kg)
>
> 4½ lb (2 kg) fresh peas, shelled
> baking soda (bicarbonate of soda), for the jar
> salt

Choose early-harvest peas that are not too young (these have too high a water content) nor too ripe (these can be starchy and often maggoty). Ideally, they should be harvested in the early morning before sunrise, and the preparation should be carried out as soon as you are finished picking.

—

Have ready a large bowl filled halfway with ice cubes and enough cold water to cover the ice. Bring a large pan of salted water to a boil. Carefully add the peas and blanch for 2 minutes. Remove the peas with a slotted spoon or skimmer and plunge into the ice-cold water. Leave for 1 minute, then drain.

—

Transfer the peas to sterilized jars (SEE p. 40). Bring enough salted water to a boil (1 teaspoon salt per 4¼ cups/34 fl oz/1 liter water) in a pan, adding enough baking soda (bicarbonate of soda) (just under 1 teaspoon per 4¼ cups/34 fl oz/1 liter water) to keep the peas green, and use to top off the jars. Seal with sterilized lids.

—

Process in a pressure canner (SEE p. 53 and follow the manufacturer's instructions) for 40 minutes.

## DRIED PEAS

Let the pods dry and turn yellow on the plant, and harvest in mid to late fall (autumn). Make sure you harvest them before the end of the dry season.

—

Thread the pods together with strong thread with a large needle and hang these garlands up to dry in a cool and well-ventilated place.

—

To shell, place the peas in a cloth bag, tie it off with a string, and hit with a stick. The pods will open and the peas will fall into the bag. Sort the peas from the pods and stems, and place them in a large-mesh strainer to rid them of chaff.

—

Store the peas in bags or crates, exposing them to air regularly.

—

Dried peas should not be kept for more than two years, or they will take too long to cook and will remain tough.

## SPLIT PEAS

Pick very ripe peas that are starting to go yellow on the plant and shell them.

—

Put the peas out to dry in the sun until the outer skin covering the two inner halves of the pea can be removed easily without damaging (sometimes the skin is easy to remove at the shelling step). Do this by hand, delicately.

—

Dry the split peas for a few more days in the sun.

—

Complete the drying process in a low oven with the door ajar, or in a dehydrator.

# LEEKS

## LEEKS, STORED FRESH IN THE GROUND

Leeks stand the cold well. Cover the leek bed with a thick bed of leaves.

## STORED FRESH IN THE CELLAR

Fill some crates 12–16 inches/30–40 cm deep with sand or moist earth. Trim off part of the green leaves from the leeks, and push the leeks into the earth quite deeply, so the white part is entirely buried (FIG. 8).

Leeks are readily available throughout the year, so there is no real merit in canning them.

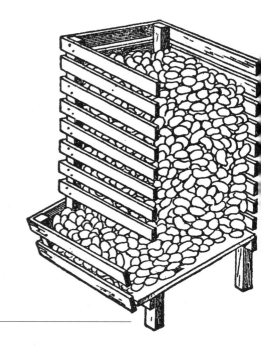

Fig.9

12–16 inches (30–40 cm)

Sand or moist earth

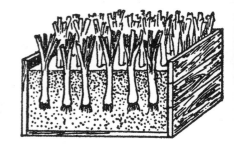

Fig.8

# POTATOES

## POTATOES, STORED FRESH

To store for winter, choose late-harvest potatoes ready for picking in mid fall (autumn).

—

Potatoes should never be left in sacks, and should be sorted carefully; remove any that are shriveled or bruised. Make sure you remove any eyes, which will sprout tubers.

—

The best place to store them is in the cellar or cupboard, provided it is dark and cool. It should be well ventilated, too, but any vent or opening should be closed off with rags or straw in case of frost.

—

If the potatoes have been picked from your own garden or backyard, leave them out to air-dry for a few days first, in a sheltered spot.

—

Germinating potatoes produce solanine, which is poisonous and is found in the green parts of potatoes exposed to the sun. Any potato that has germinated should be peeled entirely before using.

## STORED FRESH IN A STACK

Arrange the potatoes on a bed of dry straw or dry sand, forming piles no larger than 3 feet/ 1 m across or 3 feet/1 m high. Go through the stack two or three times over the course of the winter to remove the sprouts and reposition the potatoes.

## STORED FRESH IN A VENTILATED BIN

Potatoes can be stored in a bin with ventilated sides, as is done in Switzerland; the potatoes are collected from an opening at the bottom (FIG. 9).

## STORED FRESH IN A SILO

For perfect keeping until early to mid spring, and if you have enough space in your garden or backyard, store your potato harvest in a silo.

—

Take advantage of a spell of dry weather in October to arrange the potatoes in a pile, about 5 feet/1.5 m high, and let them air for a few days.

—

Next, cover the pile with a layer of straw (8 inches/20 cm thick) and a layer of earth (8 inches/20 cm thick). Follow with a thinner layer of straw (2 inches/5 cm thick) and a thinner layer of earth (4 inches/10 cm thick). Create a ventilation duct at the top that you will stopper with straw.

—

If the soil is damp, take the precaution of digging a channel all around the silo to catch rainwater.

# PUMPKIN

## PUMPKINS, STORED FRESH

For winter storage, pick pumpkins in late fall (autumn).

—

Cut the stems to separate from the vine and leave in place in the sun for a few days before removing them to the cellar or larder, on a bed of straw or wooden boards. Some varieties are smaller than others, and these are easier to move and store.

—

Pumpkins should be kept out of reach of frost.

## PUMPKIN JAM

Preparation time 30 minutes
Steeping time 24 hours
Cooking time 45 minutes
Canning time 5 minutes
Makes 3 x 1 lb (450 g) jars

1 small pumpkin, peeled, seeded, and finely diced
2½ cups (1 lb 2 oz/500 g) sugar
2 lemons, finely diced

You need 2¼ lb (1 kg) peeled pumpkin flesh.

—

Put the pumpkin, sugar and lemons in a large bowl and mix together to combine. Cover with plastic wrap (clingfilm) and steep for 24 hours.

—

The next day, put a small plate or saucer in the freezer to chill. Put the mixture into a large preserving pan and cook over low heat for 45 minutes. To test for a set, pour several drops of jam onto the chilled plate and when you tip the plate the juice should not run.

—

Transfer the jam to sterilized jars (SEE p. 40) and seal with sterilized lids.

—

Process in a boiling-water canner (SEE pp. 52–3 and follow the manufacturer's instructions) for 5 minutes.

## PUMPKIN AND DRIED APRICOT JAM

Preparation time 30 minutes
Soaking time 24 hours
Cooking time 50 minutes
Canning time 5 minutes
Makes 10–12 x 1 lb (450 g) jars

5¾ cups (2¼ lb/1 kg) unsulfured dried apricots, rinsed and cut into strips
4½ lb (2 kg) pumpkin, peeled, seeded, and diced
13½ cups (6 lb/2.7 kg) sugar

Put the apricot strips in a bowl, cover with 6¼ cups (53 fl oz/1.5 liters) water, and soak for 24 hours. Strain, setting the water aside.

—

Put a small plate or saucer in the freezer to chill. Pour the apricot soaking water into a large preserving pan, add the diced pumpkin, and bring to a boil. Boil for 15 minutes. Remove from the heat and pass the pumpkin through a fine strainer, then return the pumpkin to the pan, add the sugar, and cook for another 15 minutes. Add the apricots and cook for 15 minutes. To test for a set, pour several drops of jam onto the chilled plate and when you tip the plate the juice should not run.

—

Transfer the jam to sterilized jars (SEE p. 40) and seal with sterilized lids.

—

Process in a boiling-water canner (SEE pp. 52–3 and follow the manufacturer's instructions) for 5 minutes.

# SALSIFY

## SALSIFY, STORED FRESH IN THE CELLAR

Salsify is picked from early winter to mid spring, but can't be harvested during cold weather when the ground is too hard, so it is good to keep a supply in the cellar.

———

Gather the salsify in bundles. Arrange a layer of moist sand in the cellar and lay the salsify on it at a slight angle, to let the leaves sprout; these can be eaten in salads.

# TOMATOES

## WHOLE TOMATOES AU NATUREL

**Preparation time 20 minutes**
**Canning time 15–45 minutes**
**Makes 6½ lb (3 kg)**

**6½ lb (3 kg) tomatoes**
**bottled lemon juice or citric acid, for the jars**
**salt**

For preserving, choose tomatoes that are not too watery, favoring those picked early in the season (around mid summer). Select tomatoes of the same size if you can; they should be freshly picked and unblemished.

———

Peel the tomatoes. If the skin doesn't peel off easily, poach the tomatoes in a pan of boiling water for 30 seconds to loosen, then drain and peel. Carve a hole on the stalk side, and run a small spoon inside to remove the seeds.

———

Add 2 tablespoons bottled lemon juice (or just under ⅓ teaspoon/1.5 g citric acid) to each sterilized jar (SEE p. 40) and add the tomatoes, packing them as much as possible. Bring enough salted water to a boil (1 teaspoon salt per 4¼ cups/34 fl oz/1 liter water) in a pan and use to top off the jars. Seal with sterilized lids.

———

Process in a boiling-water canner (SEE p. 52 and follow the manufacturer's instructions) for 45 minutes, or in a pressure canner (SEE p. 53) for 15 minutes.

———

These whole tomatoes can be served as a side, cooked with onions and garlic as is traditional in Provence, or used as a garnish.

## TOMATO PUREE

Preparation time 30 minutes
Cooking time 20-30 minutes
Canning time 15-40 minutes
Makes 1 lb 2 oz (500 g)

6 lb (2.7 kg) ripe tomatoes, cut into quarters
bottled lemon juice or citric acid, for the jars
salt and freshly ground black pepper

Crush the tomatoes in a large nonreactive pan and cook over medium heat for 20–30 minutes until the puree has reduced by one third to one half. Push the puree through a strainer or food mill to remove the skins and seeds. Season the remaining mixture with salt and pepper.

—

Add 2 tablespoons bottled lemon juice (or just under ⅓ teaspoon/1.5 g citric acid) to each 1 lb 2 oz (500-g) sterilized jar (SEE p. 40), add the puree, and seal with sterilized lids.

Process in a boiling-water canner (SEE p. 52 and follow the manufacturer's instructions) for 40 minutes, or in a pressure canner (SEE p. 53) for 15 minutes.

—

This puree can be used for sauces and soups; bring to a simmer again in a pan before using.

## TOMATO SAUCE

Preparation time 30 minutes
Cooking time 1 hour 20 minutes
Canning time 15-40 minutes
Makes 8½ cups (68 fl oz/2 liters)

11 lb (5 kg) tomatoes, cored and cut into
    quarters
2¼ lb (1 kg) onions, sliced
1 large bouquet garni (SEE p. 273)
bottled lemon juice or citric acid, for the
    jarssalt and freshly ground black pepper

Crush the tomatoes into a nonreactive pan with the onions and bouquet garni. Cook over medium heat for 30–40 minutes, stirring frequently. Remove and discard the bouquet garni. Press the tomatoes through a strainer or food mill to remove the skins and seeds. Return the puree to the pan and cook for 40 minutes, or until it reaches a fairly thick consistency.

—

Add 2 tablespoons bottled lemon juice (or just under 1 teaspoon/1.5 g citric acid) to each sterilized preserving bottle or jar (SEE p. 40). Add the sauce and seal with sterilized lids.

—

Process in a boiling-water canner (SEE p. 52 and follow the manufacturer's instructions) for 40 minutes, or in a pressure canner (SEE p. 53) for 15 minutes.

## SALTED TOMATOES

Preparation time 20 minutes
Cooking time 2 minutes
Brining time 3-4 weeks
Makes 6½ lb (3 kg)

6½ lb (3 kg) small not overly ripe tomatoes
⅔ cup (3½ oz/100 g) coarse salt

Poke each tomato with a large needle in five or six places.

—

Have ready a large bowl filled halfway with ice cubes and enough cold water to cover the ice. Bring a large pan of salted water to a boil. Carefully add the tomatoes and blanch for 2 minutes. Remove the tomatoes with a slotted spoon and plunge into the ice-cold water. Leave for 1 minute, then drain.

—

Transfer to sterilized ceramic pots or glass jars (SEE p. 40). Make a brine using ⅔ cup (3½ oz/100 g) coarse salt per 4¼ cups (34 fl oz/ 1 liter) water. Boil for 10 minutes, then remove from the heat, cool, and pour over the tomatoes.

—

Push down using a small wooden plate (like the ones used for sauerkraut), place a weight on it, and cover with a clean cloth.

—

Pickle for 3–4 weeks. Rinse in several changes of water before use to remove excess salt. Eat raw or use in soups and sauces.

## GREEN TOMATOES IN VINEGAR

Preparation time 20 minutes, plus cooling
Cooking time 10 minutes
Pickling time 24 hours, plus 1-2 months
Makes 1¼ lb (500 g)

1 lb 2 oz (500 g) very small green tomatoes
4 sprigs tarragon
6 oz (175 g) pearl (baby) onions
3 red chiles
1¼ cups (10 fl oz/300 ml) distilled vinegar
4 sprigs chervil
1 teaspoon black peppercorns
salt

Cherry or plum tomatoes are ideal for preserving in vinegar.

—

Bring a large pan of salted water to a boil. Carefully add the tomatoes and blanch for 1 minute, then drain.

—

Transfer the tomatoes to a large sterilized jar (SEE p. 40), arranging the tomatoes with alternating layers of tarragon, pearl (baby) onions, and chiles.

—

Bring the vinegar to a boil in a medium pan and boil for 5 minutes, then carefully pour it into the jar. Cover with a sterilized lid and pickle for 24 hours.

—

Remove the tomatoes from the jar, setting the vinegar aside. Pour the vinegar into a medium pan and bring to a boil again, then remove from the heat and cool.

—

Pack the tomatoes down into the jar, adding the chervil and peppercorns. Top off with the cooled vinegar and seal with a sterilized lid.

—

Pickle for 1–2 months before eating, and use as you would gherkins.

## TOMATO JUICE

Preparation time 30 minutes
Cooking time 5 minutes
Canning time 15–40 minutes
Makes 2 x 17 fl oz (500 ml) bottles

4 tablespoons bottled lemon juice or citric
 acid, for the bottles
5 lb (2.3 kg) unblemished ripe tomatoes, cored
 and cut into quarters
ground spices, to serve

Have ready some 18-fl-oz (500-g) sterilized
preserving bottles (SEE p. 40) and add
2 tablespoons bottled lemon juice (or just under
⅓ teaspoon/1.5 g citric acid) to each.
—
Crush the tomatoes into a large nonreactive
pan. Bring to a boil, then reduce the heat and
simmer for 5 minutes as you continue to crush
the tomatoes. Press the tomatoes through
a strainer or food mill so you are left with
the juice and pulp only, then transfer even
amounts of the juice and pulp to the prepared
bottles. Seal with sterilized lids.
—
Process in a boiling-water canner (SEE p. 52
and follow the manufacturer's instructions) for
40 minutes, or in a pressure canner (SEE p. 53)
for 15 minutes.
—
Serve chilled, seasoned with ground spices.

## RED TOMATO JAM

Preparation time 30 minutes
Cooking time 2 hours
Canning time 5 minutes
Makes 1 lb 5 oz (600 g)

1 lb 2 oz (500 g) tomatoes, cut into chunks
2½ cups (1 lb 2 oz/500 g) sugar
¼ cup (2 fl oz/60 ml) dark rum

Put a small plate or saucer in the freezer to
chill. Push the tomatoes through a strainer or
food mill, then transfer the pulp and juice to a
large preserving pan and add the sugar. Bring
to a boil over low heat and cook at a low but
steady boil for 1 hour, skimming off any foam
that forms on the surface. Add the rum and
cook for another hour. To test for a set, pour
several drops of jam onto the chilled plate and
when you tip the plate the juice should not run.
—
Transfer the jam to sterilized jars (SEE p. 40)
and seal with sterilized lids.
—
Process in a boiling-water canner (SEE p. 52
and follow the manufacturer's instructions) for
5 minutes.

## GREEN TOMATO JAM

Preparation time 30 minutes
Steeping time 24 hours
Cooking time 1 hour
Canning time 5 minutes
Makes 1 lb 5 oz (600 g)

1 lb 2 oz (500 g) green tomatoes, thinly sliced
2½ cups (1 lb 2 oz/500 g) sugar
finely grated zest and juice of 1 lemon

Arrange the tomatoes in a deep ceramic or glass dish, alternating layers of tomatoes and sugar. Cover with plastic wrap (clingfilm) and steep for 24 hours.

—

Put a small plate or saucer in the freezer to chill. Transfer the tomatoes and sugar to a large preserving pan, adding the lemon zest and juice. Bring to a boil over low heat and cook at a low but steady boil for 1 hour, skimming off any foam that forms on the surface. To test for a set, pour several drops of jam onto the chilled plate and when you tip the plate the juice should not run.

—

Transfer the jam to sterilized jars (SEE p. 40) and seal with sterilized lids.

—

Process in a boiling-water canner (SEE p. 52 and follow the manufacturer's instructions) for 5 minutes.

# MIXED VEGETABLES

## JULIENNE AU NATUREL

Preparation time 30 minutes
Cooking time 5 minutes
Canning time 90 minutes
Makes 6½ lb (3 kg)

2 lb (900 g) carrots, cut into thin strips
1 lb (450 g) turnips, cut into thin strips
2 large leeks, cut into thin strips
2 large onions, chopped
2 lb (900 g) cabbage, cut into thin strips
salt

This is made with a mix of carrots, turnips, leeks, onions, and cabbage, and can be used in soups.

—

Have ready a large bowl filled halfway with ice cubes and enough cold water to cover the ice. Arrange a cloth at the bottom of a large pan (so the vegetables are easy to remove), then bring enough salted water to a boil. Carefully add the vegetables and blanch for 5 minutes. Remove them by carefully pulling all four corners of the cloth. Drain and plunge into the ice-cold water. Leave for 1 minute, then drain again.

—

Transfer the vegetables to sterilized jars (SEE p. 40). Bring enough salted water to a boil (1 teaspoon salt per 4¼ cups/34 fl oz/1 liter water) in a pan and use to top off the jars. Seal with sterilized lids.

—

Process in a pressure canner (SEE p. 53 and follow the manufacturer's instructions) for 90 minutes.

# VEGETABLE MACÉDOINE

**Preparation time 40 minutes**
**Cooking time 5 minutes**
**Canning time 90 minutes**
**Makes 5¼ lb (2.4 kg)**

12 oz (350 g) artichoke hearts, cut into
    ½-inch/1-cm cubes
10 oz (275 g) carrots, cut into ½-inch/
    1-cm cubes
7 oz (200 g) turnips, cut into ½-inch/
    1-cm cubes
14 oz (400 g) green beans, cut into ½-inch/
    1-cm cubes
11 oz (300 g) fresh peas, shelled
14 oz (400 g) lima (butter) beans, shelled
11 oz (300 g) cauliflower florets
salt

Such mixed vegetables can be prepared in any season, but they take a while to prepare, so if you find yourself with volunteer helpers (such as children on summer vacation) you can put up a few jars that will no doubt come in handy.

—

Have ready a large bowl filled halfway with ice cubes and enough cold water to cover the ice. Place each vegetable into a separate cheesecloth (muslin) bag.

—

Bring a large pan of salted water to a boil. Carefully add the vegetables and blanch for 5 minutes, then remove the vegetables with a slotted spoon and plunge into the ice-cold water. Leave for 1 minute, then drain well.

—

Transfer the vegetables to sterilized jars (SEE p. 40), arranging them in alternating layers of color (or any artistic arrangement you please).

Bring enough salted water to a boil (1 teaspoon salt per 4¼ cups/34 fl oz/1 liter water) in a pan and use to top off the jars. Seal with sterilized lids.

—

Process in a pressure canner (SEE p. 53 and follow the manufacturer's instructions) for 90 minutes.

—

NOTE: If you don't mind having all the vegetables mixed in the jar, you can blanch them all together.

# PRESERVED TURNIPS

Fall-harvest (autumn-harvest) turnips can be
stored fresh in the cellar. Cut off the leaves
and trim the stalk base to prevent sprouting.
Arrange on a board slightly raised from the
ground, and cover with straw. Those turnip
varieties whose entire root bulb remains below
ground can be kept there through the winter.
Simply cover with a thick bed of dry leaves.
Since turnips are easily available throughout
the winter, and spring turnips appear in the
stores while winter ones are still available,
there is little point in canning them. If you are
absolutely determined to do so, however, use
spring-harvest varieties

**Preparation time 15 minutes**
**Cooking time 10 minutes**
**Canning time 30 minutes**
**Makes 1¾ lb (800 g)**

**1¾ lb (800 g) turnips**
**salt**

Have ready a large bowl filled halfway with ice
cubes and enough cold water to cover the ice.
Place the turnips in a large pan of salted water,
Bring to a boil, reduce the heat, and simmer for
10 minutes. Remove the turnips with a slotted
spoon and plunge into the ice-cold water.
Leave for 1 minute, then drain.

—

Arrange the turnips in sterilized jars (SEE
p. 40). Bring enough salted water to a boil (1
teaspoon salt per 4¼ cups/34 fl oz/1 liter water)
in a pan and use to top off the jars. Seal with
sterilized lids.

—

Process in a pressure canner (SEE p. 53 and
follow the manufacturer's instructions) for
30 minutes.

—

Before serving, place the turnips with the
canning liquid in a large pan and bring
to a simmer over medium heat. Simmer for
10 minutes.

FRUITS

During the summer period, fruit are both abundant and varied (SEE Kitchen Garden calendar, pp. 18–20), and preserving them will make it easier to prepare varied, fruit-based desserts for the remaining months of the year.

There are many ways of preserving fruit, which require more or less work, and a short to long cooking time: fruit may be canned, dried, candied (crystallized), or made into jam.

Jam is especially versatile and can be enjoyed on many occasions during the day, for breakfast, as a snack, or for dessert. It brightens up a wide range of dishes, too, such as yogurt, cheese, rice and semolina cakes, desserts, pancakes, tarts, sponge cakes, shortbread cookies (biscuits), etc.

### GENERAL NOTES

- Sort the fruit with care and use only those that are both ripe and in perfect condition.
- Work in a perfectly clean environment, with perfectly clean utensils.
- Fruit is high in acid, so use a stainless steel knife to prevent the fruit blackening.
- For canning and jam-making, please refer to the full instructions given on pp. 35–55. The processing times are indicated for jars no larger than 1 lb 2 oz (500 g) in capacity; processing time must be increased if using larger jars.
- When making preserves, use granulated or preserving sugar as both have large grains that dissolve easily.
- For jam-making we've given indicative cooking times, but you should always test for a set before putting into jars, as explained on p. 41.
- When testing jams and jellies for set (SEE p.41, always take the pan off the heat while the test is done. If the correct temperature hasn't been reached, return the pan to the heat and test again in 5 minutes.
- For best canning results, use fruit that was freshly picked from the backyard or garden, ideally early in the morning.
- During the canning process, berries and fruit chunks tend to rise to the surface. While this cannot be totally avoided, heating very slowly until boiling point gives the jars a better appearance.
- You will find instructions referring to sugar syrup and its various stages on pp. 36–8.
- If you wish to store fresh fruit, do so in a well-aired spot with a constant temperature of 39–42.8°F/4–6°C. Always place the fruit on open shelves, without the fruit touching, sitting on their least ripe side, and keep the ripest fruit at the front. Check on them and remove any spoilt fruit on a daily basis.

# APRICOTS

## APRICOTS, STORED FRESH

For storing, pick apricots before they are fully ripe and arrange them on a layer of well-dried straw, leaving some room between each, in a dry place and away from the light. Keep for no longer than 10 days.

## APRICOTS AU NATUREL

**Preparation time 20 minutes**
**Canning time 40 minutes**
**Makes 3 x 1 lb 2 oz (500 g) jars**

4½ lb (2 kg) apricots, halved and pitted
3 tablespoons sugar
3 tablespoons bottled lemon juice

Choose quality, unblemished apricots.

—

Arrange the apricot halves in sterilized jars (SEE p.40), skin side up, packing them in well. Add 1 tablespoon sugar and 1 tablespoon bottled lemon juice to each jar. Seal with sterilized lids.

—

Process in a boiling-water canner (SEE p. 53 and follow the manufacturer's instructions) for 40 minutes.

## APRICOTS IN SYRUP

Preparation time 20 minutes
Cooking time 5 minutes
Canning time 40 minutes
Makes about 3 x 1 lb 2 oz (500 g) jars

4½ lb (2 kg) apricots, halved and pitted
3 tablespoons sugar, plus extra for making
   the syrup
3 tablespoons bottled lemon juice

Arrange the apricot halves in sterilized jars
(SEE p. 40), skin side up, packing them in well.
Add 1 tablespoon sugar and 1 tablespoon
bottled lemon juice to each jar.
—
For the sugar syrup, bring 2 cups (14 oz/400 g)
sugar per 4¼ cups (34 fl oz/1 liter) water to a
boil in a pan. Boil for 2–3 seconds, then remove
from the heat. Carefully top off the jars with
the boiling syrup, then seal with sterilized lids.
—
Process in a boiling-water canner (SEE p. 53
and follow the manufacturer's instructions)
for 40 minutes.

## APRICOT JAM

Preparation time 20 minutes
Cooking time 30 minutes
Canning time 5 minutes
Makes about 4 x 1 lb 2 oz (500 g) jars

2¼ lb (1 kg) apricots, halved and pitted,
   setting the pits aside
5 cups (2¼ lb/1 kg) sugar

The advantage of this recipe is the fruit halves
are candied whole, but it does require you to
prepare a small pearl syrup.
—
Weigh the halved apricots. Crack 12 of the pits
and remove the kernels. Bring a large pan of
water to a boil over high heat. Add the kernels
and blanch for 2 minutes, then drain, peel, and
set aside.
—
Heat the sugar and water (10¾ cups /90 fl
oz/2.5 liters) gently in a pan, stirring until
the sugar has dissolved, then bring to a boil
and boil rapidly until it reaches the small
pearl stage (232°F/111°C), or when tiny round
beads form at the surface of the syrup, and
when dropped into a glass of cold water it
forms threads of about 1½–2 inches/4–5 cm
in length. Lower in the fruit and, as soon as
the syrup boils again, lift them out with a
slotted spoon and set aside. Skim the syrup if
necessary with a slotted spoon.
—
Boil the syrup to the small pearl stage again.
Put the apricots back in and bring to a boil.
Add the peeled kernels and remove the pan
from the heat. Pour the mixture into sterilized
jars (SEE p. 40) and seal with sterilized lids.
—
Process in a boiling-water canner (SEE p. 53
and follow the manufacturer's instructions)
for 5 minutes.

## CANDIED APRICOTS

Preparation time 40 minutes
Soaking time 30 minutes
Cooking time 1 hour
Steeping time 48 hours
Makes about 3 lb (1.4 kg)

2 tablespoons distilled vinegar
4½ lb (2 kg) apricots, halved and pitted
sugar

Fill a large bowl with 2 tablespoons distilled vinegar per 4¼ cups/34 fl oz/1 liter water. Add the apricots and soak in the acidulated water for 30 minutes. Drain and put the fruit in a saucepan and pour in enough cold water to cover. Have ready a large bowl filled halfway with ice cubes and enough cold water to cover the ice. Place the pan with the apricots over high heat and heat until the fruit bobs to the surface, then drain and plunge the fruit into the ice-cold water. Leave for 1 minute, then drain again.

—

Put the same weight of sugar as the fruit in a pan, adding a scant ½ cup (3½ fl oz/100 ml) water per ⅓ cup (2¼ oz /60 g) sugar. Heat gently, stirring until the sugar has dissolved, then bring to a boil and boil rapidly until it reaches the small thread stage (225°F/107°C), or when the syrup thickens and the bubbles grow larger, and when a teaspoon of the syrup is dropped into a glass of cold water it forms thin threads that cannot be rolled into small balls when lifted out. Lower in the fruit and bring back to a boil. Remove from the heat and leave the fruit in the syrup overnight.

The next day, carefully remove the fruit with a slotted spoon and set aside. Heat the syrup until it reaches the large thread stage (228–230°F/109–110°C), or when dropped into a glass of water, it forms threads of about about ¾–1¼ inches/2–3 cm long. Lower in the fruit and bring back to a boil. When the syrup boils, remove from the heat and leave the fruit in the syrup overnight.

—

Repeat the process over the next four days, increasing the sugar concentration by 1.8°F/1°C each day until the syrup reaches the large pearl stage (237°F/114°C), or when small beads form on the surface of the syrup, and if you blow on a skimmer coated with the syrup, bubbles form at the edges.

—

Remove the fruit from the syrup with a slotted spoon and drain well. Place the fruit on a rack, standing the rack on a tray, sheet of parchment paper, or aluminum foil to catch any drips, and leave to dry in a well-ventilated place.

## APRICOT FRUIT PASTE

**Preparation time 30 minutes**
**Cooking time 1 hour 10 minutes**
**Drying time 4-5 days**
**Makes about 50 pieces**

2¼ lb (1 kg) apricots, halved and pitted
1 lb 2 oz (500 g) sugar, plus extra for dusting
a little tasteless oil, for oiling

Choose ripe apricots with no blemishes.
—
Put the apricots in a large pan, cover with
cold water, bring to the boil and cook for 30
minutes, or until the fruit is soft.
—
Using a wooden spoon, push the fruit through
a strainer (or process in a food processor) to
form a puree.
—
Weigh the pureed fruit and return it to the pan
with the same weight in sugar. Put the pan over
medium heat and cook, stirring constantly
for about 40 minutes, or until the mixture
becomes thick enough that it pulls away from
the bottom of the pan. At this point, the water
will have completely evaporated.
—
Pour the paste onto an oiled marble slab, or
oiled pie dishes, dust the surface with sugar,
and dry for 4-5 days in a cool place.
—
Cut the paste into the shapes of your choice
(such as squares, diamonds, rounds, half-
moons, etc.) and dust the cut surfaces with
more sugar until they are coated.
—
They will keep for months in an airtight
container, with a sheet of parchment paper
between each layer.

## SUNDRIED APRICOTS

These can only be prepared in a very warm
and dry climate, which will result in naturally
sweet apricots with very little water content.
—
Halve and pit the apricots. Place the fruit
halves on racks and leave in the sun all day.
Bring back inside at night.
—
Repeat several days in a row, flipping the
apricots daily.
—
Complete the drying process by placing the
fruit in a low oven preheated to 122–140°F/50–
60°C/lowest possible Gas Mark setting. The
fruit halves must be dark red in color and
wrinkled. Flatten each half to give it a regular
shape.
—
Before using, soak in a bowl of cold water for
12 hours to plump up.

## DEHYDRATED APRICOTS

Drying time 12 hours

---

Halve and pit the apricots. Place the apricot halves in a dehydrator for 12 hours, at a temperature that increases progressively from 104–158°F/40°C–70°C.

## APRICOTS IN EAU-DE-VIE, PLUS COOLING

Preparation time 30 minutes, plus cooling
Cooking time 1 hour
Steeping time 6 days plus 2 months
Makes about 2 x 4¼ cups (34 fl oz/1 liter) jars

4½ lb (2 kg) apricots, wiped
6⅔ cups (3 lb/1.32 kg) sugar
4¼ cups (34 fl oz/1 liter) eau-de-vie at 45%

---

Prick the apricots to the pit with a large sewing needle.

—

Heat the sugar and water (2½ cups/ 21 fl oz/600 ml) gently in a large pan, stirring until the sugar has dissolved, then bring to a boil and boil rapidly until it reaches the small thread stage (225°F/107°C), or when the syrup thickens and the bubbles grow larger, and when a teaspoon of the syrup is dropped into a glass of cold water it forms thin threads that cannot be rolled into small balls when lifted out. Lower in the apricots, boil for 5 minutes, then transfer them to a terrine dish or bowl, cover with plastic wrap (clingfilm), and steep overnight in the refrigerator.

—

Strain the apricots and arrange in sterilized jars (SEE p. 40).

—

Pour the syrup into a pan and heat over high heat to large pearl stage (237°F/114°C), or when small beads form on the surface of the syrup, and if you blow on a skimmer coated with the syrup, bubbles form at the edges. Remove from the heat and cool for 20 minutes, then pour over the apricots. Seal with sterilized lids and set aside for 4–5 days.

—

Pour the alcohol over the apricots in the jars, stirring it into the syrup to mix. Seal again and steep in a cool, dark place for two months before serving.

## APRICOTS IN VINEGAR

This is a good recipe to make use of green apricots. When a tree bears plenty of fruit, which you can tell about one month after blossoming, removing a portion is recommended to ensure a harvest of beautiful and ripe fruit. Size and quality will easily make up for quantity.

—

The green, almond-shaped apricots you will prune can be preserved in vinegar and served as a condiment, like gherkins.

**Preparation time 20 minutes**
**Pickling time 24 hours, plus 10 weeks**
**Makes about 4¼ cup (34 fl oz/1 liter) jar**

3 lb (1.4 kg) green apricots
2 cups (11 oz/300 g) coarse salt
20 pearl (baby) onions, peeled
1 shallot, sliced
10 cloves garlic
8 sprigs tarragon, or to taste
6¼ cups (53 fl oz/1.5 liters) cold distilled vinegar
   at 8°

Place the apricots in a clean coarse cloth with a handful of the salt. Tie the cloth into a bundle and shake vigorously. Untie the cloth, remove the apricots and wipe each one. Place in a large ceramic or other nonmetallic bowl. Sprinkle with the remaining salt, then cover and steep for 24 hours.

—

Drain the apricots, wipe them individually with paper towels, and pack them tightly into a large sterilized jar (SEE p. 40), alternating with the onions, shallot, garlic, and tarragon. Pour in cold vinegar to cover. Seal tightly with a sterilized lid and leave for three weeks in a cool, dark place.

Drain the vinegar from the jar and cover again with fresh vinegar. Cover and steep for another three weeks.

—

Drain the vinegar from the jar one more time, and cover again with fresh vinegar. Seal tightly with a sterilized lid.

—

Pickle for one month before eating. Always use clean wooden tongs to remove the apricots from the jar.

# ALMONDS

## ALMONDS AU NATUREL

Pick almonds when they are fully ripe; their hulls will be split open and easy to remove then.

—

Hull the almonds and leave them out in their shells for two weeks, exposed to the air but in the shade. Store them in the shell or shelled in an airtight container. Almonds will keep for up to a year and may go rancid after that.

## ALMOND PASTE

**Preparation time 20 minutes**
**Makes 1 lb 2 oz (500 g)**

2¾ cups (9 oz/250 g) ground almonds
1¼ cups (9 oz/250 g) confectioners' (icing) sugar
2 medium egg whites, lightly beaten
kirsch or coffee extract, to taste (optional)

Work the ground almonds and confectioners' (icing) sugar in a mortar with a pestle to remove any lumps. Transfer to a bowl and add the egg whites, a little at a time, stirring until it forms a soft, but not sticky, paste—you may not need to use all the egg whites.

—

This paste can be flavored by kneading in a little kirsch or coffee extract to taste and also tinted with paste or gel (but not liquid) food colorings to make a wide range of petits fours.

# PINEAPPLE

## PINEAPPLE AU NATUREL

Preparation time 40 minutes
Cooking time 1 hour
Canning time 20 minutes
Makes 1 large or 2 smaller jars, depending on
   the size of the pineapple

1 large, ripe pineapple, peeled and 'eyes'
   removed
sugar

Cut the pineapple into round slices, about
½ inch/1 cm thick, then stamp out the cores
using a small, round cookie cutter. Weigh the
slices and stack them in 1 large or 2 smaller
sterilized jars (SEE p. 40), depending on the size
of the pineapple.
—
Put the same weight of sugar as the pineapple
in a pan, adding a scant ½ cup (3½ fl oz/
100 ml) water per ⅓ cup (2¼ oz/60 g) sugar.
Heat gently in a pan, stirring until the sugar
has dissolved. Bring to a boil and boil rapidly
until it reaches large pearl stage (237°F/114°C),
or when small beads form on the surface of the
syrup, and if you blow on a skimmer coated
with the syrup, bubbles form at the edges.
—
Pour the sugar syrup into the jars to cover the
pineapple slices and seal with sterilized lids.
—
Process in a boiling-water canner (SEE p. 53
and follow the manufacturer's instructions) for
20 minutes.
—
NOTE: If the pineapple slices are too wide to
fit inside your jars, cut them into cubes and
proceed as above.

## PINEAPPLE JAM

Preparation time 40 minutes
Cooking time 1 hour
Canning time 5 minutes
Makes about 3 x1 lb 2 oz (500 g) jars

2 ripe pineapples, peeled and 'eyes' removed,
   about 3 lb (1.4 kg) in total, with leaves
sugar

Slice and core the pineapple, cut the flesh into
cubes, and weigh.
—
Put the same weight of sugar as the fruit in a
pan, adding a scant ½ cup (3½ fl oz/100 ml)
water per ⅓ cup (2¼ oz/60 g) sugar. Heat
gently, stirring until the sugar has dissolved,
then bring to a boil and boil rapidly until it
reaches the small thread stage (225°F/107°C),
or when the syrup thickens and the bubbles
grow larger, and when a teaspoon of the syrup
is dropped into a glass of cold water it forms
thin threads that cannot be rolled into small
balls when lifted out.
—
Lower the pineapple cubes into the syrup,
bring back to a boil, and boil for 20 minutes,
or until the pineapple cubes are thoroughly
cooked and translucent, and the syrup is thick.
—
Pour into sterilized jars (SEE p. 40) and seal with
sterilized lids.
—
Process in a boiling-water canner (SEE p. 53
and follow the manufacturer's instructions) for
5 minutes.

## CANDIED PINEAPPLE

**Preparation time 50 minutes**
**Soaking time 30 minutes**
**Cooking time 1 hour**
**Steeping time 48 hours**
**Makes about 8 slices or 32 quarter slices**

2 tablespoons distilled vinegar
1 pineapple, peeled and 'eyes' removed
sugar

Cut the pineapple into round slices, about ½ inch/1 cm thick, then stamp out the cores using a small, round cookie cutter. Leave the slices as they are or cut each into four sections.

—

Fill a large bowl with 2 tablespoons distilled vinegar per 4¼ cups/34 fl oz/1 liter water Add the pineapple and soak in the acidulated water for 30 minutes. Drain and put the fruit in a saucepan and pour in enough cold water to cover. Have ready a large bowl filled halfway with ice cubes and enough cold water to cover the ice. Place the pan with the pineapple over high heat and heat until the fruit bobs to the surface, then drain and plunge the fruit into the ice-cold water. Leave for 1 minute, then drain again.

—

Weigh the fruit. Put the same weight of sugar as the fruit in a pan, adding a scant ½ cup (3½ fl oz/100 ml) water per ⅓ cup (2¼ oz/ 60 g) sugar. Heat gently, stirring until the sugar has dissolved, then bring to a boil and boil rapidly until it reaches the small thread stage (225°F/107°C), or when the syrup thickens and the bubbles grow larger, and when a teaspoon of the syrup is dropped into a glass of cold water it forms thin threads that cannot be rolled into small balls when lifted out. Lower in the fruit and bring back to a boil. Remove

from the heat and leave the fruit in the syrup overnight.

—

The next day, carefully remove the fruit with a slotted spoon and set aside. Heat the syrup until it reaches the large thread stage (228–230°F/109–110°C), or when the syrup forms firmer threads when dropped into cold water, about ¾–1¼ inches/2–3 cm long. Lower in the fruit and bring back to a boil. When the syrup boils, remove from the heat and leave the fruit in the syrup overnight.

—

Repeat the process over the next four days, increasing the sugar concentration by 1.8°F/1°C each day until the syrup reaches the large pearl stage (237°F/114°C), or when small beads form on the surface of the syrup, and if you blow on a skimmer coated with the syrup, bubbles form at the edges.

—

Remove the pineapple from the syrup with a slotted spoon and drain well, then place the fruit on a rack to dry in a well-ventilated place.

## PINEAPPLE SYRUP

**Preparation time 30 minutes**
**Cooking time 1 hour**
**Resting time 24 hours**
**Canning time 5 minutes**
**Makes about 8¼ cups (70 fl oz/2 liters)**

1 pineapple, peeled, cored and flesh grated
5 cups (2¼ lb/1 kg) sugar

Put the grated pineapple in a pan with water
3 cups (26 fl oz/750 ml) and simmer over low
heat for 40 minutes. Remove the pan from the
heat and strain to collect the juice into a clean
pitcher (jug), squeezing all the liquid out of the
pulp. Cover and rest for 24 hours.

—

The next day, put the pineapple juice and
sugar into a pan and heat gently, stirring until
the sugar has dissolved, then bring to a boil
and boil rapidly until it reaches the small pearl
stage (232°F/111°C), or when tiny round beads
form at the surface of the syrup, and when
dropped into a glass of water, it form threads of
about 1½–2 inches/4–5 cm in length.

—

Remove the pan from the heat and cool
slightly, then pour into sterilized bottles (SEE
p. 40) and seal.

—

Process in a boiling-water canner (SEE p. 53
and follow the manufacturer's instructions) for
5 minutes.

# ANGELICA

## PEELING ANGELICA

Bring a large pan of water to a boil. Plunge the angelica into a bowl of cold water, then add to the boiling water. Boil for 1 minute, then remove the pan from the heat and soak for 1 hour. The stems are then soft enough for easy peeling. Using a small knife, strip away the fibers on the outer part of the stem and the thin skin on the inside. The fruit is ready for use.

## ANGELICA JAM

**Preparation time 40 minutes**
**Cooking time 1 hour 5 minutes**
**Canning time 5 minutes**
**Makes about 3 x 1 lb 2 oz (500 g) jars**

**4½ lb (2 kg) angelica, peeled (SEE previous entry) and cut into segments, about 2 inches (5 cm) in length**
**sugar**

Weigh the angelica and place in a large preserving pan with the same weight of sugar, plus scant ½ cup (3½ fl oz/100 ml) water per 2¼ lb (1 kg) angelica. Bring to a boil, then reduce the heat to low and cook for 1 hour, or until the angelica is soft.

---

Pour into sterilized jars (SEE p. 40) and seal with sterilized lids.

---

Process in a boiling-water canner (SEE p. 53 and follow the manufacturer's instructions) for 5 minutes.

## CANDIED ANGELICA

Preparation time 40 minutes
Cooking time 3 hours
Resting time 1 hour
Steeping time 4 days
Drying time several days
Makes about 1¾ lb (800 g)

2¼ lb (1 kg) angelica, peeled (SEE p. 159) and
    sliced into segments, about 4-6 inches
    (10-15 cm) in length
handful of coarse salt
sugar

Place each segment as it is peeled into a
nonreactive pan with enough water to cover.
Bring to a boil, then reduce the heat and
cook for 1 hour, or until the segments are soft.
The angelica will have turned yellow during
cooking, so add a handful of coarse salt to
turn it green again. Remove the pan from the
heat and rest for 1 hour, then strain. Weigh
the amount of angelica and place in a large,
nonreactive, heatproof bowl.

—

Put the same weight of sugar as the angelica
in a pan, adding a scant ½ cup (3½ fl oz/
100 ml) water per ⅓ cup (2¼ oz/60 g)
sugar. Heat gently, stirring until the sugar
has dissolved, then bring to a boil and boil
rapidly until it reaches the small thread stage
(225°F/107°C), or when the syrup thickens
and the bubbles grow larger, and when a
teaspoon of the syrup is dropped into a glass
of cold water it forms thin threads that cannot
be rolled into small balls when lifted out. Pour
the boiling syrup over the angelica, cover with
plastic wrap (clingfilm), and steep for 24 hours.

—

The next day, drain the syrup back into the
pan and bring to a boil, then boil rapidly until

it reaches the small pearl stage (232°F/111°C),
or when tiny round beads form at the surface
of the syrup, and when dropped into a glass of
water it forms threads of about 1½–2 inches
(4–5 cm) in length. Pour over the angelica,
cover again, and leave for another 24 hours.

—

The next day, drain the syrup into a pan and
bring to a boil rapidly until it reaches large
pearl stage (237°F/114°C), or when small beads
form on the surface of the syrup, and if you
blow on a skimmer coated with the syrup,
bubbles form at the edges. Pour over the
angelica, cover again, and leave for another 24
hours.

—

The next day, drain the syrup back into the
pan and bring to a boil, then remove the pan
from the heat, pour over the angelica, cover,
and leave for a final 24 hours.

—

The next day, drain the angelica and dry on
a rack, standing the rack on a tray, sheet of
parchment paper, or aluminum foil to catch
any drips, for several days. If necessary,
complete the drying process by placing the
fruit in a low oven preheated to 122–140°F/
50–60°C/lowest Gas Mark setting. The
angelica should remain soft.

# NECTARINES

## NECTARINES AU NATUREL

Preparation time 30 minutes
Canning time 40 minutes
Makes about 2 x 4¼ cup (34 fl oz/1 liter) jars

8-10 nectarines, ripe but firm
2 tablespoons sugar
2 tablespoons bottled lemon juice

Prick the whole nectarines to the pit with a large sewing needle.

—

Pack them into sterilized jars (SEE p. 40), and add 1 tablespoon sugar and 1 tablespoon bottled lemon juice per jar. Seal with sterilized lids.

—

Process in a boiling-water canner (SEE p. 53 and follow the manufacturer's instructions) for 40 minutes.

## NECTARINES IN SYRUP

Preparation time 40 minutes
Cooking time 5 minutes
Canning time 30 minutes
Makes 2 x 4¼ cup (34 fl oz/1 liter) jars

8-10 nectarines, ripe but firm
sugar

Prick the whole nectarines to the pit with a large sewing needle. Pack them into sterilized jars (SEE p. 40).

—

For the sugar syrup, bring 2 cups (14 oz/400 g) sugar per 4¼ cups (34 fl oz/1 liter) water to a boil in a pan. Boil for 2-3 seconds, then remove from the heat. Carefully top off the jars with the boiling syrup, then seal with sterilized lids.

—

Process in a boiling-water canner (SEE p. 53 and follow the manufacturer's instructions) for 30 minutes.

# BLACK CURRANTS

## BLACK CURRANT JELLY

Preparation time 40 minutes
Cooking time 30 minutes
Canning time 5 minutes
Makes about 3 x 1 lb 2 oz (500 g) jars

5 lb (2.2 kg) black currants
scant 2 cups (13 oz/375 g) sugar per 2¼ cups
    (17 fl oz/500 ml) juice

Keep the black currants on their stalks and
weigh the fruit.

—

Place the black currants in a large preserving
pan, adding ½ cup (4 fl oz/125 ml) water per
1 lb 2 oz (500 g) black currants and heat gently
for about 10 minutes, or until the fruits split and
render their juice.

—

Remove the pan from the heat and strain, but
don't crush or push through the strainer as this
would cloud the juice.

—

Put a small plate or saucer into the freezer to
chill. Measure the juice and pour back into
the clean pan. Add scant 2 cups (13 oz/375 g)
sugar per 2¼ cups (17 fl oz/500 ml) juice. Bring
to a boil, then reduce the heat and simmer for
15–20 minutes, skimming with a slotted spoon
to get rid of any scum as needed.

—

Take the pan off the heat. To test for a set, pour
several drops of jam onto the chilled plate and
when you tip the plate the juice should not run.
If it does, heat a little longer and test again. Pour
the jelly into sterilized jars (SEE p. 40) and seal with
sterilized lids.

—

Process in a boiling-water canner (SEE p. 53
and follow the manufacturer's instructions) for
5 minutes.

NOTE: Black currants have a very high pectin
content, so do not overcook the jelly or it will
dry up in the jars.

## BLACK CURRANT AND WHITE CURRANT JELLY

Preparation time 40 minutes
Cooking time 30 minutes
Canning time 5 minutes
Makes about 4 x 1 lb 2 oz (500 g) jars

2¼ lb (1 kg) white currants
5 lb (2.2 kg) black currants
scant 2 cups (13 oz/375 g) sugar per 2¼ cups
    (17 fl oz/500 ml) juice

Using a mixture of currants gives a lighter-
colored jelly. Keep the currants on their stalks
and weigh the fruit.

—

Place the currants in a large preserving pan,
adding ½ cup (4 fl oz/125 ml) water per
1 lb 2 oz (500 g) currants and heat gently for
about 10 minutes, or until the fruits split and
render their juice.

—

Remove the pan from the heat and strain, but
don't crush or push through the strainer as this
would cloud the juice.

—

Put a small plate or saucer into the freezer to
chill. Measure the juice and pour back into
the clean pan. Add scant 2 cups (13 oz/375 g)
sugar per 2¼ cups (17 fl oz/500 ml) juice. Bring
to a boil, then reduce the heat and simmer for
15–20 minutes, skimming with a slotted spoon
to get rid of any scum as needed.

—

Take the pan off the heat. To test for a set, pour
several drops of jam onto the chilled plate and
when you tip the plate the juice should not run.
If it does, heat a little longer and test again. Pour
the jelly into sterilized jars (SEE p. 40) and seal with
sterilized lids.

—

Process in a boiling-water canner (SEE p. 53
and follow the manufacturer's instructions) for
5 minutes.

## BLACK CURRANT FRUIT PASTE

Preparation time 30 minutes
Cooking time 1 hour 10 minutes
Drying time 4-5 days
Makes about 40 pieces

1¾ lb (800 g) black currants, stripped from
    stalks
sugar, plus extra for dusting
a little tasteless oil, for oiling

Black currant paste sets easily thanks to the
high pectin content of the fruit.

—

Put the black currants in a large pan, add scant
½ cup (3½ fl oz/100 ml) water per 1 lb 2 oz
(500 g) fruit and cook over high heat for about
10 minutes, or with until the fruit splits.

—

Remove the pan from the heat and strain
through a strainer, pounding the berries
vigorously with a wooden spoon to extract all
the pulp.

—

Weigh the pulp and return it to the pan with
the same weight in sugar. Put the pan over
medium heat and cook, stirring constantly
for about 40 minutes, or until the mixture
becomes thick enough that it pulls away from
the bottom of the pan. At this point, the water
will have completely evaporated.

—

Pour the paste onto an oiled marble slab, or
oiled pie dishes, dust the surface with sugar,
and dry for 4–5 days in a cool place.

—

Cut the paste into the shapes of your choice
(such as squares, diamonds, rounds, half-
moons, etc.) and dust the cut surfaces with
more sugar until they are coated.

—

They will keep for months in an airtight
container, with a sheet of parchment paper
between each layer.

## BLACK CURRANT LIQUEUR

Preparation time 20 minutes
Cooking time 5 minutes
Steeping time 2 months
Makes about 6¼ (53 fl oz/1.5 liters)

2¼ lb (1 kg) black currants, plus a few clean
    leaves
4¼ cups (34 fl oz/ 1 liter per 2¼ lb/1 kg fruit)
    eau-de-vie at 45%
scant 2 cups (13 oz/375 g) sugar per 2¼ cups
    (17 fl oz/500 ml) water per 2¼ lb/1 kg fruit

Put the black currants with a few black currant
leaves into a large sterilized jar (SEE p. 40).

—

Pour in the alcohol and seal with a sterilized
lid. Steep in a cool, dark place for 2 months.

—

Strain the fruit through a strainer to collect the
alcohol in a clean pitcher (jug). The alcohol
should have turned a nice shade of red.

—

For the sugar syrup, bring scant 2 cups
(13 oz/375 g) sugar per 2¼ cups (17 fl oz/
500 ml) water per 2¼ lb/1 kg alcohol to a boil in
a pan. Boil for 2–3 seconds, then remove from
the heat. Carefully add the syrup to the alcohol
and then pour into a sterilized bottle (SEE p. 40)
with an airtight seal or stopper.

—

NOTE: White currants, while a rare variety,
have a particularly refined taste, and are well
suited to making this liqueur.

# CHERRIES

Pick cherries just before they are fully ripe and place them in a single layer and nicely spaced on a bed of straw or fern, in a cool and airy place. The cherries will keep for a few days, a week at the most.

## CHERRIES AU NATUREL

Preparation time 15 minutes
Canning time 30 minutes
Makes about 2 x 1 lb 2 oz (500 g) jars

3 lb (1.4 kg) cherries, stalks and pits removed
2 tablespoons sugar

Use good-quality, fresh and clean cherries.

—

Arrange the cherries in sterilized jars (SEE p. 40), packing them well with a spatula or banging the pot on a folded cloth on the counter (work surface). Sprinkle each jar with 1 tablespoon sugar and seal with sterilized lids.

—

Process in a boiling-water canner (SEE p. 53 and follow the manufacturer's instructions) for 30 minutes.

NOTE: You can leave the pits in. This will give the cherries a unique taste that some people prefer.

## CHERRIES IN SYRUP

Preparation time 10 minutes
Cooking time 1 hour
Canning time 30 minutes
Makes about 2 x 1 lb 2 oz (500 g) jars

3 lb (1.4 kg) cherries, stalks and pits removed
2 cups (14 oz/400 g) sugar per 4¼ cups (34 fl oz/1 liter) water

Arrange the cherries in sterilized jars (SEE p. 40), packing them well with a spatula or banging the pot on a folded cloth on the counter (work surface).

—

For the sugar syrup, bring 2 cups (14 oz/400 g) sugar per 4¼ cups (34 fl oz/1 liter) water to a boil in a pan. Boil for 2–3 seconds, then remove from the heat and top the jars off with the boiling syrup. Seal with sterilized lids.

—

Process in a boiling-water canner (SEE p. 53 and follow the manufacturer's instructions) for 30 minutes.

## CHERRY JAM

**Preparation time 20 minutes**
**Cooking time 1 hour**
**Canning time 5 minutes**
**Makes about 4 x 1 lb 2 oz (500 g) jars**

4½ lb (2 kg) cherries, stalks and pits removed
about 1⅔ cups (14 fl oz/400 ml) red currant
    juice
sugar

Put a small plate or sauce into the freezer to
chill. Pit the cherries with a cherry pitter,
working over a large preserving pan to collect
all the juices. Add generous ¾ cup (7 fl oz/
200 ml) red currant juice per 2¼ lb (1 kg) fruit,
bring to a boil, and boil for 20 minutes.

—

Remove the pan from the heat and weigh the
fruit and the juice. Return the fruit and juice
to the pan and add 3¾ cups (1 lb 10 oz/750 g)
sugar per 2¼ lb (1 kg) fruit and juice. Bring to a
boil and boil for 30 minutes, skimming with a
slotted spoon to remove any scum at the end of
the cooking time. To test for a set, pour several
drops of jam onto the chilled plate and when
you tip the plate the juice should not run.

—

Pour the jam into sterilized jars (SEE p. 40) and
seal with sterilized lids.

—

Process in a boiling-water canner (SEE p. 53
and follow the manufacturer's instructions) for
5 minutes.

—

NOTE: The red currant juice, which has a high
pectin content, helps the jam set faster and
better.

## POACHED CHERRY JAM

**Preparation time 40 minutes**
**Cooking time 50 minutes–1 hour**
**Canning time 5 minutes**
**Makes about 3 x 1 lb 2 oz (500 g) jars**

4½ lb (2 kg) cherries, stalks and pits removed
sugar

This jam uses equal weights of sugar and fruit.

Weigh the cherries and put the same quantity
of sugar in a large pan, add 2¼ cups (17 fl oz/
500 ml) water and heat gently, stirring until
the sugar has dissolved. Bring to a boil and
boil rapidly until it reaches large pearl stage
(237°F/114°C), or when small beads form on
the surface of the syrup, and if you blow on a
skimmer coated with the syrup, bubbles form
at the edges.

—

Add the cherries and simmer over low heat
for about 30–40 minutes, or until they turn
translucent. Remove the pan from the heat
and strain, keeping the syrup.

—

Arrange the cherries in sterilized jars (SEE
p. 40). Return the syrup to the pan and heat
it to 235°F/113°C (halfway between the small
and large pearl stages). Carefully pour the
syrup into the jars and seal with sterilized lids.

—

Process in a boiling-water canner (SEE p. 53
and follow the manufacturer's instructions) for
5 minutes.

—

NOTE: You can make vanilla cherry jam by
adding 2–3 fresh vanilla beans (pods), split
open lengthwise and seeds scraped out, to the
syrup and cherries before cooking. Remove
the beans (pods) when pouring the jam into
the jars.

## CANDIED CHERRIES

**Preparation time 50 minutes**
**Soaking time 30 minutes**
**Cooking time 3 hours 40 minutes**
**Drying time several days**
**Makes about 1¾ lb (800 g)**

**2¼ lb (1 kg) sour cherries, such as**
**    Montmorency, stalks removed and pitted**
**juice of about 2 lemons**
**sugar**

Use large cherries that are firm and not
too ripe.

—

Fill a large bowl with cold water and add the
juice of 1 lemon per 4¼ cups (34 fl oz/1 liter)
water. Soak the cherries in the acidulated
water for 30 minutes.

—

Drain the cherries and cook them in a steamer
for about 40 minutes, or until soft. Meanwhile,
have ready a large bowl filled halfway with ice
cubes and enough cold water to cover the ice.
Remove the cherries and plunge them into
the ice-cold water and leave for 1 minute, then
drain.

—

Weigh the drained cherries and put the same
quantity of sugar in a pan, add a scant ½ cup
(3½ fl oz/100 ml) water per ⅓ cup (2¼ oz/
60 g) sugar and heat gently, stirring until the
sugar has dissolved. Bring to a boil and boil
rapidly until it reaches the small thread stage
(225°F/107°C), or when the syrup thickens and
the bubbles grow larger, and when dropped
into a glass of cold water, it forms a thin and
flexible thread about ½-inch/1-cm long, which
breaks easily. Lower in the fruit and bring back
to a boil. Remove from the heat and leave the
fruit in the syrup overnight.

The next day, carefully remove the fruit
with a slotted spoon and set aside. Heat the
syrup until it reaches the large thread stage
(228–230°F/109–110°C), or when the syrup
forms firmer threads when dropped into a
glass of water, about ¾–1¼ inches/2–3 cm
long. Lower in the fruit and bring back to a
boil. When the syrup boils, remove from the
heat and leave the fruit in the syrup overnight.

—

Repeat the process over the next 5–6 days,
increasing the sugar concentration by
1.8°F/1°C each day until the syrup reaches the
large pearl stage (237°F/114°C), or when small
beads form on the surface of the syrup, and if
you blow on a skimmer coated with the syrup,
bubbles form at the edges.

—

Remove the fruit from the syrup with a slotted
spoon and drain well, then place the fruit on a
rack to drain, standing the rack on a tray, sheet
of parchment paper, or aluminum foil to catch
any drips, and dry in a well-ventilated place.
To speed up the process, you can transfer
the cherries, still on the rack, to a low oven
preheated to 122–140°F/50–60°C/lowest
possible Gas Mark setting with the door
held ajar.

## SUN- OR OVEN-DRIED CHERRIES

If you live in a hot climate then you can alternate drying the cherries between sun- and oven-drying.

—

Preheat the oven to its lowest setting. Remove the stalks and pits from the cherries. Bring a large pan of water to a boil. Carefully add the cherries and poach for 1 minute, then drain and place on wire racks, setting the racks over trays, sheets of parchment paper, or aluminum foil to catch any drips, inside the oven with the door held ajar, until the fruit releases no juice when pressed between your fingers. The cherries should not shrivel up. You will need to continue the drying process over the course of several days, pausing during the night.

—

Dried cherries keep for a long time in an airtight container in a dry place. Soak in cold water for 12 hours before using.

## CHERRIES DRIED IN THE DEHYDRATOR

Pit and cook the cherries in a steamer for 3 minutes then dry well.

—

Place the cherries on racks in a dehydrator for 10–12 hours, at a temperature that increases progressively from 104–158°F/40°C–70°C.

## CHERRIES IN EAU-DE-VIE

Preparation time 20 minutes
Steeping time 2–4 months
Makes 3 jars, 1 lb 2 oz (500 g)

2¼ lb (1 kg) sour cherries, stalks trimmed to
    ¾ inch/1.5 cm
½ cup (3½ oz/100 g) sugar
3½ cups (28 fl oz/800 ml) eau-de-vie at 45%

Make sure the cherries are in perfect shape
and not too ripe.

—

Arrange the cherries in a sterilized jar (SEE
p. 40), sprinkle with the sugar, and top off with
the alcohol. Seal with a sterilized lid.

—

During the first week, swish the preserving jar
around every day or so to ensure that the sugar
dissolves evenly. Steep for at least two months,
ideally three or four.

—

NOTE: To make spiced cherries in alcohol, add
a small cheesecloth (muslin) bag containing a
cinnamon stick and some cloves to each jar.

## CHERRIES IN VINEGAR

Preparation time 20 minutes, plus cooling
Cooking time 20 minutes
Steeping time 2 days, plus 2 weeks
Makes 3 jars, 1 lb 2 oz (500 g)

3 lb (1.4 kg) cherries, washed, stalks trimmed to
    ¾ inch/1.5 cm, and dried thoroughly
8 sprigs tarragon
1 tablespoon white peppercorns
6 cloves
6¼ cups (53 fl oz/1.5 liters) distilled vinegar
Salt

Arrange the cherries in a sterilized jars (SEE
p. 40), adding the tarragon, white
peppercorns, and cloves.

—

Bring the vinegar with some salt (4¼ cups/
34 fl oz/1 liter vinegar and 1 teaspoon salt per
2¼ lb/1 kg fruit) to a boil in a pan. Once it is
boiling, remove the pan from the heat and
cool, then pour over the cherries. Seal with a
sterilized lid and steep in a cool, dark place for
two days.

—

Carefully pour the vinegar from the jar into a
pan without touching the cherries. Bring to a
boil and boil for 10 minutes, then remove from
the heat and cool. Pour over the cherries and
seal the jar with a sterilized lid.

—

Steep for 2 weeks in a cool, dark place before
serving with game, stewed meats, and
charcuterie. Always use a stainless steel spoon
or wooden tongs to pick up the cherries.

# QUINCES

## QUINCES, STORED FRESH

Quinces can only be eaten after cooking. They don't do well in frosts, so they usually need to be picked before they are fully ripe.

—

Store quinces in the cellar on a bed of straw until yellow in color. Do not allow the quinces to overripen, otherwise the jams and jellies you make from them will not set well.

## QUINCES AU NATUREL

These can be used in tarts, or eaten as they are with a little sugar. When peeling quince, use a stainless-steel knife to avoid blackening the fruit.

---

**Preparation time 20 minutes, plus cooling**
**Cooking time 20 minutes**
**Canning time 30 minutes**
**Makes 3 x 1 lb 2 oz (500 g) jars**

**4½ lb (2 kg) quinces, peeled, cored, and cut into quarters (or smaller if quince are large)**
**juice of 1 lemon**
**Sugar**

---

Fill a large pan with water, add the lemon juice and quinces, and bring to a boil. Boil for 15 minutes, then remove the pan from the heat, drain the quince, and cool.

—

Arrange the quinces in sterilized jars (SEE p. 40). For the sugar syrup, bring 3¾ cups (1 lb 10 oz/750 g) sugar per 4¼ cups (34 fl oz/1 liter) water to a boil in a pan. Boil for 2–3 seconds, then remove from the heat and top the jars off with the boiling syrup. Seal with sterilized lids.

—

Process in a boiling-water canner (SEE p. 53 and follow the manufacturer's instructions) for 30 minutes.

## QUINCE JAM

Preparation time 30 minutes
Cooking time 1 hour 20 minutes
Canning time 5 minutes
Makes about 6 x 1 lb 2 oz (500 g) jars

6 lb (2.75 kg) quinces, wiped and quartered (no
 need to peel or core)
sugar

Place the quinces in a large preserving pan,
cover with water, and simmer over low heat for
about 30 minutes, or until softened. Drain the
quinces, setting the cooking juices aside. Peel
the skin and carve out the cores.

—

Put a small plate or saucer into the freezer to
chill. Weigh the cooking juices and fruit, then
return them to the pan with 3¾ cups
(1 lb 10 oz/750 g) sugar per 2¼ lb (1 kg) fruit and
juice. Bring to a boil, then reduce the heat and
simmer for 45 minutes. Mash up any large
lumps of fruit. To test for a set, pour several
drops of jam onto the chilled plate and when
you tip the plate the juice should not run.

—

Arrange the fruit in sterilized jars (SEE p. 40)
and seal with sterilized lids.

—

Process in a boiling-water canner (SEE p. 53
and follow the manufacturer's instructions) for
5 minutes.

## QUINCE JELLY

Preparation time 30 minutes
Cooking time 1 hour
Canning time 5 minutes
Makes about 3 x 1 lb 2 oz (500 g) jars

4½ lb (2 kg) quinces, wiped
sugar

Put a small plate or saucer into the freezer to
chill.

—

Quarter the quinces without peeling, then
carve out the cores and seeds (pips) and place
them in a small cheesecloth (muslin) bag.

—

Put the quinces in a large preserving pan,
cover with water, and simmer for 30 minutes,
or until the fruit is soft. Remove the pan from
the heat and, using a slotted spoon, remove the
fruit and set aside for another recipe. Measure
the cooking juices and return them to the
clean pan with the same weight in sugar and
the cheesecloth (muslin) bag. Simmer for 30
minutes. To test for a set, pour several drops of
jelly onto the chilled plate and when you tip the
plate the juice should not run.

—

Pour the mixture into sterilized jars (SEE p. 40)
and seal with sterilized lids.

—

Process in a boiling-water canner (SEE p. 53
and follow the manufacturer's instructions) for
5 minutes.

## QUINCE FRUIT PASTE

Preparation time 1 hour 30 minutes
Cooking time 30 minutes
Drying time 4–5 days
Makes about 50 pieces

4–5 quinces, about 2½–3 lb (1.2–1.4 kg) in total,
  wiped
sugar, plus extra for dusting
a little tasteless oil, for oiling

Quarter the quinces without peeling, then carve out the cores and pips and place them in a small cheesecloth (muslin) bag.

—

Put the quinces in a large preserving pan, cover with water, and simmer for 30 minutes, or until the fruit is soft. Remove the pan from the heat and, using a slotted spoon, remove the fruit and place in a bowl or mortar. Crush the softened fruit pulp thoroughly with a pestle, then push through a strainer or a food mill.

—

Weigh the amount of fruit pulp and put in a large preserving pan with the same weight in sugar. Cook over medium heat for 1 hour, stirring occasionally to prevent the paste scorching on the bottom of the pan. The mixture is very hot so be careful of it spitting. The quince paste is ready when it is very thick and pulls away from the sides of the pan.

—

Pour the paste onto an oiled marble slab, or oiled pie dishes. Dust the surface with sugar and dry in a cool place for 4–5 days.

—

Cut the paste into the shapes of your choice (such as squares, diamonds, rounds, half-moons, etc.) and dust the cut surfaces with more sugar until they are coated.

—

These will keep for months in an airtight container, with a sheet of parchment paper between each layer.

## QUINCE RATAFIA (QUINCE EAU-DE-VIE)

Preparation time 20 minutes
Chilling time 3 days
Steeping time 2–3 months
Makes 7½ cups (60 fl oz/1.7 liters)

3–4 quinces, about 2½ lb (1.2 kg) in total,
  wiped and grated, discarding the pips
3¾ cups (29 fl oz/850 ml) alcohol, such as
  vodka, at 45%
1 cinnamon stick, crushed
2 cloves
sugar

Choose ripe and unblemished quinces.

—

Place the quince pulp in a large nonreactive dish, cover with plastic wrap (clingfilm), and chill in the refrigerator for three days.

—

Place the pulp in a strainer to collect the juice. Measure the juice, then pour it and an equal amount of alcohol into a sterilized jar (SEE p. 40). Place the crushed cinnamon stick and cloves into a small cheesecloth (muslin) bag, tie, and put into the jar. Add 1½ cups (11 oz/ 300 g) sugar per 4¼ cups (34 fl oz/1 liter) juice and alcohol to the jar. Seal with a sterilized lid and steep in a cool, dark place for 2–3 months.

# DOGBERRY

Dogberries grow on dogwood trees. They are small egg-shaped berries with rather large pits, which must be removed when making jam. Pick nicely ripe dogwood fruit.

## DOGBERRY JAM

Preparation time 20 minutes
Cooking time 1 hour
Canning time 5 minutes
Makes 2 x 1 lb 2 oz (500 g) jars

4½ lb (2 kg) dogberries, pitted
sugar

Place the dogberries in a large preserving pan and pour in enough cold water to barely cover them. Bring to a boil and boil for 20–30 minutes; the fruits will split open after a few minutes.
—
Remove from the heat and press through a strainer or food mill to collect the juice. Discard the pits.
—
Put a small plate or saucer into the freezer to chill. Measure the juice and pour it back into the clean pan with the same weight in sugar. Heat gently, stirring until the sugar has dissolved, then bring to a boil and boil rapidly until the mixture reaches the small pearl stage (232°F/111°C), or when tiny round beads form at the surface of the syrup, then when dropped into a glass of cold water, it forms a wider thread of about 1½–2 inches/4–5 cm in length.
—
Remove the pan from the heat and skim with a slotted spoon to remove any scum that's on the surface. To test for a set, pour several drops of jam onto the chilled plate and when you tip the plate the juice should not run. Pour the jam into sterilized jars (SEE p. 40) and seal with sterilized lids.
—
Process in a boiling-water canner (SEE p. 53 and follow the manufacturer's instructions) for 5 minutes.

# ROSEHIP

Rosehips come from the wild rose tree. The dark red berries have the fullest flavor, and you should wait until after the first frosts to pick them.

## ROSEHIP JAM

Preparation time 30 minutes
Steeping time 1 week
Cooking time 1 hour 15 minutes
Canning time 5 minutes
Makes about 2 x 1 lb 2 oz (500 g) jars

4½ lb (2 kg) rosehips, black pods removed and fruit cut in half
dry white wine, to cover
sugar

Place the berries in a terrine dish or a large, nonreactive bowl. Cover with white wine and steep for one week in the refrigerator, stirring the fruit daily with a wooden spatula.
—
Pour the fruit and wine into a large preserving pan, bring to a boil, and boil for 1 hour, stirring frequently to prevent the mixture sticking to the bottom of the pan, until the fruit is very soft.
—
Remove the pan from the heat and push this puree through a strainer or food mill to remove the pips and the fuzz that's inside the fruit. Weigh the puree and return it to the clean pan with the same weight in sugar. Bring to a boil, stirring constantly, then reduce the heat and simmer for 10 minutes. Skim with a slotted spoon to remove any scum floating on the surface. To test for a set, pour several drops of jam onto a chilled plate and when you tip the plate the juice should not run. Transfer the mixture to sterilized jars (SEE p. 40). Seal with sterilized lids.
—
Process in a boiling-water canner (SEE p. 53 and follow the manufacturer's instructions) for 5 minutes.

# BARBERRY

The barberry shrub bears small, red, tart berries that are used to make jam after the first frosts.

## BARBERRY JAM

Preparation time 20 minutes
Cooking time 30 minutes
Canning time 5 minutes
Makes 2 x 1 lb 2 oz (500 g) jars

4½ lb (2 kg) barberries, stripped from stalks
sugar

Put a small plate or sauce into the freezer to chill. Place the berries in a large preserving pan, pour in enough cold water to barely cover the berries, then bring to a boil. Boil over high heat for 20 minutes.

—

Remove the pan from the heat and crush the mixture in the pan with a pestle. Strain through a strainer to collect the juice.

—

Measure the juice and return to the clean pan with the same weight in sugar. Bring back to a boil and cook for 8 minutes. Skim with a slotted spoon to remove any scum on the surface. To test for a set, pour several drops of jam onto the chilled plate and when you tip the plate the juice should not run. Pour the mixture into sterilized jars ( see p. 40) and seal with sterilized lids.

—

Process in a boiling-water canner (SEE p. 53 and follow the manufacturer's instructions) for 5 minutes.

# FIG

## FIGS AU NATUREL

Preparation time 30 minutes
Cooking time 10 minutes
Canning time 45 minutes
Makes 3 x 1 lb 2 oz (500 g) jars

4½ lb (2 kg) figs
3 tablespoons sugar

Leave the fruit whole but prick them a few times with a needle. Have ready a large bowl filled halfway with ice cubes and enough cold water to cover the ice. Bring a large pan of water to a boil over high heat. Carefully add the figs and blanch for 5 minutes, or until tender. Remove the figs with a slotted spoon and plunge into the ice-cold water. Leave for 1 minute, then drain.

—

Arrange the figs in sterilized jars (SEE p. 40), adding 1 tablespoon sugar to each jar. Seal with sterilized lids.

—

Process in a boiling-water canner (SEE p. 53 and follow the manufacturer's instructions) for 45 minutes.

## FIG JAM

**Preparation time 20 minutes**
**Cooking time 1 hour 10 minutes**
**Soaking time 32 hours**
**Canning time 5 minutes**
**Makes 2 x 1 lb 2 oz (500 g) jars**

**2¼ lb (1 kg) green figs**
**sugar**
**grated zest of 2 lemons**

Fig jam is generally very sweet, and is often livened up with finely grated lemon zest.

—

Have ready a large bowl filled halfway with ice cubes and enough cold water to cover the ice. Bring a large pan of water to a boil over high heat. Carefully add the figs and blanch for 3 minutes, or until tender. Remove the figs with a slotted spoon and plunge into the ice-cold water. Leave the figs in the cold water for 24 hours.

—

When ready, make a light sugar syrup. Weigh the figs, then place the same weight of sugar as the figs in a large pan and pour in 2¼ cups (17 fl oz/500 ml) water per 5 cups (2¼ lb/1 kg) sugar and bring to a boil. Boil for 2–3 seconds, then remove from the heat and carefully lower the figs into the syrup. Add the lemon zest and bring to a boil. Boil for 5 minutes, then remove the pan from the heat, cover with a lid, and leave the fruit in the syrup overnight in a cool, dark place.

—

The next day, put a small plate or saucer into the freezer to chill. Drain the figs from the syrup, putting the syrup in a clean pan. Bring the syrup to a boil and boil rapidly until it reaches the small pearl stage (232°F/111°C), or

when tiny round beads form at the surface of the syrup, and when dropped into cold water it forms threads about 1½–2 inches/4–5 cm in length. Carefully add the figs and heat the syrup until it reaches the large pearl stage (237°F/114°C), or when small beads form on the surface of the syrup, and if you blow on a skimmer coated with the syrup, bubbles form at the edges. Skim with a slotted spoon. To test for a set, pour several drops of jam onto the chilled plate and when you tip the plate the juice should not run.

—

Pour the jam into sterilized jars (SEE p. 40) and seal with sterilized lids.

—

Process in a boiling-water canner (SEE p. 53 and follow the manufacturer's instructions) for 5 minutes.

## SUNDRIED FIGS

This preservation technique can only be done in regions where the sun is very hot as the process must be completed over just a few days.

—

Check the figs carefully and remove any that are spoiled. Place the fruit on racks and leave in the sun all day. Bring the racks indoors at night. Repeat several days in a row, turning the figs over daily.

—

When the figs are nearly dry, place the figs on a table, stalks facing upwards. Using a rolling pin and exerting even pressure, gently flatten the figs to to give them a regular shape. Return the figs to the racks to complete the drying process.

—

Store in airtight containers with a few bay leaves, and eat as they are.

# STRAWBERRIES

## STRAWBERRIES, STORED FRESH

Strawberries are very juicy, and are best eaten fresh and within 24 hours of picking or purchasing.

## STRAWBERRIES AU NATUREL

**Preparation time 20 minutes**
**Canning time 15 minutes**
**Makes 2 x 1 lb 2 oz (500 g) jars**

2¼ lb (1 kg) strawberries, washed, dried, and hulled
sugar, for dusting

Use smaller strawberries with a dense, not watery flesh.

—

Arrange the strawberries in layers inside sterilized jars (SEE p. 40), dusting each layer with sugar. Seal with sterilized lids.

—

Process in a boiling-water canner (SEE p. 53 and follow the manufacturer's instructions) for 15 minutes.

## STRAWBERRY SYRUP

**Preparation time 20 minutes**
**Cooking time 40 minutes**
**Canning time 5 minutes**
**Makes 3 x 1 lb 2 oz (500 g) jars**

**4½ lb (2 kg) strawberries, hulled**
**10 cups (4½ lb/2 kg) sugar**

Make a sugar syrup. Heat the same weight of sugar as the fruit weight and 1 cup (9 fl oz/250 ml) water per 5 cups (2¼ lb/1 kg) sugar gently in a large pan, stirring until the sugar has dissolved, then bring to a boil and boil rapidly until it reaches the small pearl stage (232°F/111°C), or when tiny round beads form at the surface of the syrup, then when dropped into a glass of water, it forms threads of about 1½–2 inches/4–5 cm in length.

—

Carefully lower the strawberries into the syrup and return to a boil. Boil for 1 minute. Strain the strawberries, setting the syrup aside. Add the strawberries to sterilized jars (SEE p. 40), filling the jars by half.

—

Put the syrup into a clean pan and bring to a boil. Boil for 20 minutes, then carefully pour the hot syrup into the jars. Seal with sterilized lids.

—

Process in a boiling-water canner (SEE p. 53 and follow the manufacturer's instructions) for 5 minutes.

## STRAWBERRY MARMALADE

**Preparation time 20 minutes**
**Steeping time 12 hours**
**Cooking time 1 hour**
**Canning time 5 minutes**
**Makes 4 x 1 lb 2 oz (500 g) jars**

**strawberries, hulled**
**sugar**

Place the strawberries in a large preserving pan with 4 cups (1¾ lb/800 g) sugar per 2¼ lb (1 kg) fruit, cover with a lid, and steep for 12 hours.

—

When ready, place the pan over low heat to melt any remaining sugar crystals, then increase the heat and bring to a boil. Boil for 20–25 minutes. Skim with a slotted spoon.

—

Strain the strawberries, setting the syrup aside, and add the strawberries to sterilized jars (SEE p. 40). Seal with sterilized lids.

—

Put the syrup in a clean pan and bring to a boil. Boil for 20 minutes, then carefully pour the hot syrup into the jars. Seal with sterilized lids.

—

Process in a boiling-water canner (SEE p. 53 and follow the manufacturer's instructions) for 5 minutes.

—

NOTE: Using wild strawberries is not recommended for jam-making: the fruit are too small and tend to become dry or bitter.

# RASPBERRIES

## RASPBERRIES AU NATUREL

Preparation time 20 minutes
Standing time 1 hour
Canning time 20 minutes
Makes 3 x 1 lb 2 oz (500 g) jars

3¼ lb (1.5 kg) raspberries
about 1¼ cups (9 oz/250 g) sugar

Use ripe raspberries.

—

Arrange the raspberries in sterilized jars
(SEE p. 40), with alternating layers of sugar
after each 1¼-inch/3-cm layer of fruit. Leave
for 1 hour.

—

Top off with an extra layer of fruit and sugar
and seal with sterilized lids.

—

Process in a boiling-water canner (SEE p. 53
and follow the manufacturer's instructions) for
20 minutes.

## RASPBERRIES IN SYRUP

Preparation time 20 minutes
Standing time 1 hour
Cooking time 5 minutes
Canning time 20 minutes
Makes 3 x 1 lb 2 oz (500 g) jars

3¼ lb (1.5 kg) raspberries
about 1¼ cups (9 oz/250 g) sugar, plus extra for
the syrup

Arrange the raspberries in sterilized jars
(SEE p. 40), with alternating layers of sugar after
each 1¼-inch/3-cm layer of fruit. Leave for
1 hour.

—

While the raspberries are settling in the jars,
make a sugar syrup. Bring 3¾ cups (1 lb 10 oz/
750 g) sugar per 3¾ cups (34 fl oz/1 liter) water
to a boil in a pan. Boil for 2–3 seconds, then
remove from the heat and pour over the fruit to
cover. Seal with sterilized lids.

—

Process in a boiling-water canner (SEE p. 53
and follow the manufacturer's instructions) for
20 minutes.

## RASPBERRY JAM

Preparation time 15 minutes
Steeping time 12 hours
Cooking time 20 minutes
Canning time 5 minutes
Makes 4 x 1 lb 2 oz (500 g) jars

6 lb (2.75 kg) raspberries
13¾ cups (6 lb/2.75 kg) sugar

This jam is used in pastries, in the Austrian Linzertorte in particular.
—
Put the raspberries into a terrine dish or large nonreactive bowl and add the same weight of sugar as fruit. Cover with a lid or plastic wrap (clingfilm) and steep in a cool place for 12 hours.
—
When ready, put a small plate or saucer into the freezer to chill. Transfer the sugar and fruit to a large preserving pan, bring to a boil, and boil for 15 minutes. Skim with a slotted spoon to remove any scum floating on the surface. To test for a set, pour several drops of jam onto the chilled plate and when you tip the plate the juice should not run.
—
Pour the jam into sterilized jars (SEE p. 40) and seal with sterilized lids.
—
Process in a boiling-water canner (SEE p. 53 and follow the manufacturer's instructions) for 5 minutes.

## RASPBERRY JELLY

Preparation time 30 minutes
Cooking time 10 minutes
Canning time 5 minutes
Makes 2 x 1 lb 2 oz (500 g) jars

2¼ lb (1 kg) raspberries
9 oz (250 g) white currants, stripped from stalks
sugar

Mixing white currants with raspberries (9 oz/250 g white currants per 2¼ lb/1 kg raspberries) ensures that the jelly will set correctly. White currants are preferred over red currants as their taste is both sweeter and more neutral.
—
Put the fruit in a terrine dish or large nonreactive bowl and crush with a pestle. Using a spoon, scoop the fruit out into a clean, damp dishtowel (tea towel), gather into a bundle, and wring over a large bowl to squeeze out all the juice.
—
Put a small plate or saucer into the freezer to chill. Measure the juice and pour into a large preserving pan with the same weight of sugar as the juice. Bring to a boil, skim with a slotted spoon to remove any scum floating on the surface, and boil for 3 minutes. To test for a set, pour several drops of jam onto the chilled plate and when you tip the plate the juice should not run.
—
Transfer the jelly to sterilized jars (SEE p. 40) and seal with sterilized lids.

Process in a boiling-water canner (SEE p. 53 and follow the manufacturer's instructions) for 5 minutes.

NOTE: Raspberry juice is difficult to remove from fabrics once dried, so make sure you clean the dishtowel (tea towel) straightaway, and use one that you don't mind staining.

## RASPBERRY SYRUP

Preparation time 20 minutes
Canning time 5 minutes
Makes 4¼ cups (34 fl oz/1 liter)

3 lb (1.4 kg) raspberries
sugar

Put the raspberries in a terrine dish or large nonreactive bowl and crush with a pestle. Using a spoon, scoop the fruit out into a clean, damp dishtowel (tea towel), gather into a bundle, and wring over a large bowl to squeeze out all the juice.

—

Measure the juice and pour into a large preserving pan with 8 cups (3½ lb/1.6 kg) sugar per 4¼ cups (34 fl oz/1 liter) juice. Bring to a boil, skim with a slotted spoon to remove any scum on the surface, and boil rapidly until it reaches the coated or nappé stage (221°F/105°C), or when small bubbles form at the surface of the syrup, which thinly coats the back of a skimmer dipped into the syrup.

—

Pour into sterilized bottles (SEE p. 40) and seal.

—

Process in a boiling-water canner (SEE p. 53 and follow the manufacturer's instructions) for 5 minutes.

—

NOTE: Raspberry juice is difficult to remove from fabrics once dried, so make sure you clean the dishtowel (tea towel) straightaway, and use one that you don't mind staining.

## RASPBERRY EAU-DE-VIE

Preparation time 20 minutes
Cooking time 5 minutes
Steeping time 8 days, plus 1 month
Makes 4¾ cups (40 fl oz/1.15 liters)

1 lb 2 oz (500 g) raspberries
2½ cups (1 lb 2 oz/500 g) sugar
4¼ cups (34 fl oz/1 liter) flavorless alcohol, such as vodka, at 45%

Put the raspberries in a large ceramic or nonreactive bowl and crush with a pestle. Transfer to a sterilized jar (SEE p. 40).

—

For the sugar syrup, bring the sugar and 2¼ cups (17 fl oz/500 ml) water to a boil in a pan. Boil for 2–3 seconds, then remove from the heat and pour over the raspberries. Stir to combine, cover with a sterilized lid, and steep in a cool place for eight days.

—

Strain the fruit and discard, then pour the syrup into a clean sterilized jar. Pour in the alcohol, mix well, seal with a sterilized lid, and steep for one month.

## RASPBERRY VINEGAR

Preparation time 15 minutes
Steeping time 15 days
Makes 6¼ cups (53 fl oz/1.5 liters)

12 oz (350 g) raspberries
4¼ cups (34 fl oz/1 liter) white vinegar
sugar

Place the raspberries and vinegar in a
nonreactive container and stir to combine,
then cover with a lid or plastic wrap (clingfilm)
and steep in a cool, dark place for 15 days.
—
Strain the mixture through a strainer to collect
the juice, then measure the juice and pour into
a sterilized bottle (SEE p. 40). Add double the
weight in sugar before sealing.
—
This refreshing syrup is ready to serve when
the sugar has completely dissolved.

# BLACK CURRANTS

## BLACK CURRANTS AU NATUREL

Preparation time 20 minutes
Standing time 1 hour
Canning time 20 minutes
Makes about 3 x 1 lb 2 oz (500 g) jars

3¼ lb (1.5 kg) black currants, stripped from
    stalks
about 1½ cups (11 oz/300 g) sugar

Black currants are not typically preserved
because of their thick skin and strong flavour.
—
Arrange the black currants in sterilized jars
(SEE p. 40), with alternating layers of sugar after
each 1¼-inch/3-cm layer of fruit. Leave for
1 hour.
—
Top off with an extra layer of fruit and sugar
and seal with sterilized lids.
—
Process in a boiling-water canner (SEE p. 53
and follow the manufacturer's instructions) for
20 minutes.

# RED CURRANTS

## RED CURRANTS AU NATUREL

**Preparation time 20 minutes**
**Standing time 1 hour**
**Canning time 20 minutes**
**Makes 3 x 1 lb 2 oz (500 g) jars**

3¼ lb (1.5 kg) red currants, stripped from stalks
  (for best results when working with red
  currants, combine with ⅓ white currants if
  possible, with white currants for ⅔ red
  currants)
sugar

Use a stainless steel fork to remove the fruit from the stalks as other metals may react and darken the juice of the fruit.

—

Arrange the red currants in sterilized jars (SEE p. 40), with alternating layers of sugar after each 1¼-inch/3-cm layer of fruit. Leave for 1 hour.

—

Top off with an extra layer of fruit and sugar and seal with sterilized lids.

—

Process in a boiling-water canner (SEE p. 53 and follow the manufacturer's instructions) for 20 minutes.

## RED CURRANT JELLY

Preparation time 15 minutes
Cooking time 25 minutes
Canning time 5 minutes
Makes about 2 x 1 lb 2 oz (500 g) jars

4½ lb (2 kg) red currants, washed
sugar

Place the red currants, still on their stalks, in a large preserving pan with a little water (¼ cup/2 fl oz/60 ml water per 4½ lb/2 kg fruit) and heat for 5 minutes, or until the fruit splits. Bring to a boil and boil for 8 minutes, stirring constantly.
—
Strain the mixture through a strainer to collect the juice. Do not push or squeeze the fruit or the jelly will be cloudy.
—
Put a small plate or saucer into the freezer to chill. Measure the juice and pour it into a clean pan and add the same weight of sugar. Heat over low heat, stirring constantly until the sugar dissolves. Bring to a boil and just as it is boiling stop stirring. Boil for exactly 3 minutes. This is the time it takes the pectin in the red currants to set into a jelly. To test for a set, pour several drops of jam onto the chilled plate and when you tip the plate the juice should not run.
—
Pour the jelly into sterilized jars (SEE p. 40) and seal with sterilized lids.
—
Process in a boiling-water canner (SEE p. 53 and follow the manufacturer's instructions) for 5 minutes.

## RASPBERRY AND RED CURRANT JELLY

Preparation time 15 minutes
Cooking time 25 minutes
Canning time 5 minutes
Makes 2 x 1 lb 2 oz (500 g) jars

1 lb 5 oz (600 g) red currants, washed
9 oz (250 g) white currants, washed
7 oz (200 g) raspberries, stalks removed
sugar

Place the currants, still on their stalks, and the raspberries, in a large preserving pan with a little water (¼ cup/2 fl oz/60 ml water per 4½ lb/2 kg fruit) and heat for 5 minutes, or until the fruit splits. Bring to a boil and boil for 8 minutes, stirring constantly.
—
Strain the mixture through a strainer to collect the juice. Do not push or squeeze the fruit or the jelly will be cloudy.
—
Put a small plate or saucer into the freezer to chill. Measure the juice and pour it into a clean pan and add the same weight of sugar. Heat over low heat, stirring until the sugar dissolves completely. Bring to a boil and just as it is boiling stop stirring. Boil for exactly 3 minutes. This is the time it takes the pectin in the red currants to set into a jelly. To test for a set, pour several drops of jam onto the chilled plate and when you tip the plate the juice should not run.
—
Pour the jelly into sterilized jars (SEE p. 40) and seal with sterilized lids.
—
Process in a boiling-water canner (SEE p. 53 and follow the manufacturer's instructions) for 5 minutes.

## RED CURRANT SYRUP

Preparation time 20 minutes
Canning time 5 minutes
Makes 4¼ cups (34 fl oz/1 liter)

3 lb (1.4 kg) red currants, stripped from stalks
(for best results when working with red
currants, combine with white currants if
possible, with 1/3 white currants for 2/3 red
currants)
sugar

Use a stainless steel fork to remove the fruit
from the stalks as other metals may react and
darken the juice of the fruit.

—

Put the red currants in a large ceramic or
nonreactive bowl and crush with a pestle.
Using a spoon, scoop the fruit out into a clean,
damp dishtowel (tea towel), gather into a
bundle, and wring over a large bowl to squeeze
out all the juice.

—

Measure the juice and pour into a large
preserving pan with 8 cups (3½ lb/1.6 kg)
sugar per 4¼ cups (34 fl oz/1 liter) juice. Bring
to a boil, skim with a slotted spoon to remove
any scum on the surface, and boil rapidly
until it reaches the coated or nappé stage
(221°F/105°C), or when small bubbles form at
the surface of the syrup, which thinly coats the
back of a skimmer dipped into the syrup.

—

Pour into sterilized bottles (SEE p. 40) and seal.

—

Process in a boiling-water canner (SEE p. 53
and follow the manufacturer's instructions) for
5 minutes.

# GOOSEBERRIES

## GOOSEBERRY JELLY

Preparation time 20 minutes
Cooking time 30 minutes
Canning time 5 minutes
Makes about 2 x 1 lb 2 oz (500 g) jars

4½ lb (2 kg) gooseberries, trimmed
sugar

Gooseberries have a wonderful flavor, but they have thick skins and pips, which makes them less suited to jam. Gooseberry jelly can often provide better results.

—

Put a small plate or saucer into the freezer to chill. Put the gooseberries in a large pan with ¼ cup (2 fl oz/60 ml) water per 2¼ lb (1 kg) fruit and heat for about 5 minutes, or until the skins split.

—

Strain the gooseberries through a strainer to collect the juice, pressing the fruit with a wooden spoon. Measure the juice, pour into a large preserving pan and add the same weight in sugar as the juice. Bring to a boil and boil for 20 minutes. Skim with a slotted spoon to remove any scum floating on the surface. To test for a set, pour several drops of jam onto the chilled plate and when you tip the plate the juice should not run.

—

Pour the jelly into sterilized jars (SEE p. 40) and seal with sterilized lids.

—

Process in a boiling-water canner (SEE p. 53 and follow the manufacturer's instructions) for 5 minutes.

## GOOSEBERRY JAM

Preparation time 20 minutes
Resting time 12 hours
Cooking time 30-35 minutes
Makes about 6 x 1 lb 2 oz (500 g) jars

4 lb (1.8 kg) gooseberries, trimmed
sugar

The jam can have an uneven consistency due to pips and skins in it. Most people will probably prefer gooseberry jelly (SEE left) but if you like jams with a thicker consistency and less smooth texture then goosberry jam works well.

—

Put the gooseberries in a large ceramic or nonreactive bowl with scant 2 cups (13 oz/375 g) sugar per 1 lb 2 oz (500 g) of fruit. Cover with a lid or plastic wrap (clingfilm) and leave overnight.

—

The next day, put a small plate or saucer into the freezer to chill. Transfer the fruit and sugar to a large preserving pan and bring to a boil. Boil for 25–30 minutes. Skim with a slotted spoon to remove any scum floating on the surface. To test for a set, pour several drops of jam onto the chilled plate and when you tip the plate the juice should not run.

—

Pour the jam into sterilized jars (SEE p. 40) and seal with sterilized lids.

—

Process in a boiling-water canner (SEE p. 53 and follow the manufacturer's instructions) for 5 minutes.

# MANDARINS

## CANDIED MANDARIN (OR TANGERINE) PEEL

**Preparation time 30 minutes**
**Cooking time 1 hour**
**Steeping time 6-72 hours**
**Makes 2¼ lb (1 kg)**

10-12 mandarins, peeled, white pith removed
    and either left whole if small or quartered
sugar
salt

Bring a large pan of salted water to a boil over high heat. Carefully add the manadarin peel and blanch for 4 minutes, then drain and set aside.

—

Make a sugar syrup. Heat 8 cups (3½ lb/1.6 kg) sugar per 4¼ cups (34 fl oz/1 liter) water gently in a pan, stirring until the sugar has dissolved, then bring to a boil and boil rapidly until it reaches the small thread stage (225°F/107°C), or when the syrup thickens and the bubbles grow larger, and when pulled apart, it forms a thin and flexible thread about ½ inch/1 cm long, which breaks easily. Carefully lower in the peel and return to a boil. When the syrup comes back to a boil, remove the pan from the heat, cover with a lid, and leave the peel in the syrup for 1 hour, or overnight.

—

When ready, carefully remove the peel with a slotted spoon and set aside. Heat the syrup until it reaches the large thread stage (228–230°F/109–110°C), or when dropped into a glass of water, it forms threads of about ¾–1¼ inches/2–3 cm long. Carefully lower in the peel and return to a boil. When the syrup comes back to a boil, remove the pan from the heat and leave the peel in the syrup for 1 hour, or overnight.

Repeat the process another four times, increasing the sugar concentration by 1.8°F/1°C each day until the syrup reaches the large pearl stage (237°F/114 °C), or when small beads form on the surface of the syrup, and if you blow on a skimmer coated with the syrup, bubbles form at the edges.

—

Remove the peel from the syrup with a slotted spoon and drain well. Place on a rack, standing the rack on a tray, sheet of parchment paper, or aluminum foil to catch any drips, and dry in a well-ventilated place. When dry cut the peel into strips.

## MANDARIN (OR TANGERINE) JAM

Preparation time 30 minutes
Cooking time 1 hour 30 minutes
Resting time 6–72 hours
Canning time 5 minutes
Makes 6 x 1 lb 2 oz (500 g) jars

4½ lb (2 kg) mandarins, peeled, white pith
    removed and either left whole if small or
    quartered
sugar
salt

Mandarins are best preserved freshly picked at
their peak of ripeness.

—

To candy the peel, see page 185.

—

To make the jam, put a small plate or saucer
into the freezer to chill. Put the mandarins and
3¾ cups (1 lb 10 oz/750 g) sugar per 2¼ lb (1 kg)
fruit into a large preserving pan. Bring to a
boil and boil for 20–25 minutes. The juice will
thicken. Add the candied peel strips and cook
for another 5 minutes. To test for a set, pour
several drops of jam onto the chilled plate and
when you tip the plate the juice should not run.

—

Pour the jam into sterilized jars (SEE p. 40) and
seal with sterilized lids.

—

Process in a boiling-water canner (SEE p. 53
and follow the manufacturer's instructions) for
5 minutes.

# CHESTNUTS

## CHESTNUTS, STORED FRESH

Chestnuts for storing are best harvested in
early winter. Remove their spiky casing and let
them dry for a few days, in the sun if possible,
or in a well-ventilated place.

—

To store, bury the chestnuts in a container of
sand mixed with dry earth. You can also place
them in a crate, with alternating layers of dried
leaves. They will keep for 2–3 months.

## CHESTNUT JAM

**Preparation time 30 minutes plus cooling**
**Cooking time 1 hour 30 minutes**
**Canning time 5 minutes**
**Makes 5 x 1 lb 2 oz (500 g) jars**

4½ lb (2 kg) chestnuts, washed
sugar
1 vanilla bean (pod), split open lengthwise and
   seeds scraped out

---

Chestnut jam is best made in small batches of 4½ lb (2 kg) fruit at the most.

—

Using a knife, score the chestnuts' skins to form an "X" on the rounded side. Place in a large pan, pour in enough cold water to cover, and bring to a boil. Boil for 3–4 minutes. Remove the pan from the heat and, protecting your hands with heat-resistant gloves or a thick dishtowel (tea towel), peel off the skins immediately, without cooling.

—

Discard the cooking water and fill the pan back up with hot water. Lower in the chestnuts while still hot, and bring to a boil. Cook for 15–20 minutes, or until soft. Drain, reserving the cooking water.

—

Grind the chestnuts to a fine meal in a mortar or food mill. Add a little of the reserved cooking water and grind or process to make a puree. Weigh the puree.

—

Make a sugar syrup. Heat the same weight of sugar as the puree weight with ½ cup (4 fl oz/125 ml) water per 5 cups (2¼ lb/1 kg) sugar gently in a pan, stirring until the sugar has dissolved, then bring to a boil and boil rapidly until it reaches the small pearl stage (232°F/111°C), or when tiny round beads form at the surface of the syrup, and when dropped in a glass of water it forms threads of about 1½–2 inches/4–5 cm in length.

—

Stir in the chestnut puree together with the vanilla bean (pod) and seeds. Bring to a boil, stirring constantly, and cook for 30 minutes, stirring constantly to prevent the puree sticking to the bottom of the pan. Be careful as the hot mixture may spit and sputter.

—

Remove the pan from the heat, take out the vanilla bean (pod) and cool the mixture for 15 minutes.

—

Pour the jam into sterilized jars (SEE p. 40) and seal with sterilized lids.

—

Process in a boiling-water canner (SEE p. 53 and follow the manufacturer's instructions) for 5 minutes.

## CANDIED CHESTNUTS

Preparation time 1 hour
Cooking time 50 minutes
Steeping time 6 days
Canning time 5 minutes
Makes about 2 x 1 lb 2 oz (500 g) jars

2 lb (900 g) chestnuts
4½ cups (2 lb/900 g) sugar
1 vanilla bean (pod), split open lengthwise and
  seeds scraped out

Use plump chestnuts with tight, shiny, dark brown skins that feel heavy for their size.

—

Using a knife, score the chestnuts' skins to form an "X" on the rounded side. Place in a large pan, pour in enough cold water to cover, and bring to a boil. Boil for 3–4 minutes. Remove the pan from the heat and protecting your hands with heat-resistant gloves or a thick dishtowel (tea towel), peel off the skins immediately, without cooling.

—

Bring another large pan of water to a boil, add the chestnuts, and simmer for 15 minutes until the chestnuts are soft; they should be easy to prick to the core with a needle. Have ready a large bowl filled halfway with ice cubes and enough cold water to cover the ice. Drain the chestnuts and peel off the thin inner skin carefully. Plunge them into the ice-cold water, leave for 1 minute, then drain.

—

Make a sugar syrup. Bring 3¾ cups (1 lb 10 oz/750 g) sugar per 4¼ cups (34 fl oz/1 liter) water with the vanilla bean (pod) and seeds to a boil in a pan. Boil for 2–3 seconds, carefully add the chestnuts, then remove from the heat. Cover with a lid and steep in a cool, dark place for two days.

Remove the chestnuts from the syrup with a nonreactive slotted spoon and set aside. Bring the syrup to a boil and boil for 3 minutes. Add the chestnuts, remove from the heat, cover with a lid, and steep for another two days.

—

Remove the chestnuts from the syrup again, and set aside. Bring the syrup to a boil and boil rapidly until it reaches the coated or nappé stage (221°F/105°C), or when small bubbles form at the surface of the syrup, which thinly coats the back of a skimmer dipped into the syrup. Add the chestnuts, remove the pan from the heat, and steep for two more days.

—

Remove the chestnuts from the syrup again and set aside. Bring the syrup to a boil and boil rapidly until it reaches the small pearl stage (232°F/111°C), or when tiny round beads form at the surface of the syrup, then when held between the fingers it forms a wider thread of about 1½–2 inches/4–5 cm in length. Add the chestnuts and boil for 2 minutes.

—

Strain the chestnuts and arrange in sterilized jars (SEE p. 40) and seal with sterilized lids.

—

Process in a boiling-water canner (SEE p. 53 and follow the manufacturer's instructions) for 5 minutes.

## MARRONS GLACÉS

Preparation time 1 hour
Cooking time 1¼-1½ hours
Steeping time 6 days
Drying time 30 minutes
Makes about 2 lb (900 g)

2 lb (900 g) chestnuts
4½ cups (2 lb/900 g) sugar
1 vanilla bean (pod), split open lengthwise and
    seeds scraped out

Using a knife, score the chestnuts' skins to
form an "X" on the rounded side. Place in a
large pan, pour in enough cold water to cover,
and bring to a boil. Boil for 3–4 minutes.
Remove the pan from the heat and, protecting
your hands with heat-resistant gloves or a
thick dishtowel (tea towel), peel off the skins
immediately, without cooling.

—

Bring another large pan of water to a boil, add
the chestnuts, and simmer for 15 minutes until
the chestnuts are soft; they should be easy to
prick to the core with a needle. Have ready a
large bowl filled halfway with ice cubes and
enough cold water to cover the ice. Drain
the chestnuts and peel off the thin inner skin
carefully. Plunge them into the ice-cold water,
leave for 1 minutes, then drain.

—

Make a sugar syrup. Bring 3¾ cups (1 lb
10 oz/750 g) sugar per 4¼ cups (34 fl oz/1 liter)
water with the vanilla bean (pod) and seeds
to a boil in a pan. Boil for 2–3 seconds, carefully
add the chestnuts, then remove from the heat.
Cover with a lid and steep in a cool, dark place
for two days.

—

Remove the chestnuts from the syrup with a
nonreactive slotted spoon and set aside. Bring

the syrup to a boil and boil for 3 minutes. Add
the chestnuts, remove from the heat, cover with
a lid, and steep for another two days.

—

Remove the chestnuts from the syrup again,
and set aside. Bring the syrup to a boil and boil
rapidly until it reaches the coated or nappé stage
($221°F/105°C$), or when small bubbles form at
the surface of the syrup, which thinly coats the
back of a skimmer dipped into the syrup. Add
the chestnuts, remove the pan from the heat,
and steep for two more days.

—

Preheat the oven to $250°F/120°C$/Gas Mark ½.

—

Remove the chestnuts from the syrup again
and set aside. Bring the syrup to a boil and
boil rapidly until it reaches the small pearl
stage ($232°F/111°C$), or when tiny round beads
form at the surface of the syrup, then when
dropped into a glass of water it forms threads of
about 1½–2 inches/4–5 cm in length. Add the
chestnuts and boil for 2 minutes.

—

Strain the chestnuts and set aside. Heat the
syrup again until it reaches large pearl stage
($237°F/114°C$), or when small beads form on
the surface of the syrup, and if you blow on a
skimmer coated with the syrup, bubbles form
at the edges. Stir the syrup with a spatula until
it turns white. Add the chestnuts and stir gently
to coat.

—

Strain the chestnuts, place them on a baking
sheet, and place in the oven for 15–30 minutes,
or until dry. Remove from the oven and cool,
then store in an airtight container in a dry place.

# MELONS

## MELONS, STORED FRESH

Ripe melons are best eaten immediately, but they will also keep in the refrigerator for a week. However, their strong scent can permeate other foods.

—

Melons picked just before they are fully ripe can be stored for 1–2 months: keep the stems on and leave the melons in the open air for a day before burying them in a crate of fine, dry sand in a cool, dark place.

## MELON JAM

Preparation time 15 minutes
Cooking time 20 minutes
Canning time 5 minutes
Makes 2 x 1 lb 2 oz (500 g) jars

1 melon, peeled, seeded, and cut into
    ½-inch/1-cm cubes (prepared weight of
    melon cubes about 2¼ lb/1 kg)
equal weight of sugar to melon cubes
1 vanilla bean (pod), split open lengthwise and
    seeds scraped out
lemon juice

Put a small plate or saucer into the freezer to chill. Put the melon into a large preserving pan with the sugar, vanilla bean (pod) and seeds, and scant ½ cup (3½ fl oz/100 ml) lemon juice per 2¼ lb (1 kg) fruit. Bring to a boil over gentle heat, and simmer for 15 minutes. To test for a set, pour several drops of jam onto the chilled plate and when you tip the plate the juice should not run.

—

Pour the jam into sterilized jars (SEE p. 40) and seal with sterilized lids.

—

Process in a boiling-water canner (SEE p. 53 and follow the manufacturer's instructions) for 5 minutes.

## SMALL MELONS IN VINEGAR

Preparation time 30 minutes
Resting time 12 hours
Steeping time 3 weeks
Makes 2 x 1 lb 2 oz (500 g) jars

1½ lb (675 g) walnut-sized melons
few clean grape (vine) leaves
2 onions, finely chopped
9 sprigs tarragon
1 tablespoon black peppercorns
2 shallots, sliced (optional)
4 garlic cloves (optional)
about 2¼ cups (17 fl oz/500 ml) cold distilled
    vinegar
coarse salt

Gardeners generally prune some of the young melons that start to form to enable others to grow larger. This pickle makes use of the discarded melons, which are about the size of a walnut. The pickle can be used in the same way as gherkins.

—

Rub the melons with coarse salt and place in a large ceramic or nonreactive bowl for 12 hours, coated evenly with the salt.

—

Arrange a few clean vine leaves in the bottom of your sterilized jars (SEE p. 40).

—

Wipe off the excess salt from the melons and fill the jars in layers, alternating with the chopped onions, tarragon, and pepper. Add a few sliced shallots and garlic cloves, if liked.

—

Top off with cold vinegar, seal tightly with sterilized lids, and steep for three weeks in a cool, dark place.

# MIRABELLE PLUMS

## MIRABELLE PLUMS AU NATUREL

Preparation time 20 minutes
Cooking time 2 minutes
Canning time 20 minutes
Makes 2 x 1 lb 2 oz (500 g) jars

1¾ lb (800 g) Mirabelle plums, washed, with
   the pits in
2 tablespoons sugar

Mirabelles are tiny plums that are greenish-yellow in color and exceptionally flavorful. Most Mirabelle plums are grown in Lorraine and Alsace in France, and their season is short. Pick Mirabelle plums that are not too ripe.
—
Have ready a large bowl filled halfway with ice cubes and enough cold water to cover the ice. Bring a large pan to a simmer over low-medium heat. Prick each fruit with a stainless-steel needle until you reach the pit, then lower the plums into the pan of simmering water and cook for 2 minutes, until they rise to the surface. Remove the plums with a slotted spoon and plunge into the ice-cold water. Leave for 1 minute, then drain.
—
Arrange the fruit in sterilized jars (SEE p. 40). Sprinkle with 1 tablespoon sugar per jar and seal with sterilized lids.
—
Process in a boiling-water canner (SEE p. 53 and follow the manufacturer's instructions) for 20 minutes.

## MIRABELLE PLUMS IN SYRUP

Preparation time 30 minutes
Cooking time 10 minutes
Canning time 20 minutes
Makes 2 x 1 lb 2 oz (500 g) jars

1¾ lb (800 g) Mirabelle plums, washed, with
   the pits in
sugar

Have ready a large bowl filled halfway with ice cubes and enough cold water to cover the ice. Bring a large pan to a simmer over low-medium heat. Prick each fruit with a stainless-steel needle until you reach the pit, then lower the plums into the pan of simmering water and cook for 2 minutes until they rise to the surface. Remove the plums with a slotted spoon and plunge into the ice-cold water, leave for 1 minute, then drain.
—
Arrange the fruit in sterilized jars (SEE p. 40).
—
Make a sugar syrup. Bring 2 cups (14 oz/400 g) sugar per 4¼ cups (34 fl oz/1 liter) water to a boil in a pan. Boil for 2–3 seconds then remove from the heat. Carefully top off the jars with the syrup. Seal with sterilized lids.
—
Process in a boiling-water canner (SEE p. 53 and follow the manufacturer's instructions) for 20 minutes.

## MIRABELLE PLUM JAM

Preparation time 20 minutes
Steeping time 12 hours
Cooking time 25 minutes
Canning time 5 minutes
Makes 4 x 1 lb 2 oz (500 g) jars

6 lb (2.75 kg) Mirabelle plums, halved and pitted
sugar

Put the plums in a large preserving pan, add
2½ cups (1 lb 2 oz/500g) sugar per 2¼ lb (1 kg)
fruit, cover with a lid, and steep for 12 hours.
—
The next day, put a small plate or saucer into
the freezer to chill. Bring the plums and sugar
to a boil and cook for 20 minutes. Mirabelle
plums do not release much juice, so watch the
jam carefully as it cooks to make sure it doesn't
stick to the bottom of the pan. To test for a set,
pour several drops of jam onto the chilled plate
and when you tip the plate the juice should not
run.
—
Pour the jam into sterilized jars (SEE p. 40) and
seal with sterilized lids.
—
Process in a boiling-water canner (SEE p. 53
and follow the manufacturer's instructions) for
5 minutes.

## MIRABELLE PLUMS IN EAU-DE-VIE

Preparation time 20 minutes
Cooking time 2 minutes
Drying time 30 minutes
Steeping time 1–3 months
Makes 2 x 1 lb 2 oz (500 g) jars

2¼ lb (1 kg) Mirabelle plums, stalks rimmed by
half
sugar
about 1¼ cups (10 fl oz/300 ml) eau-de-vie at
45%

Have ready a large bowl filled halfway with ice
cubes and enough cold water to cover the ice.
Bring a large pan of water to a boil over high
heat. Carefully add the plums and blanch for
2 minutes. Remove the plums with a slotted
spoon and plunge them into the ice-cold water.
Leave for 1 minute, then drain and set on a
clean cloth to dry, about 30 minutes.
—
Arrange the fruit in a sterilized jar (SEE p. 40)
with 1¼ cups (9 oz/250 g) sugar per 2¼ lb (1 kg)
fruit. Top off with the eau-de-vie. Seal with a
sterilized lid and steep in a cool, dark place for
at least one month, preferably three, shaking
the jar daily for the first few days to make sure
the alcohol and sugar mix well.

# BLACKBERRIES

## WHOLE BLACKBERRY JAM

Preparation time 20 minutes
Steeping time 12 hours
Cooking time 30-35 minutes
Canning time 5 minutes
Makes 4 x 1 lb 2 oz (500 g) jars

6 lb (2.75 kg) blackberries, stalks removed
sugar

Put the blackberries in a large preserving pan with 3¾ cups (1 lb 10 oz/750 g) sugar per 2¼ lb (1 kg) fruit, cover with a lid, and steep for 12 hours.

—

The next day, put a small plate or saucer into the freezer to chill. Bring the blackberries and sugar slowly to a boil and cook for 25–30 minutes. Skim with a slotted spoon to remove any scum floating on the surface. To test for a set, pour several drops of jam onto the chilled plate and when you tip the plate the juice should not run.

—

Pour the jam into sterilized jars (SEE p. 40) and seal with sterilized lids.

—

Process in a boiling-water canner (SEE p. 53 and follow the manufacturer's instructions) for 5 minutes.

—

NOTE: It is important not overcook this jam: the blackberries will lose their juice and dry out, and you would be left with pips in syrup.

## BLACKBERRY JELLY

Preparation time 30 minutes
Cooking time 35 minutes
Canning time 5 minutes
Makes about 3 x 1 lb 2 oz (500 g) jars

4½ lb (2 kg) blackberries, stalks removed
sugar

Use very ripe blackberries, which will be very black in color.

—

Put the blackberries in a terrine or a large nonreactive bowl and crush with a pestle. Using a spoon, scoop the fruit out into a clean, damp dishtowel (tea towel), gather into a bundle, and wring over a large bowl to squeeze out all the juice.

—

Put a small plate or saucer into the freezer to chill. Measure the juice, pour it into a large preserving pan and add the same weight in sugar. Bring to a boil and cook for 30 minutes. Skim with a slotted spoon to remove any scum floating on the top. To test for a set, pour several drops of jam onto the chilled plate and when you tip the plate the juice should not run.

—

Pour the jelly into sterilized jars (SEE p. 40) and seal with sterilized lids.

—

Process in a boiling-water canner (SEE p. 53 and follow the manufacturer's instructions) for 5 minutes.

—

NOTE: Blackberry juice is difficult to remove from fabrics once dried, so make sure you clean the cloth straightaway, and use one you don't mind staining.

## BLACKBERRY AND APPLE JELLY

Preparation time 30 minutes
Cooking time 45 minutes
Canning time 5 minutes
Makes about 3 x1 lb 2 oz (500 g) jars

4½ lb (2 kg) blackberries, stalks removed
9 oz (250 g) cooking apples, unpeeled and
    thickly sliced, no need to core
sugar

---

Put the blackberries and apples in a large preserving pan with ¼ cup (2 fl oz/60 ml) water per 2¼ lb (1 kg) berries and cook over low heat for 10 minutes, or until soft.
—
Strain through a strainer to collect the juice, Don't press the fruit through the strainer otherwise the jelly will be cloudy.
—
Put a small plate or saucer into the freezer to chill. Measure the juice and pour into a clean preserving pan and add the same weight in sugar. Bring to a boil and cook for 30 minutes. Skim with a slotted spoon to remove any scum floating on the top. To test for a set, pour several drops of jam onto the chilled plate and when you tip the plate the juice should not run.
—
Pour the jelly into sterilized jars (see p. 40) and seal with sterilized lids.
—
Process in a boiling-water canner (see p. 53 and follow the manufacturer's instructions) for 5 minutes.

## BLACKBERRY SYRUP

Preparation time 30 minutes
Steeping time 24 hours
Cooking time 20 minutes
Canning time 5 minutes
Makes about 4¼ cups (34 fl oz/1 liter)

3 lb (1.4 kg) blackberries, stalks removed
sugar

---

Put the blackberries into a large ceramic or nonreactive bowl and crush with a pestle. Cover with a lid or plastic wrap (clingfilm) and steep in the refrigerator for 24 hours.
—
Strain through a strainer to collect the juice, Don't press the fruit through the strainer otherwise the jelly will be cloudy.
—
Measure the juice and pour into a large preserving pan with 8 cups (3½ lb/1.6 kg) sugar per 4¼ cup (34 fl oz/1 liter) juice. Heat gently, stirring until the sugar has dissolved, then bring to a boil and boil rapidly until it reaches the coated or nappé stage (221°F/105°C), or when small bubbles form at the surface of the syrup, which thinly coats the back of a skimmer dipped into the syrup. Skim with a slotted spoon to remove any scum floating on the surface.
—
Pour the syrup into sterilized bottles (see p. 40), and seal.
—
Process in a boiling-water canner (see p. 53 and follow the manufacturer's instructions) for 5 minutes.

# BLUEBERRIES

## BLUEBERRIES AU NATUREL

Preparation time 15 minutes
Canning time 25 minutes
Makes about 2 x 1 lb 2 oz (500 g) jars

2 lb (900 g) blueberries
Sugar

Arrange the fruit in sterilized jars (SEE p. 40), packing them in well. Dust with ¾ cup (5 oz/140 g) sugar for each 4¼-cup (34 fl oz/1 liter) jar. Seal with sterilized lids.

—

Process in a boiling-water canner (SEE p. 53 and follow the manufacturer's instructions) for 25 minutes.

## BLUEBERRY JAM

Preparation time 15 minutes
Steeping time 12 hours
Cooking time 25–30 minutes
Canning time 5 minutes
Makes about 3 x 1 lb 2 oz (500 g) jars

4½ lb (2 kg) blueberries
sugar

Put the blueberries in a large preserving pan with the same weight in sugar, cover with a lid, and steep for 12 hours.

—

The next day, put a small plate or saucer into the freezer to chill. Bring the fruit and sugar to a boil and cook for 20–25 minutes. To test for a set, pour several drops of jam onto the chilled plate and when you tip the plate the juice should not run.

—

Pour the jam into sterilized jars (SEE p. 40) and seal with sterilized lids.

—

Process in a boiling-water canner (SEE p. 53 and follow the manufacturer's instructions) for 5 minutes.

## BLUEBERRY JELLY

Preparation time 30 minutes
Cooking time 45–55 minutes
Canning time 25 minutes
Makes about 3 x 1 lb 2 oz (500 g) jars

4½ lb (2 kg) blueberries

For the apple juice
6 large cooking apples

First, make the apple juice. Cut the apples into quarters without peeling or removing the cores. Put in a pan with enough water to cover and bring to a simmer. Cook for 10–15 minutes, or until the apples are very soft. Strain and collect the juice.

—

Put the blueberries in a pan. Add just enough water to cover them and bring to a boil so the berries burst. Strain, collect the juice, and measure it.

—

Add the blueberry juice to the same quantity of apple juice. Simmer together for 25–30 minutes, or until a teaspoonful dropped onto a chilled saucer does not run and turns to jelly on cooling.

—

Pour into sterilized jars (SEE p. 40) and seal with sterilized lids.

—

Process in a boiling-water canner (SEE p. 53 and follow the manufacturer's instructions) for 25 minutes.

# MEDLARS

## MEDLARS AU NATUREL

Preparation time 20 minutes
Cooking time 1 hour 30 minutes
Canning time 5 minutes
Makes about 2 x 1 lb 2 oz (500 g) jars

4½ lb (2 kg) medlars, unpeeled and roughly
  chopped
sugar

Medlars grow on shrubby trees and are only
edible once they have turned brown and soft. If
you pick them when they are hard and green,
store in a cool, dark place until soft and brown.
You can also wait and pick them after the first
hard frost, which has the same bletting effect.

—

Put the unpeeled, roughly chopped fruit in a
large pan and simmer over low heat for 1 hour,
or until very soft and pulpy. Drain and press
through a strainer to reduce to a puree.

—

Weigh the puree and put it in a large
preserving pan with 3¾ cups (1 lb 10 oz/
750 g) sugar per 2¼ lb (1 kg) puree. Cook for
30 minutes.

—

Pour into sterilized jars (SEE p. 40) and seal with
sterilized lids.

—

Process in a boiling-water canner (SEE p. 53
and follow the manufacturer's instructions) for
5 minutes.

# HAZELNUTS

## HAZELNUTS, STORED FRESH

Pick hazelnuts when the first ones start to fall
from the tree. Remove the outer coverings,
but leave the nuts in the shells and store
in stoneware pots containing dry sand or
sawdust. This will prevent the hazelnuts from
turning rancid.

# WALNUTS

## GREEN WALNUTS IN VINEGAR

Preparation time 10 minutes
Cooking time 7 minutes
Pickling time 6 months
Makes 1 x 4½ cups (34 fl oz/1 liter) jar

1¾ lb (800 g) green walnuts
1¼ cups (10 fl oz/300 ml) distilled vinegar

Use very young green walnuts picked in late spring, before the shell and kernels have had a chance to form and harden for pickling.

—

Have ready a large bowl filled halfway with ice cubes and enough cold water to cover the ice. Prick the walnuts with a needle. Bring a large pan of water to a boil over high heat. Carefully add the walnuts and blanch for 2 minutes, or until tender. Remove the walnuts with a slotted spoon and plunge into the ice-cold water. Leave for 1 minute, then drain.

—

Arrange the walnuts in a sterilized jar (SEE p. 40). Top off with the distilled vinegar and seal with a sterilized lid.

—

Pickle for six months before serving.

## GREEN WALNUT LIQUEUR

Preparation time 30 minutes
Cooking time 5 minutes
Steeping time 5 months
Makes 2¼ UK pints (1.25 liters)

20 green walnuts, quartered
4¼ cup (34 fl oz/1 liter) flavorless alcohol, such as vodka, at 45%
sugar

Use barely formed walnuts harvested in early summer, which can be pricked right through with a pin, for this wine.

—

Put the walnuts into a mortar and crush with a pestle, then place in a nonreactive container, pour in the alcohol, 4¼ cups (34 fl oz/1 liter) per 20 kernels, cover tightly with a clean cloth, and steep for two months in a cool, dark place.

—

Strain to collect the alcohol into a clean container. Make a light sugar syrup. Bring 1¼ cups (9 oz/250 g) sugar per 1 cup (9 fl oz/250 ml) water per 4¼ cups (34 fl oz/1 liter) alcohol to a boil in a pan. Boil for 2–3 seconds, then remove from the heat and carefully pour it into the container. Leave to cool.

—

Pour the liqueur into sterilized bottles (SEE p. 40) and seal. Steep for another three months before drinking; the liqueur will get better and better as it ages.

# ORANGES

## SWEET ORANGE JAM

Preparation time 30 minutes
Steeping time 24 hours
Cooking time 1 hour 30 minutes
Canning time 5 minutes
Makes 12 x 1 lb 2 oz (500 g) jars
5¼ lb (2.4 kg) oranges
2 lemons
10 cups (4½ lb/2 kg) sugar

---

To make this jam, choose sweet oranges with a thin skin and a vibrant orange color.

—

Squeeze the juice of 2 oranges and set aside. Wash the others and slice them thinly, then put into a large preserving pan with 8½ cups (70 fl oz/2 liters), the juice of the reserved oranges, and the juice of the lemons. Cover with a lid and steep for 24 hours.

—

When ready, put a small plate or saucer into the freezer to chill. Add the sugar to the pan, then bring to a boil over low heat, and cook for 1½ hours. Skim with a slotted spoon to remove any scum floating on the surface. To test for a set, pour several drops of jam onto the chilled plate and when you tip the plate the juice should not run.

—

Pour the jam into sterilized jars (SEE p. 40) and seal with sterilized lids.

—

Process in a boiling-water canner (SEE p. 53 and follow the manufacturer's instructions) for 5 minutes.

## ORANGE MARMALADE

Preparation time 30 minutes
Steeping time 24 hours
Cooking time 2 hours
Canning time 5 minutes
Makes 10 x 1 lb 2 oz (500 g) jars

4½ lb (2 kg) bitter oranges
17½ cups (7¾ lb/3.5 kg) sugar

---

Peel the oranges deeply to expose the pulp of the fruit. Slice the pulp thinly and chop the peel finely in a food processor. Put the peel into a terrine or large nonreactive bowl, add 5¼ quarts (8¾ UK pints/5 liters) water, cover with a lid or plastic wrap (clingfilm), and steep for 24 hours.

—

When ready, put a small plate or saucer into the freezer to chill. Transfer the mixture to a large preserving pan with the sugar and slowly bring to a boil and cook over low heat for 2 hours. To test for a set, pour several drops of jam onto the chilled plate and when you tip the plate the juice should not run.

—

Pour the marmalade into sterilized jars (SEE p. 40) and seal with sterilized lids.

—

Process in a boiling-water canner (SEE p. 53 and follow the manufacturer's instructions) for 5 minutes.

## ORANGE AND APPLE JELLY

Preparation time 30 minutes
Cooking time 1 hour
Canning time 5 minutes
Makes 4 x 1 lb 2 oz (500 g) jars

10 large oranges
sugar

For the apple juice
6 large cooking apples, quartered

The day before, prepare the apple juice.
—
For the apple juice, put the apples in a large preserving pan with just enough cold water to cover. Bring to a simmer and cook for 10 minutes until tender.
—
Strain to collect the juice, and use for the jelly.
—
Cut the oranges in half and squeeze their juice, then measure the juice.
—
Put a small plate or saucer into the freezer to chill. Combine the orange juice with the apple juice and some sugar, allowing 1¼ cups (10 fl oz/300 ml) apple juice and 6½ cups (3 lb/1.3 kg) sugar per 4¼ cups (34 fl oz/1 liter) juice in a large preserving pan. Bring to a boil and cook for 40 minutes. To test for a set, pour several drops of jam onto the chilled plate and when you tip the plate the juice should not run.
—
Pour the jelly into sterilized jars (SEE p. 40) and seal with sterilized lids.
—
Process in a boiling-water canner (SEE p. 53 and follow the manufacturer's instructions) for 5 minutes.

If desired, you can add very finely diced candied orange peel in the last few minutes of cooking the jam. To make the candied orange peel, peel 2 thick-skinned oranges. Using the point of a sharp knife, score through the skin of each orange five times at regular intervals, from top to bottom. Carefully peel off the skin in segments along the scored lines so the pieces are similar in shape to the outer rind of melon wedges. Place the peel in a large pan and pour in enough cold water to cover. Bring to a boil and boil for 5 minutes, then remove the pan from the heat and cool in the water for 2–3 hours. Drain, return the peel to a clean pan and cover with fresh cold water. Simmer over low heat for 30 minutes until softened, then drain.
—
Make a sugar syrup. Bring 3⅓ cups (1½ lb /660 g) sugar per 4¼ cups (34 fl oz/1 liter) water to a boil in a pan. Add the peel, reduce the heat to low, and cook for 5 minutes. Remove from the heat and leave the peel in the syrup.
—
Repeat the process every day. The syrup will gradually concentrate; stop when the syrup reaches the large pearl stage (237°F/114°C), or when small beads form on the surface of the syrup, and if you blow on a skimmer coated with the syrup, bubbles form at the edges. Drain, place the peel on a rack and leave to air-dry. Alternatively, you can keep the peel in a jar with the remaining syrup.

## ORANGE LEMONADE

Preparation time 20 minutes
Makes 3¾ cups (32 fl oz/900 ml)

2 oranges
4 oz (125 g) sugar cubes
juice of ½ lemon

Rub the skin of the oranges with the sugar cubes until they have absorbed all of the zest.

—

Squeeze the juice of the oranges, and combine it in a large bowl with the lemon juice, the sugar cubes, and 3 cups (26 fl oz/750 ml) boiling water. Stir well to dissolve the sugar, then cool.

—

Strain, pour into sterilized bottles (see p. 40), seal, and chill before serving.

## ORANGE SYRUP

Preparation time 15 minutes
Cooking time 5 minutes
Makes 5 cups (42 fl oz/1.2 liters)

16 oranges, washed
sugar

Choose oranges with quite thick skins with close-grained flesh, but with a fine grain.

—

Use a vegetable peeler to peel the zest from half the oranges in strips, taking care to leave behind the white pith. Halve the oranges and squeeze to collect their juice.

—

Measure the juice and pour it into a large pan with 8 cups (3½ lb/1.6 kg) sugar per 4¼ cups (34 fl oz/1 liter) juice. Dissolve the sugar completely and bring to a boil. Add the zest, then remove from the heat and cool slightly.

—

Pour the syrup into sterilized bottles (see p. 40) and seal.

## ORANGE WINE

Preparation time 15 minutes
Steeping time 48 hours
Makes 4¼ cups (34 fl oz/1 liter)

2 oranges, washed
3½ oz (100 g) sugar cubes
3 cups (26 fl oz/750 ml) dry white wine
generous ¾ cup (7fl oz/200 ml) flavorless
    alcohol, such as vodka at 45%

Rub the orange skin with the sugar cubes until they have absorbed all of the zest.
—
Combine the wine, alcohol and sugar cubes in a large sterilized jar (SEE p. 40). Cover with a sterilized lid and steep for 48 hours.
—
Strain and pour into sterilized bottles, then seal.

## ORANGE PEEL LIQUEUR

Preparation time 30 minutes
Steeping time 2 months
Cooking time 5 minutes
Makes 8½ cups (68 fl oz/2 liters)

4 oranges, washed
4 lemons, washed
8½ cups (68 fl oz/2 liters) eau-de-vie at 45%
sugar

Use a vegetable peeler to remove the zest of 2 of the oranges and 2 of the lemons in strips, taking care to leave behind the white pith.
—
Put the citrus zests into a sterilized jar (SEE p. 40) and pour in enough eau-de-vie to cover the zests, measuring the amount of alcohol you put in. Seal with a sterilized lid and steep for one month. Strain.
—
Peel the zest from the remaining 2 oranges and 2 lemons, put into the jar and pour over the strained eau-de-vie. Seal the jar and steep in a cool, dark place for another month.
—
After two months, make a sugar syrup. Bring 1 cup (7 oz/200 g) sugar per scant ½ cup (3½ fl oz/100 ml) water per 4¼ cups (34 fl oz/ 1 liter) alcohol to a boil in a pan. Make sure that the sugar has fully dissolved. Boil for 2–3 seconds, then remove from the heat.
—
Strain the alcohol through a strainer into a large pitcher (jug), add the sugar syrup, and mix well. Pour the liqueur into sterilized bottles (SEE p. 40) and seal.

## WHOLE ORANGE LIQUEUR

Preparation time 10 minutes
Steeping time 1 month
Makes 5 cups (42 fl oz/1.2 liters)

3 medium oranges with a fairly thin skin, sliced
4¼ cups (34 fl oz/1 liter) eau-de-vie at 45%
scant 1 cup (6 oz/175 g) sugar

Combine the orange slices with the eau-de-vie in a large sterilized jar (SEE p. 40).

—

Put the sugar in a medium bowl, pour a little water onto the sugar so it begins to melt and dissolve, then pour the sugar mixture into the jar, seal with a sterilized lid, and steep in a cool, dark place for one month.

—

Strain the liqueur, pour into sterilized bottles (SEE p. 40), and seal.

## CANDIED ORANGE PEEL

Preparation time 1 hour, plus cooling
Cooking time 1 hour
Drying time 4–5 days
Makes 2 lb (900 g)

6 large oranges
sugar

Choose oranges with thick skin. If the peel is too thin, it will harden and lose too much volume.

—

Use the point of a sharp knife to peel the oranges. Score through the skin of each orange five times at regular intervals, from top to bottom. Carefully peel off the skin in segments along the scored lines so the pieces are similar in shape to the outer rind of melon wedges. Place the peel in a large pan and pour in enough cold water to cover. Bring to a boil and boil for 5 minutes, then remove the pan from the heat and cool in the water for 2–3 hours.

—

Drain, return the peel to a clean pan and cover with fresh cold water. Simmer over low heat for 30 minutes until softened, then drain.

—

Make a sugar syrup. Bring 3⅓ cups (1½ lb /660 g) sugar per 4¼ cups (34 fl oz/1 liter) water to a boil in a pan. Add the peel, reduce the heat to low, and cook for 5 minutes. Remove from the heat and leave the peel in the syrup.

—

Repeat the process every day. The syrup will gradually concentrate; stop when the syrup reaches the large pearl stage (237°F/114°C), or when small beads form on the surface of the syrup, and if you blow on a skimmer coated with the syrup, bubbles form at the edges. Drain, place the peel on a rack and leave to air-dry. Alternatively, you can keep the peel in a jar with the remaining syrup.

# WATERMELON

## WATERMELON JAM

Preparation time 30 minutes
Cooking time 35 minutes
Steeping time 24 hours
Canning time 5 minutes
Makes 4 x1 lb 2 oz (500 g) jars

1x 4½ lb (2 kg) watermelon, peeled, then flesh
cut into ¾-inch (2-cm) cubes and seeded
sugar
few pieces of candied lemon peel (optional)
1 lemon
1 tablespoon vinegar

Have ready a large bowl filled halfway with ice cubes and enough cold water to cover the ice. Put the watermelon into a large preserving pan and pour in enough cold water to cover the fruit. Bring to a boil and boil for 5 minutes, or until soft. Remove the watermelon with a slotted spoon and plunge into the ice-cold water. Leave for 1 minute, then drain and dry with a clean cloth.

—

Weigh the watermelon pulp and measure the same weight in sugar. Put the watermelon pulp into a large ceramic or nonreactive bowl, alternating with layers of the sugar, and adding a few pieces of candied lemon peel, if desired. Squeeze over the juice of 1 lemon per watermelon, then cover with a lid or plastic wrap (clingfilm) and steep for 24 hours in a cool, dark place, stirring the mixture several times.

—

Put a small plate or saucer into the freezer to chill. Transfer the mixture to a large preserving pan, add the vinegar, and bring to a boil. Boil for 20 minutes. To test for a set, pour several drops of jam onto the chilled plate and when you tip the plate the juice should not run.

Pour the jam into sterilized jars (SEE p. 40) and seal with sterilized lids.

—

Process in a boiling-water canner (SEE p. 53 and follow the manufacturer's instructions) for 5 minutes.

# GRAPEFRUITS

## GRAPEFRUIT JAM

Preparation time 30 minutes
Steeping time 24 hours
Cooking time 1 hour 30 minutes
Canning time 5 minutes
Makes 12 x 1 lb 2 oz (500 g) jars

2½ lb (1.2 kg) oranges
2½ lb (1.2 kg) grapefruits, peeled and thinly
    sliced
2 lemons
10 cups (4½ lb/2 kg) sugar

Squeeze the juice of 2 of the oranges and set aside. Wash the other oranges and slice them thinly, then put them and the grapefruit into a large preserving pan with 8½ cups (68 fl oz/ 2 liters) water, the juice of the reserved oranges, and the juice of the lemons. Cover with a lid and steep for 24 hours.

——

When ready, put a small plate or saucer into the freezer to chill. Add the sugar to the pan, then bring to a boil over low heat, and cook for 1½ hours. Skim with a slotted spoon to remove any scum floating on the surface. To test for a set, pour several drops of jam onto the chilled plate and when you tip the plate the juice should not run.

——

Pour the jam into sterilized jars (SEE p. 40) and seal with sterilized lids.

——

Process in a boiling-water canner (SEE p. 53 and follow the manufacturer's instructions) for 5 minutes.

# PEACHES

## PEACHES, STORED FRESH

Only store peaches that are in perfect condition with no bruises or blemishes. Wrap each fruit individually in tissue paper, twisting the ends of the paper so the fruit are tightly wrapped. Store in a dry, cool place for up to two weeks.

## PEACHES AU NATUREL

Preparation time 1 hour
Cooking time 2–3 minutes
Canning time 20 minutes
Makes 2 x 4¼ cups (34 fl oz/1 liter) jars

12 peaches
sugar, for sprinkling

Pick the peaches just before they are ripe, in early morning ideally. Rub with a moist clean cloth to remove the fuzz.

—

Have ready a large bowl filled halfway with ice cubes and enough cold water to cover the ice. Put the peaches into a large pan and pour in enough cold water to cover. Cook over low heat for 2–3 minutes, or as soon as the fruit rise to the surface Remove the peaches with a slotted spoon and plunge into the ice-cold water. Leave for 1 minute, then drain. You can also put 12 peaches at once into a pan of boiling water, cook on a rolling boil for 1 minute, then plunge into the ice-cold water, leave for 1 minute, and drain.

—

Handling the fruit delicately, halve and pit. Place the peach halves in sterilized jars (SEE p. 40), round side up; a 4¼ cup (35 fl oz/1 liter) jar should hold 6 medium peaches. Sprinkle the top of the peaches in the jar with sugar and seal with sterilized lids.

—

Process in a boiling-water canner (SEE p. 53 and follow the manufacturer's instructions) for 40 minutes.

## PEACHES IN SYRUP

Preparation time 20 minutes
Cooking time 10 minutes
Canning time 40 minutes
Makes 2 x 4¼ cups (33 fl oz/1 liter) jars

12 peaches
sugar

Have ready a large bowl filled halfway with ice cubes and enough cold water to cover the ice. Put the peaches into a large pan and pour in enough cold water to cover. Cook over low heat for 2–3 minutes, or as soon as the fruit rise to the surface Remove the peaches with a slotted spoon and plunge into the ice-cold water. Leave for 1 minute, then drain. You can also put 12 peaches at once into a pan of boiling water, cook on a rolling boil for 1 minute, then plunge into the ice-cold water, leave for 1 minute, and drain.

—

Handling the fruit delicately, halve and pit. Place the peach halves in sterilized jars (SEE p. 40).

—

For the sugar syrup, bring 2 cups (14 oz/400 g) sugar per 4¼ cups (34 fl oz/1 liter) water to a boil in a pan. Boil for 2–3 seconds, then remove from the heat. Carefully top off the jars with the syrup. Seal with sterilized lids.

—

Process in a boiling-water canner (SEE p. 53 and follow the manufacturer's instructions) for 40 minutes.

—

NOTE: Preserving peaches whole with their pits is not recommended, as they would take up too much space in the jar.

## PEACH JAM

Preparation time 40 minutes
Steeping time 12 hours
Cooking time 45 minutes
Canning time 5 minutes
Makes 4 x 1 lb 2 oz (500 g) jars

12 peaches, peeled, pitted, and cut into halves
    or quarters, depending on size
sugar

Weigh 4¼ cups (1 lb 14 oz/850 g) sugar per
2¼ lb (1 kg) fruit, and arrange the fruit and
sugar in alternating layers in a large preserving
pan. Cover with a lid and steep for 12 hours.

—

The next day, bring the mixture slowly to a
boil and cook for 20–25 minutes, or until the
fruit is translucent. Remove the fruit from the
pan with a slotted spoon, leaving the syrup
behind, and arrange the fruit in sterilized jars
(SEE p. 40), filling the jars to two thirds full.

Heat the syrup until it reaches the ball stage,
(248°F/120° C): when a small amount of syrup
is dropped into a bowl of cold water, it forms a
soft ball the size of a pea. Carefully top off the
jars with the syrup. Seal with sterilized lids.

—

Process in a boiling-water canner (SEE p. 53
and follow the manufacturer's instructions) for
5 minutes.

## GLAZED PEACHES

Preparation time 40 minutes
Cooking time 20 minutes
Resting time 4-5 hours
Canning time 5 minutes
Makes 2-3 x 2¼ lb (1 kg) jars

2¼ lb (1 kg) peaches
sugar
kirsch

Pick peaches just 2–3 days shy of full maturity.

—

Bring a large pan of water to a boil over high
heat. Carefully add the peaches and blanch
for 2–3 seconds, then drain and carefully peel
off the skin as thinly as possible. Leave the fruit
whole.

Put the peaches in a large ceramic or
nonreactive bowl and pour in enough boiling
water to cover. Leave in the water for 4–5 hours.

For the sugar syrup, bring 5 cups (2¼ lb/1 kg)
sugar per 4¼ cups (34 fl oz/1 liter) water per
2¼ lb (1 kg) fruit to a boil in a large preserving
pan. Boil for 2–3 seconds, then carefully lower
the peaches into the syrup and cook slowly for
10 minutes, until tender.

—

Remove the fruit from the pan with a slotted
spoon, leaving the syrup behind. Push the
pits out, retaining the shape, and arrange in
sterilized jars (SEE p. 40). Add a little kirsch, scant
¼ cup (1¾ fl oz/50 ml) per 2¼ lb (1 kg) fruit.

Heat the syrup until it reaches the ball stage,
(248°F/120° C): when a small amount of syrup is
dropped into a bowl of cold water, it forms a soft
ball the size of a pea. Carefully top off the jars
with the syrup. Seal with sterilized lids.

—

Process in a boiling-water canner (SEE p. 53
and follow the manufacturer's instructions) for
5 minutes.

## DRIED PEACHES

Preparation time 10 minutes
Drying time several days, or 12 hours if using a
   dehydrator

peaches, halved and pitted

Dry the peaches in early summer so that the sun is still hot enough to complete the drying process quickly.

—

Place the fruit halves on racks and leave in the sun all day. Bring back inside at night. Repeat several days in a row, turning the peach halves over daily.

—

Complete the drying process by placing the fruit in a low oven preheated to its lowest setting. The fruit halves must be dark red in color and wrinkled. Flatten each half with your hand to give it a regular shape.

—

Alternatively, if drying the peaches later in the summer, place the peach halves in a dehydrator for 12 hours, at a temperature that increases progressively from 104–158°F/40°C–70°C.

—

Before using, soak in a bowl of cold water for 12 hours to plump up.

## PEACH WINE

Preparation time 40 minutes
Cooking time 25–30 minutes
Steeping time 12 hours
Makes 5¼ cups (44 fl oz/1.25 liters)

6 ripe peaches
4¼ cups (34 fl oz/1 liter) dry white wine
1 cup (7 oz/200 g) sugar
1 cup (9 fl oz/250 ml) flavorless alcohol at 45%

Bring a large pan of water to a boil over high heat. Carefully add the peaches and blanch for 2–3 seconds, then drain and carefully peel off the skin as thinly as possible, cut in half, and remove the pits.

—

Put the peaches in a large pan, add the white wine and bring to a boil. Boil for 20–25 minutes, then remove from the heat, cover with a lid, and steep overnight.

—

The next day, strain the peaches into a large pitcher (jug) or bowl, discarding the peach pulp. Add the sugar and alcohol to the liquid, stir to combine, then pour into sterilized bottles (SEE p. 40) and seal. Store in a cool dry place.

## PEACHES IN EAU-DE-VIE

**Preparation time 30 minutes, plus cooling**
**Cooking time 6–8 minutes (for each batch), plus syrup**
**Steeping time 1–2 months**
**Makes 2–3 large jars**

**2¼ lb (1 kg) peaches**
**sugar**
**eau-de-vie at 45%**

Prick each peach to the pit with a clean needle, and place in a large bowl of cold water and set aside.

—

For the sugar syrup, bring 2¾ cups (1¼ lb/ 550 g) sugar per 4¼ cups (34 fl oz/1 liter) water per 2¼ lb (1 kg) peaches to a boil in a large preserving pan. When the syrup reaches boiling point, working in small batches, carefully lower in the peaches and cook for 6–8 minutes. Remove the fruit from the pan with a slotted spoon, leaving the syrup behind to cook the remaining peaches, and arrange the peaches in sterilized jars (SEE p. 40).

—

Heat the syrup until it reaches the large thread stage (228–230°F/109–110°C), or when the syrup forms firmer threads when dropped into a glass of water, about ¾–1¼ inches/2–3 cm long. Remove the pan from the heat and cool.

—

Measure the syrup and combine with the same volume of eau-de-vie. Top off the jars with the mixture, seal with sterilized lids, and steep 1–2 months before serving.

—

NOTE: Keeping the pits in the fruit gives this eau-de-vie an excellent flavor.

# PEARS

## PEARS, STORED FRESH

Pears are picked in the fall (autumn) months, before the frosts, in mid to late fall (autumn), or early winter at the latest. They are then kept in a fruit store or in the cellar.

—

Choose fruit in perfect condition with no brown spots, bruises, or blemishes. Place the pears on racks, stem up, without them touching, in a cool, dry, and well-ventilated place. Check on them daily.

## PEARS AU NATUREL

Preparation time 1 hour 15 minutes
Cooking time 2 minutes (optional)
Canning time 30–40 minutes
Makes 2 x 3 cups (26 fl oz/750 ml) jars

2¼ lb (1 kg) pears
lemon juice, for rubbing (optional)
sugar, for dusting

Choose smaller pears for this; they should be tender, sweet, and aromatic.

—

For very small pears, peel but leave them whole, and trim the stalks if they are too long. For larger ones, peel, cut them in half, and core. Use a stainless steel knife to prevent the fruit blackening, and rub the cut sides with a bit of lemon juice as you go.

—

If the pears are firm, or if you wish to reduce the canning time, plunge the fruit in a large bowl of cold water (no need to rub with lemon), then bring a large pan of water to a boil over high heat. Carefully add the pears and blanch for 2 minutes, then remove the pears carefully, cool, and dry on a clean cloth.

—

Arrange the pears in sterilized jars (SEE p. 40), dust with sugar, and seal with sterilized lids.

—

Process in a boiling-water canner (SEE p. 53 and follow the manufacturer's instructions) for 40 minutes (30 minutes if the pears have been blanched).

## PEARS IN SYRUP

Preparation time 1 hour 15 minutes
Cooking time 5 minutes
Canning time 30–40 minutes
Makes 2 x 4¼ cups (34 fl oz/1 liter) jars

2¼ lb (1 kg) pears
sugar

For very small pears, peel but leave them whole, and cut the stalks in half if they are too long. For larger ones, peel, cut them in half, and core. Use a stainless steel knife to prevent the fruit blackening, and rub the cut sides with a bit of lemon juice as you go.

—

If the pears are firm, or if you wish to reduce the canning time, plunge the fruit in a large bowl of cold water (no need to rub with lemon), then bring a large pan of water to a boil over high heat. Carefully add the pears and blanch for 2 minutes, then remove the pears carefully, cool, and dry on a clean cloth. Arrange the pears in sterilized jars (SEE p. 40).

—

Make a sugar syrup. Bring 1½ cups (11 oz/ 300 g) sugar per 4¼ cups (34 fl oz/1 liter) water to a boil in a large preserving pan. Boil for 2–3 seconds, then remove from the heat and carefully top off the jars with the syrup. Seal with sterilized lids.

—

Process in a boiling-water canner (SEE p. 53 and follow the manufacturer's instructions) for 40 minutes (30 minutes if the pears have been blanched).

## PEARS IN WHITE WINE

Preparation time 1 hour
Cooking time 10 minutes
Canning time 30–40 minutes
Makes 4 x 4¼ cups (34 fl oz/1 liter) jars

9 lb (4 kg) pears
lemon juice, for rubbing (optional)
1¼ cups (9 oz/250 g) sugar
scant ½ cup (3½ fl oz/100 ml) dry white wine

For very small pears, peel but leave them whole, and trim the stalks if they are too long. For larger ones, peel, cut them in half, and core. Use a stainless steel knife to prevent the fruit blackening, and rub the cut sides with a bit of lemon juice as you go.

—

If the pears are firm, or if you wish to reduce the canning time, plunge the fruit in a large bowl of cold water (no need to rub with lemon), then bring a large pan of water to a boil over high heat. Carefully add the pears and blanch for 2 minutes, then remove the pears carefully, cool, and dry on a clean cloth. Arrange the pears in sterilized jars (SEE p. 40),

—

Make a sugar syrup. Bring the sugar, white wine, and scant ½ cup (3½ fl oz/100 ml) water to a boil in a large preserving pan. Boil for 2–3 seconds, then remove from the heat and carefully top off the jars with the syrup. Seal with sterilized lids.

—

Process in a boiling-water canner (SEE p. 53 and follow the manufacturer's instructions) for 40 minutes (30 minutes if the pears have been blanched).

## PEAR JAM

Preparation time 40 minutes
Steeping time 12 hours
Cooking time 1 hour
Canning time 5 minutes
Makes 5 x 1 lb 2 oz (500 g) jars

4½ lb (2 kg) pears, peeled, cored, and quartered
sugar
few cloves, or 1 vanilla bean (pod), split in half lengthwise and seeds scraped out, or finely grated lemon zest

You will find that some pears turn pink while others remain white during cooking.

—

Put the pears in a large ceramic or nonreactive bowl with alternating layers of sugar (scant 2 cups/13 oz/375 g sugar per 1 lb 2 oz/500 g fruit). Cover with a lid or plastic wrap (clingfilm) and steep for 12 hours.

—

The next day, transfer the pears to a large preserving pan and bring to a boil. Cook for 1 hour, stirring regularly to make sure the jam doesn't stick to the bottom of the pan.

—

About 15 minutes before the end of the cooking time, skim with a slotted spoon to remove any scum floating on the surface. You can enhance the flavor of the jam by adding 3–4 whole cloves, a split vanilla pod and its seeds, or the finely grated zest of a lemon.

—

Pour the jam into sterilized jars (SEE p. 40) and seal with sterilized lids.

—

Process in a boiling-water canner (SEE p. 53 and follow the manufacturer's instructions) for 5 minutes.

## CANDIED PEARS

Preparation time 1 hour
Cooking time 3-4 hours
Steeping time 73-85 hours
Draining time 1-2 days
Makes 6 candied pears

**6 firm-fleshed pears, peeled, stalks trimmed, and cored**
**juice of 1 lemon**
**sugar**

Fill a large bowl with cold water and add the lemon juice. Peel each pear, trim the stalk by half, and core then put immediately into the acidulated water to prevent it turning brown. Repeat with all the pears.

—

Make a sugar syrup. Bring 2¾ cups (1¼ lb/ 550 g) sugar per 4¼ cups (34 fl oz/1 liter) water to a boil in a large preserving pan. Carefully lower in the pears, reduce the heat to low, and cook for 15 minutes. Remove the pan from the heat, cover with a lid, and leave the fruit in the syrup overnight.

—

The next day, carefully remove the pears with a slotted spoon and set aside.

—

Bring the syrup to a boil and boil for 5 minutes, then carefully put the pears back in, reduce the heat to low, and cook for 15 minutes. Remove the pan from the heat, cover with a lid, and leave the fruit in the syrup overnight.

—

Repeat this process daily for 5–6 days. The syrup will gradually concentrate and the candied pears are ready when it reaches the large pearl stage (237°F/114°C), or when small beads form on the surface of the syrup, and if you blow on a skimmer coated with the syrup, bubbles form at the edges. Leave the pears in this syrup for 1 hour, then place on a rack to drain for 1–2 days before storing in airtight containers.

## DRIED PEARS

Preparation time 1 hour
Drying time 30 hours
Resting time 48 hours

**pears, unpeeled and quartered**

Choose fairly small, sweet pears for drying.

—

Preheat the oven to 140°F/60°C/lowest possible Gas Mark setting.

—

Arrange the pear quarters on a baking sheet and put in the oven for 10 hours with the door ajar for 10 hours.

—

Remove from the oven and leave the pears out on the counter (work surface) for 24 hours, then preheat the oven to 158–176°F/70–80°C/Gas Mark ¼ and resume drying with the door still ajar for 10 hours.

—

Leave the pears out on the counter (work surface) for another 24 hours, then preheat the oven to 176–212°F/80–100°C/Gas Mark ½ and resume drying with the door still ajar for 10 hours. Check the progress regularly: the pears must lose their moisture, but the sugar they contain should not caramelize.

—

Store the pears in an airtight container. Eat as is, or soak in a bowl of cold water for 12 hours to rehydrate before using in cooking.

## FLATTENED PEARS

Preparation time 10 minutes
Cooking time 5 minutes
Drying time 24-30 hours

pears, washed thoroughly leaving the skin and
stalks on

Use medium pears for this, as the process
causes them to shrink a lot.

—

Preheat the oven to its lowest setting.

—

Bring a large pan of water to a boil over high
heat. Carefully add the pears and blanch
for 3 minutes, or until tender, then drain.
Alternatively, put the pears in a steaming
basket set over a pan of gently simmering
water, and steam for 5 minutes until soft. A
toothpick (cocktail stick) should easily reach
the core.

—

Put the pears on a baking sheet and put in the
oven with the door ajar. Leave in the oven for
8–10 hours. Repeat daily for two more days,
until dry but still flexible. On the third day,
flatten the pears with your hand.

—

Store in an airtight container. Eat as is, or soak
in a bowl of cold water for 12 hours to rehydrate
before using in cooking.

## DEHYDRATED PEARS

Preparation time 20 minutes
Cooking time 5 minutes
Drying time 20-48 hours

pears, peeled and quartered

Put the pears in a steaming basket set over a
pan of gently simmering water and steam for
5 minutes, or until tender.

—

Process in the dehydrator for 20–48 hours,
depending on the variety's water content, at a
temperature of 158°F/70°C.

## PEARS IN EAU-DE-VIE

**Preparation time 1 hour, plus cooling**
**Cooking time 30–45 minutes**
**Steeping time 1–2 months**
**Makes 1 x 2¼ lb (1 kg) jar**

juice of 1 lemon
2¼ lb (1 kg) pears
sugar
eau-de-vie at 45%

Fill a large bowl with cold water and add the lemon juice. Peel each pear and trim the stalk by half and put immediately into the acidulated water to prevent it turning brown. Repeat with all the pears.

—

Make a sugar syrup. Bring 3 cups (1 lb 5 oz/ 600 g) sugar per 4¼ cups (34 fl oz/1 liter) water per 2¼ lb (1 kg) pears to a boil in a large preserving pan. When the syrup starts boiling, carefully lower in the pears and simmer for 10–15 minutes until the pears are translucent.

—

Remove the pears from the syrup with a slotted spoon, leaving the syrup behind, and arrange them in a large sterilized jar (SEE p. 40).

—

Heat the syrup until it reaches the ball stage, (248°F/120° C): when a small amount of syrup is dropped into a bowl of cold water, it forms a soft ball the size of a pea. Then remove from the heat and cool until lukewarm. Measure the syrup and add the same volume of eau-de-vie.

—

Pour the mixture over the pears, seal with a sterilized lid, and steep for 1–2 months before serving.

# APPLES

## APPLES, STORED IN THE CELLAR

Apples should be picked when the leaves are ready to fall.

—

Store apples that are firm with no brown spots or blemishes in a fruit store or a well-ventilated cellar, on wire racks, laying them stem side down and without touching. Check on them daily.

## APPLES, STORED IN A SILO

If the apple harvest is abundant, you can store the fruit until March in a silo similar to the ones built for vegetables (SEE p. 137).

—

Let the apples rest in the open air for 48 hours after picking.

—

Arrange the apples on a bed of dry ferns, allowing 2–3¼ inch/5–8 cm of space between each apple. Place a layer of dry fern (or dry straw) on top of the apples, and repeat with another, slightly smaller layer of apples so the construction will take on a pyramid shape. The silo should be about 3 feet/1 m wide and 4 feet/1.2 m high, and no longer than 6½–10 feet/2–3 m. Cover with a 4-inch/10-cm layer of straw, then a 10–12-inch/25–30-cm layer of earth, and arrange a "chimney" for ventilation.

—

The only drawback to this preservation method is that rodents, especially mice, may find their way inside.

## APPLES, STORED IN CRATES

Place the apples in a crate, separating the layers of apples with dry and fine sand. Close with a lid and store in a dry place, with one brick under each corner of the crate to avoid contact with the damp ground.

## APPLES AU NATUREL

**Preparation time 30 minutes**
**Cooking time 15 minutes**
**Canning time 30 minutes**
**Makes 2 x 1 lb 10 oz (750 g) jars**

**2½ lb (1.2 kg) apples**
**juice of 1 lemon**
**sugar**

---

Apples are rarely canned, as they can be found in grocery stores and supermarkets all year round. If the harvest is kept in a fruit store and properly looked after, the fruit will remain fresh, and will taste better than in jars. If, however, you have a significant glut of fruit and want to can part of it, proceed as follows.

---

Fill a large bowl with cold water and add the lemon juice. Peel each apple, quarter, and core, then put immediately into the acidulated water to prevent it turning brown. Repeat with all the apples.

---

Bring a large pan of water to a boil over high heat. Carefully add the apple quarters and blanch for 2 minutes, then drain and dry on a clean cloth. Arrange the fruit in sterilized jars (SEE p. 40).

---

Make a light sugar syrup. Bring 1¼ cups (9 oz/250 g) sugar per 4¼ cups (34 fl oz/1 liter) water to a boil in a pan. Boil for 2–3 seconds, then remove from the heat. Carefully top off the jars with the boiling syrup, then seal with sterilized lids.

---

Process in a boiling-water canner (SEE p. 53 and follow the manufacturer's instructions) for 30 minutes.

## APPLE JELLY

Preparation time 30 minutes
Cooking time 45 minutes
Canning time 5 minutes
Makes 2 x 1 lb 2 oz (500 g) jars

4½ lb (2 kg) apples, quartered, cores and pips
    removed
lemon juice
sugar

Put the apples cores and pips into a small cheesecloth (muslin) bag.

—

Put the apples into a large preserving pan with the cheesecloth (muslin) bag. Pour in enough cold water to just cover, bring to a simmer, and cook for 10 minutes until completely soft.

—

Strain the apples through a strainer to collect the juice. Discard the muslin bag. Measure the juice and add 1 tablespoon of lemon juice and 5 cups (2¼ lb/1 kg) sugar per 4¼ cups (34 fl oz/1 liter) juice. Return the mixture to the clean pan, bring to a simmer and cook for 30 minutes. The juice will be thick, but the apple jelly will not set immediately.

—

Pour the jelly into sterilized jars (SEE p. 40) and seal with sterilized lids.

—

Process in a boiling-water canner (SEE p. 53 and follow the manufacturer's instructions) for 5 minutes. The jelly will thicken after a few days.

## BUDGET APPLE JELLY

Preparation time 30 minutes
Cooking time 1 hour 20 minutes
Canning time 5 minutes
Makes 1 x 1 lb 2 oz (500 g) jar

peel and cores from 4½ lb (2 kg) apples
1 vanilla bean (pod), split open lengthwise and
    seeds scraped out
sugar

Use just the washed and peeled skin, the cores, and the pips and place them in a cheesecloth (muslin) bag. Place the bag in a large preserving pan and pour in enough cold water to just cover. Add the vanilla bean (pod) and bring to a simmer. Cook for 45 minutes, pressing on the bag occasionally to extract the pectin.

—

Strain through a strainer to collect the juice. Measure it and add the same weight in sugar, then return the mixture to the clean pan and cook for 30 minutes.

—

Pour the jelly into sterilized jars (SEE p. 40) and seal with sterilized lids.

—

Process in a boiling-water canner (SEE p. 53 and follow the manufacturer's instructions) for 5 minutes. The jelly will thicken after a few days.

## APPLE JUICE FOR JELLIES

Preparation time 10 minutes
Cooking time 15 minutes
Makes 2¼ cups (17 fl oz/500 ml)

0 large cooking apples, quartered

Apples are high in pectin, a substance that enables syrups to set. It is also a fruit whose cooked juice is light yellow or barely pink, with a rather neural taste, so it is a good addition to other jellies made from fruit less rich in pectin. This apple juice can replace the water in the syrup prepared to cook fruit or to make jelly.

—

Put the apples in a large preserving pan with just enough cold water to cover. Bring to a simmer and cook for 10 minutes until tender.

—

Strain to collect the juice, and use for jams and jellies.

## APPLE JAM

Preparation time 30 minutes
Cooking time 2½ hours
Canning time 5 minutes
Makes 2 x 1 lb 2 oz (500 g) jars

2¼ lb (1 kg) apples, peeled and thinly sliced
1¾ cups (12 oz/350 g) sugar
juice of 1 lemon

This yields a firm fruit conserve of a beautiful pink shade.

—

Put the apple slices in a large preserving pan with the sugar and lemon juice. Cover with a lid and cook over very low heat for 2½ hours, making sure the mixture does not caramelize. The mixture is very hot so be careful of it spitting while it starts to thicken.

—

Push the mixture through a strainer or food mill and pour the jam into sterilized jars (SEE p. 40). Seal with sterilized lids.

—

Process in a boiling-water canner (SEE p. 53 and follow the manufacturer's instructions) for 5 minutes.

## APPLE FRUIT PASTE

Preparation time 30 minutes
Cooking time 1 hour 30 minutes
Drying time 4–5 days
Makes about 50 pieces

3 lb (1.4 kg) apples
sugar, plus extra for dusting
1 vanilla bean (pod), split open lengthwise and
    seeds scraped out, or grated lemon zest
a little flavorless oil, for oiling

Quarter the apples without peeling, then carve out the cores and pips and place them in a small cheesecloth (muslin) bag.

—

Put the apples in a large preserving pan, cover with water, and simmer for 30 minutes, or until the fruit is soft. Remove the pan from the heat and, using a slotted spoon, remove the fruit. Crush the softened fruit pulp thoroughly with a food processor.

—

Weigh the amount of fruit pulp and put in a large preserving pan with the same weight in sugar. Add the vanilla bean (pod) and seeds or grated lemon zest and cook over medium heat for 1 hour, stirring often to prevent the paste scorching on the bottom of the pan. The mixture is very hot so be careful of it spitting. The apple paste is ready when it is very thick and pulls away from the sides of the pan.

—

Pour the paste onto an oiled marble slab, or oiled pie dishes. Dust the surface with sugar and dry in a cool place for 4–5 days.

—

Cut the paste into the shapes of your choice (such as squares, diamonds, rounds, half-moons, etc.) and dust the cut surfaces with more sugar until they are coated.

—

These will keep for months in an airtight container, with a sheet of parchment paper between each layer.

## NORMANDY-STYLE APPLE JAM

Preparation time 30 minutes
Cooking time 2 hours 15 minutes
Canning time 5 minutes
Makes 10 x 1 lb 2 oz (500 g) jars

15 cups (6½ lb/3 kg) sugar
9 lb (4 kg) peeled apples, thinly sliced
¾ cup (3½ oz/100 g) raisins
scant ½ cup (3½ oz/100 g) currants
3½ oz (100 g) candied orange or orange peel,
    finely chopped
scant ¼ cup (1¾ fl oz/50 ml) Calvados

This makes a full-flavored and caramelized jam.

—

Heat the same amount of sugar as the weight of the fruit with 3 cups (26 fl oz/750 ml) water gently in a large preserving pan, stirring until the sugar has dissolved, then bring to a boil and boil rapidly until it reaches the small pearl stage (232°F/111°C), or when tiny round beads form at the surface of the syrup, then when held between the fingers it forms a wider thread of about 1½–2 inches/4–5 cm in length.

—

Add the apples, raisins, currants, and peel and cook over low heat for 2 hours; the apples will turn brown and shiny. Add the Calvados.

—

Pour the jam into sterilized jars (SEE p. 40) and seal with sterilized lids.

—

Process in a boiling-water canner (SEE p. 53 and follow the manufacturer's instructions) for 5 minutes.

## BRITTANY-STYLE APPLE JAM

Preparation time 30 minutes
Cooking time 3 hours 20 minutes
Canning time 5 minutes
Makes 8 x 1 lb 2 oz (500 g) jars

9 lb (4 kg) apples, unpeeled and sliced
8½ cups (70 fl oz/2 liters) hard (dry) cider

This jam is dark red in color and quite thick.

—

Put the apples in a large preserving pan with
2¼ cups (17 fl oz/500 ml) hard (dry) cider per
2¼ lb (1 kg) apples and bring to a simmer. Cook
for 15–20 minutes, or until the apples are soft.
Using a wooden spoon, push the mixture
through a strainer to collect the apple puree.

—

Put the puree into a clean pan and cook over
very low heat for 3 hours.

—

Pour the jam into sterilized jars (SEE p. 40) and
seal with sterilized lids.

—

Process in a boiling-water canner (SEE p. 53
and follow the manufacturer's instructions) for
5 minutes.

## APPLE SYRUP

Preparation time 30 minutes
Cooking time 40 minutes
Canning time 5 minutes
Makes 5 cups (42 fl oz/1.2 liters)

4 lb (1.8 kg) apples, quartered, cored, and
    seeded, and cores and seeds set aside
sugar

Put the apples cores and pips in a small
cheesecloth (muslin) bag.

—

Place the apples in a large preserving pan
with the cheesecloth (muslin) bag and pour
in enough cold water to just cover the apples.
Bring to a simmer and cook for about 20
minutes, or until the apples are completely soft.

—

Strain through a strainer to collect the juice.

—

Measure the juice and pour it into a clean pan
and add 6 cups (2½ lb/1.2 kg) sugar per 4¼
cups (34 fl oz/liter) apple juice. Bring to a boil
and boil rapidly until it reaches the coated
or nappé stage (221°F/105°C), or when small
bubbles form at the surface of the syrup, which
thinly coats the back of a skimmer dipped into
the syrup.

—

Pour into sterilized bottles (SEE p. 40) and seal.

—

Process in a boiling-water canner (SEE p. 53
and follow the manufacturer's instructions) for
5 minutes.

## DRIED APPLE SLICES

Preparation time 20 minutes
Drying time 36–48 hours
Resting time 72–96 hours

apples, peeled if sour, unpeeled if sweet, cored,
   pips removed, and cut into vertical slices,
   about ½ inch/1 cm in thickness.

This process is generally used for fallen apples
that are partially bruised.

—

Preheat the oven to 140°F/60°C/lowest
possible Gas Mark setting.

Arrange the apple slices on broiler (grill) racks
without overlapping and place in the oven.
Dry with the door slightly ajar for 12 hours.
Remove the apples from the oven and leave on
the counter (work surface) for 24 hours.

—

Repeat this process 2–3 times, or until the
apples are completely dried.

## DRIED APPLE ROUNDS

Preparation time 30 minutes
Soaking time 1 hour
Drying time 24 hours
Resting time 48 hours

juice of 1 lemon
apples, peeled, left whole, cored, and cut into
   horizontal slices, about ½ inch/1 cm in
   thickness

Fill a large bowl with cold water and add the
lemon juice. Add the apple slices and soak for
1 hour, then drain and dry on clean cloths.

—

Preheat the oven to 140°F/60°C/lowest
possible Gas Mark setting.

—

Arrange the apple slices on broiler (grill) racks
without overlapping and place in the oven.
Dry with the door slightly ajar for 12 hours.
Remove the apples from the oven and leave on
the counter (work surface) for 24 hours.

—

Repeat this process once, then thread the
apple slices on a piece of kitchen string. Hang
the string in a well-ventilated, warm place to
finish drying.

## FLATTENED APPLES

Preparation time 20 minutes
Cooking time 3–20 minutes
Drying time 24–30 hours

apples, washed thoroughly leaving the skin on

Preheat the oven to 176°F/80°C/Gas Mark ¼.

Bring a large pan of water to a boil over high heat. Carefully add the apples and blanch for 3 minutes, or until tender, then drain. Alternatively, put the apples in a steaming basket set over a pan of gently simmering water, and steam for 15–20 minutes, or until soft. A toothpick (cocktail stick) should easily reach the core.

—

Put the apples on a baking sheet and put in the oven with the door ajar. Leave in the oven for 8–10 hours. Repeat daily for two more days, until dry but still flexible. On the third day, place the apples between two small wooden boards and press to flatten them evenly.

—

Store in an airtight container. Eat as is, or soak in a bowl of cold water for 12 hours to rehydrate before using in cooked dishes.

## DEHYDRATED APPLES

Preparation time 20 minutes
Soaking time 1 hour
Drying time 12–16 hours

juice of 1 lemon
apples, cut into vertical or horizontal slices, about ¾ inch/1.5 cm thick

Fill a large bowl with cold water and add the lemon juice. Add the apple slices and soak for 1 hour, then drain and dry on clean cloths.

—

Place the apples in a dehydrator and dry for for 12–16 hours at 158°F/70°C.

# PLUMS

## PLUMS, STORED FRESH

Plums have a high moisture content and can only be stored for a short time, about a week. Pick just before the peak of ripeness and lay them in a single layer, without touching, in a shady, cool place.

## WHOLE PLUMS AU NATUREL

**Preparation time 20 minutes**
**Cooking time 10 minutes**
**Canning time 30 minutes**
**Makes 3 x 1 lb 2 oz (500 g) jars**

4½ lb (2 kg) small purple plums
3 tablespoons sugar

---

Choose plums that are not completely ripe.

—

Prick the plums a few times with a large needle, around the stem and on the line that runs down the side of the fruit.

—

Put the plums in a large pan and pour in enough cold water to cover. Heat slowly for 5–8 minutes until the fruit rises to the surface.

—

Arrange the fruit in sterilized jars (SEE p. 40) and sprinkle with 1 tablespoon sugar per jar. Seal with sterilized lids.

—

Process in a boiling-water canner (SEE p. 53 and follow the manufacturer's instructions) for 30 minutes.

## PLUM HALVES AU NATUREL

**Preparation time 15 minutes**
**Canning time 45 minutes**
**Makes 1 x 1 lb 11 oz (750 g) jar**

4½ lb (2 kg) small purple plums, halved and pitted
sugar, for dusting

---

Arrange the plum halves in sterilized jars (SEE p. 40), round side up, and pack well with a spatula. Dust with sugar and seal with sterilized lids.

—

Process in a boiling-water canner (SEE p. 53 and follow the manufacturer's instructions) for 45 minutes.

## PLUMS IN SYRUP

Preparation time 20 minutes
Cooking time 20 minutes
Canning time 30–45 minutes
Makes 3 x 1 lb 2 oz (500 g) jars

4½ lb (2 kg) whole plums
sugar

Prick the plums a few times with a large needle, around the stem and on the line that runs down the side of the fruit.

—

Put the plums in a large pan and pour in enough cold water to cover. Heat slowly for 5–8 minutes until the fruit rises to the surface. Arrange the fruit in sterilized jars (SEE p. 40).

—

Make a sugar syrup. Bring 1½ cups (11 oz/ 300 g) sugar per 4¼ cups (34 fl oz/1 liter) water to a boil in a pan. Boil for 2–3 seconds, then remove from the heat. Carefully top off the jars with the boiling syrup, then seal with sterilized lids.

—

Process in a boiling-water canner (SEE p. 53 and follow the manufacturer's instructions) for 30 minutes.

## PLUM JAM

Preparation time 30 minutes
Steeping time 12 hours
Cooking time 30 minutes
Canning time 5 minutes
Makes 5 x 1 lb 2 oz (500 g) jars

4½ lb (2 kg) plums, halved and pitted
sugar

Most plums are very sweet and 2½ cups (1 lb 2 oz/500 g) sugar per 2¼ lb (1 kg) fruit is enough. If the plums you are using are not very sweet, use the same weight of sugar as fruit.

—

Place the plums in a large preserving pan with alternating layers of sugar. Cover with a lid and steep for 12 hours.

—

When ready to cook, put a small plate or saucer into the freezer to chill. Bring the plums to a simmer and cook for 25 minutes, skimming with a slotted spoon to remove any scum floating on the surface. Test for a set, by pouring several drops of jam onto the chilled plate and when you tip the plate the juice should not run. If it does run, heat a little longer and test again.

—

Pour the jam into sterilized jars (SEE p. 40) and seal with sterilized lids.

—

Process in a boiling-water canner (SEE p. 53 and follow the manufacturer's instructions) for 5 minutes.

## CANDIED PLUMS

**Preparation time** 20 minutes
**Cooking time** 20–30 minutes
**Steeping time** 1 hour, plus 3 days
**Drying time** several hours
**Makes** 1¾ lb (800 g)

2¼ lb (1 kg) plums
1 teaspoon salt
sugar

Choose plums just 1–2 days shy of full ripeness; they should still be firm and crisp.

—

Trim the stems by half and prick each fruit a few times around the stalk and along the line that runs down the side of the fruit with a needle.

—

Place the fruit in a large pan and pour in enough cold water to cover. Heat, without boiling, until the water reaches 176–194°F/ 80–90°C measured wth a candy (sugar) thermometer.

—

Remove the pan from the heat and add 1 teaspoon salt per 2¼ lb (1 kg) fruit. Steep for 1 hour.

—

Have ready a large bowl filled halfway with ice cubes and enough cold water to cover the ice. Heat the plums again, without boiling, for 5–8 minutes, or until they rise to the surface. Drain and plunge the plums into the ice-cold water. Leave for 1 minute, then drain again and dry on a clean cloth. Put the plums in a terrine or large nonreactive bowl and set aside.

—

Heat the same weight of sugar as the fruit weight per scant ½ cup (3½ fl oz/100 ml)

water gently in a pan, stirring until the sugar has dissolved, then bring to a boil and boil rapidly until it reaches the small thread stage (225°F/107°C), or when the syrup thickens and the bubbles grow larger, and when a teaspoon of syrup is dropped into a glass of water it forms thin threads that cannot be rolled into small balls when lifted out.

—

Pour the hot sugar syrup over the plums and steep for 24 hours.

—

Carefully remove the fruit with a slotted spoon and set aside. Heat the syrup in a pan until it reaches the large thread stage (228–230°F/109–110°C), or when the syrup forms firmer threads when dropped into a glass of water, about ¾–1¼ inches/2–3 cm long. Pour the syrup over the fruit and steep for another 24 hours.

—

Repeat the process, reaching the small pearl stage (232°F/111°C), or when tiny round beads form at the surface of the syrup, then it forms a wider thread of about 1½–2 inches/4–5 cm in length. Pour the syrup over the plums and steep for another 24 hours.

—

Carefully remove the fruit with a slotted spoon and set aside. Bring the syrup to a boil. When it boils, add the plums and cook very slowly for 5–10 minutes. Drain the plums and place on a rack to dry for several hours. Alternatively, you can speed up the process in an oven preheated to 122–140°F/50–60°C/lowest possible Gas Mark setting.

—

Store in an airtight container in a dry place.

## PLUMS IN EAU-DE-VIE

Preparation time 20 minutes, plus cooling
Cooking time 20 minutes
Steeping time 1–2 months
Makes 3 x 1 lb 2 oz (500 g) jar

2¼ lb (1 kg) plums
sugar
colorless eau-de-vie at 45%

Choose healthy fruit with no signs of bruising.
—
Trim the stalks to leave just ½ inch/1 cm,
and prick the plums with a needle 8–10 times
around the stalk.
—
Have ready a large bowl filled halfway with ice
cubes and enough cold water to cover the ice.
Bring a large pan of water to a boil over high
heat. Carefully add the plums and blanch for
1 minute, then remove the plums with a slotted
spoon and plunge into the ice-cold water.
Leave for 1 minute, then drain and dry on a
clean cloth.
—
Arrange the fruit in a large, sterilized jar (SEE p.
40), without filling it to the top so there is room
left for the sugar syrup and alcohol.
—
Heat 2½ cups (1 lb 2 oz/500 g) sugar per 2¼
cups (17 fl oz/500 ml) water per 2¼ lb (1 kg) fruit
gently in a pan, stirring until the sugar has
dissolved, then bring to a boil and boil rapidly
until it reaches the coated or nappé stage
(221°F/105°C), or when small bubbles form at
the surface of the syrup, which thinly coats the
back of a skimmer dipped into the syrup. Cool
until it is lukewarm, then combine it with the
eau-de-vie, allowing 4¼ cups (34 fl oz/1 liter)
alcohol per 2¼ lb (1 kg) fruit.
—
Pour over the plums, seal with a sterilized lid,
and steep for 1–2 months before serving.

## PRUNES IN EAU-DE-VIE

Preparation time 15 minutes
Steeping time 48 hours, plus 2–3 months
Makes 1 x 1 lb 2 oz (500 g) jar

2¼ lb (1 kg) prunes, pitted
7¼ cups (60 fl oz/1.7 liters) hot strong black tea
½ cup + 2 tablespoons (4 oz/125 g) sugar
1¼ cups (10 fl oz/300 ml) colorless eau-de-vie
   at 45%

Put the prunes in a large heatproof bowl. Pour
the hot black tea over the prunes and leave for
24 hours until plumped up.
—
Drain the prunes and pat dry with a clean
cloth and place in a sterilized jar (SEE p. 40)
with the sugar. Steep for 24 hours.
—
Pour the eau-de-vie over the fruit in the jar to
cover. Seal with a sterilized lid and steep in a
cool, dark place for 2–3 months.

## PLUM FRUIT PASTE

Preparation time 30 minutes
Cooking time 1 hour 10 minutes
Drying time 4–5 days
Makes about 50 pieces

3 lb (1.4 kg) plums, halved and pitted
sugar, plus extra for dusting
a little flavorless oil, for oiling

Put the plums into a pan, add a few tablespoons water and cook gently for 30 minutes, or until the plums are completely soft. Drain and press the pulp through a fine strainer to get a puree.
—
Weigh the puree and put it back into the pan with the same weight of sugar. Cook over medium heat, stirring frequently for 40 minutes, or until all the moisture has evaporated and the paste turns translucent and pulls away from the bottom of the pan.
—
Pour the paste onto an oiled marble slab, or oiled pie dishes, dust the surface with sugar, and dry for 4–5 days in a cool place.
—
Cut the paste into the shapes of your choice (squares, diamonds, rounds, half-moons, etc.) and dust the cut surfaces with more sugar until they are coated.
—
They will keep for months in an airtight container, with a sheet of parchment paper between each layer.

## DRIED PLUMS (PRUNES)

Preparation time 10 minutes
Drying time 6–24 hours, plus extra if necessary
Resting time 48 hours

ripe plums, halved and pitted

Choose ripe plums.
—
Arrange the plums on racks without the plums touching each other.
—
If you live in a region that is still sunny and hot in September when plums are ripe, dry the plums in the sun. Dry for 6–8 hours during the day, and bring indoors at night.
—
If not drying in the sun, preheat the oven to 104°F/40°C/lowest possible Gas Mark setting, arrange the plum halves on broiler (grill) racks without touching and place in the oven. Dry with the door slightly ajar for 12 hours. Remove the plums from the oven and leave on the counter (work surface) for 24 hours.
—
The next day, preheat the oven to 140°F/60°C/lowest possible Gas Mark. Put the plum halves in the oven and dry with the door slightly ajar for 12 hours. Remove the plums from the oven and leave on the counter (work surface) for 24 hours.
—
Repeat until the prunes are dried, but not hard. Dried plums burn easily, so watch them carefully if using the oven. Store in an airtight container.

## DEHYDRATED PLUMS

Preparation time 10 minutes
Drying time 24–30 hours

plums, halved and pitted

Place the plum halves in a dehydrator for 24–30 hours, at a temperature of 158°F/70°C.

Fig. 10

# GRAPES

### GRAPES, STORED FRESH
### DRY-STALK METHOD

This process does not require any particular equipment. Choose perfectly healthy bunches, with grapes that are not too tightly packed together.
—
When picking the grapes, leave a good length of stalk on each cluster. Hang the clusters by the stalk on wires or wooden slats (FIG. 10). The temperature of the room must remain constant throughout, and shouldn't be too cold.
—
Grapes suspended in this way lose water by evaporation: they shrivel, but their sweetness concentrates, and they will keep for several months.

### GRAPES, STORED FRESH
### WET-STALK METHOD

Choose perfectly healthy clusters, with grapes that are not too tightly packed together.
—
When picking the grapes, leave a good length of stalk on each cluster, and place each stalk in a small bottle containing a little charcoal and filled with water. Tilt the bottle slightly so the cluster can fall vertically (FIG. 11). The other end of the vine shoot should be coated with paraffin wax to prevent water evaporation.
—
This should be kept at a constant temperature (35.6–39.2°F/2–4°C) in a dry place with low lighting.
—
Because this is a rather complex installation, it is mainly set up in large fruit stores equipped for expensive and rare grapes.

Fig. 11

## GRAPES AU NATUREL

Preparation time 30 minutes
Canning time 30 minutes
Makes 2 x 1 lb 2 oz (500 g) jars

1¾ lb (800 g) grapes, picked off stems
2 tablespoons sugar

Arrange the grapes in sterilized jars (SEE p. 40) and dust with 1 tablespoon sugar each. Seal with sterilized lids.

—

Process in a boiling-water canner (SEE p. 53 and follow the manufacturer's instructions) for 30 minutes.


## GRAPES IN SYRUP

Preparation time 30 minutes
Cooking time 5 minutes
Canning time 30 minutes
Makes 2x 1 lb 2 oz (500 g) jars

1¾ lb (800 g) grapes, picked off stems
2 tablespoons sugar, plus extra for dusting

Arrange the grapes in sterilized jars (SEE p. 40) and dust with 1 tablespoon sugar each. Seal with sterilized lids.

—

Make a sugar syrup. Bring 2 cups (14 oz/400 g) sugar per 4¼ cups (34 fl oz/1 liter) water to a boil in a pan. Boil for 2–3 seconds, then remove from the heat. Carefully top off the jars with the boiling syrup, then seal with sterilized lids.

—

Process in a boiling-water canner (SEE p. 53 and follow the manufacturer's instructions) for 30 minutes.

## GRAPE JAM

Preparation time 30 minutes
Steeping time 12 hours
Cooking time 1 hour
Canning time 5 minutes
Makes 4 x 1 lb 2 oz (500 g) jars

6 lb (2.75 kg) grapes, picked off stems
sugar

Put the grapes into a large ceramic or nonreactive bowl, dusting with 2½ cups (1 lb 2 oz/500 g) sugar per 2¼ lb (1 kg) fruit. Cover with a lid or plastic wrap (clingfilm) and steep overnight.

—

The next day, put the grape mixture into a large preserving pan and bring to a boil over low heat. Cook for 1 hour, stirring occasionally and skimming several times with a slotted spoon; this will allow you to remove most of the seeds that float up. When the mixture reaches the small thread stage (225°F/107°C), or when a teaspoon of syrup dropped into a glass of water it forms thin threads that cannot be rolled into small balls when lifted out, the jam is cooked.

—

Pour the jam into sterilized jars (SEE p. 40) and seal with sterilized lids.

—

Process in a boiling-water canner (SEE p. 53 and follow the manufacturer's instructions) for 5 minutes.

—

NOTE: Some people remove the pips from the fresh fruit one by one, using a sharpened knife. The process is long and delicate, but yields perfect results.

## GRAPE JELLY

Preparation time 30 minutes
Cooking time 30–45 minutes
Canning time 5 minutes
Makes 3x 2 lb ¼ oz (500 g) jars

4½ lb (2 kg) grapes picked off stems
sugar

Heat the grapes in a large preserving pan, without water, for 10–15 minutes, or until the grape skins split open. Using a wooden spoon, push the grapes through a strainer to collect the juice.

—

Put a small plate or saucer into the freezer to chill. Measure the juice and pour it back into the clean pan with 1¼ cups (9 oz/250 g) sugar per 4¼ cups (34 fl oz/1 liter) juice, and heat gently in a pan, stirring until the sugar has dissolved, then bring to a boil and boil rapidly until it reaches the small pearl stage (232°F/111°C), or when tiny round beads form at the surface of the syrup and when dropped into a glass of water it forms threads of about 1½–2 inches (4–5 cm). Skim with a slotted spoon to remove any scum floating on the surface. Test for a set, by pouring several drops of jam onto the chilled plate and when you tip the plate the juice should not run. If it does it's ready, if not heat a little longer and test again.

—

Pour the jelly into sterilized jars (SEE p. 40) and seal with sterilized lids.

—

Process in a boiling-water canner (SEE p. 53 and follow the manufacturer's instructions) for 5 minutes.

## GRAPE AND APPLE JELLY

Preparation time 40 minutes
Cooking time 50–55 minutes
Canning time 5 minutes
Makes 3 x 1 lb 2 oz (500 g) jar

2¼ lb (1 kg) apples, quartered
3¼ lb (1.5 kg) grapes, picked off stems
sugar

Put the apples in a large preserving pan with just enough cold water to cover. Bring to a simmer and cook for 10 minutes until tender. Strain to collect the juice and measure it. Set aside.

—

Heat the grapes in a large preserving pan, without water, for 10–15 minutes, or until the grape skins split open and release the juice. Using a wooden spoon, push the grapes through a strainer to collect the juice. Measure the juice.

—

Combine the apple juice and grape juice in a large preserving pan with 3¾ cups (1 lb 10 oz/ 750 g) sugar per 4¼ cups (34 fl oz/1 liter) juice. Heat for 30 minutes, or until the juice starts to set; apple jelly only thickens after a few days.

—

Pour the jelly into sterilized jars (SEE p. 40) and seal with sterilized lids.

—

Process in a boiling-water canner (SEE p. 53 and follow the manufacturer's instructions) for 5 minutes.

## FRUIT PRESERVED IN GRAPE SYRUP

Preparation time 50 minutes
Cooking time 45 minutes
Canning time 5 minutes
Makes 3 x 1 lb 2 oz (500 g) jar

4½ lb (2 kg) grapes, picked off stems
4½ lb (2 kg) of one or all of pears, apples,
    quince, or pumpkins, peeled, cored, seeded,
    and cut into ½ inch (1 cm) pieces

---

This jam recipe uses grape juice instead of
sugar. Use black grapes if possible, or a mix of
sweet white and black grapes. The recipe can
be used to preserve a mix of seasonal fruit:
pears, apples, quince, and even pumpkins
and carrots. If you want to add carrots,
choose soft ones and cook them in the grape
juice as it is reducing, i.e. well before the rest
of the fruit. You may also use fallen fruit that
is beginning to bruise.

—

Put the grapes into a fruit press or food mill
and crush to collect the juice, then push
through a fine strainer to remove the pips and
skin, and extract the last of the juice.

—

Pour the juice into a large preserving pan and
cook over high heat, stirring occasionally for
20 minutes, or until the juice is reduced by
half.

—

Lower your chosen fruit into the reduced
juice, adding only as much as the juice can
cover. Return to a boil, then reduce the
heat to low and cook for 20 minutes stirring
occasionally, until the raisiné is reduced by
a third of its initial volume. You should get a
thick puree that holds its shape when spooned
onto a plate.

Pour into sterilized jars (SEE p. 40) and seal with
sterilized lids.

—

Process in a boiling-water canner (SEE p. 53
and follow the manufacturer's instructions) for
5 minutes.

## GRAPES IN EAU-DE-VIE

Preparation time 20 minutes, plus cooling
Cooking time 5 minutes
Steeping time 2 months, plus 3 weeks
Makes 1 x 2¼ lb (1 kg) jar

2 lb (900 g) muscat grapes, snipped off their
stems but with 1 inch (2.5 cm) of the stalk
still attached
1⅔ cups (14 fl oz/400 ml) eau-de-vie at 45%, for
covering
sugar

Use white muscat grapes.
—
Place the grapes in a large sterilized jar (SEE
p. 40) without filling it entirely, and pour
in enough eau-de-vie to cover. Seal with a
sterilized lid and steep in a cool, dark place for
two months.
—
Make a sugar syrup. Bring ¾ cup (5 oz/150 g)
sugar per 1 cup (9 fl oz/250 ml) water to a boil
in a pan. Boil for 2–3 seconds, then remove
from the heat and cool.
—
Carefully top off the jar with the cold syrup,
then seal with a sterilized lid and leave for
three weeks before serving.

## GRAPE JUICE

Preparation time 20 minutes
Cooking time 25–35 minutes
Canning time 30 minutes
Makes 14 fl oz (400 ml)

2 lb (900 g) ripe white grapes, picked from the
stems

Heat the grapes in a large preserving pan,
without water, for 10–15 minutes, or until the
grape skins split open and release the juice.
Bring to a boil and cook for 10–15 minutes until
the skins and pips float to the surface.
—
Push through a fine strainer to collect all the
juice, then pour the juice into a clean pan
and bring to a boil. Cook for 1 minute, then
carefully pour into sterilized bottles (SEE p. 40)
and seal.
—
Process in a boiling-water canner (SEE p. 53
and follow the manufacturer's instructions) for
30 minutes.

# RHUBARB

## RHUBARB MARMALADE

Preparation time 30 minutes
Steeping time 12 hours
Cooking time 10 minutes
Canning time 5 minutes
Makes 4 x 1 lb 2 oz (500 g) jars

4½ lb (2 kg) rhubarb, leaves cut off and
    discarded, peeled if necessary, and cut into
    ¾–1¼ inch/2–3 cm pieces
4½ lb (2 kg) sugar

If the rhubarb is a nice red color, do not peel so
the jam will be a beautiful dark red.

—

Put the rhubarb into a large preserving pan
with alternating layers of sugar, using the same
weight in sugar as fruit. Cover with a lid and
steep for 12 hours.

—

When ready to cook, put a small plate or saucer
into the freezer to chill. Cook over medium
heat for 10 minutes, checking carefully as
the juice reduces quickly and the jam has a
tendency to caramelize. Skim with a slotted
spoon to remove any scum floating on the
surface. To test for a set, pour several drops of
jam onto the chilled plate and when you tip the
plate the juice should not run. If it does run,
heat a little longer and test again.

—

Pour the jam into sterilized jars (SEE p. 40) and
seal with sterilized lids.

—

Process in a boiling-water canner (SEE p. 53
and follow the manufacturer's instructions) for
5 minutes.

—

NOTE: You can add lemon juice and grated
lemon zest, to taste, if liked.

## RHUBARB JAM

Preparation time 30 minutes
Cooking time 1 hour
Canning time 5 minutes
Makes 4 x 1 lb 2 oz (500 g) jars

4½ lb (2 kg) rhubarb, trimmed, peeled, and cut
    into ¾–1¼ inch/2–3 cm pieces
sugar

Place the rhubarb into a large pan and pour in
enough cold water to cover. Bring to a boil and
cook for 5–8 minutes, then drain and set aside.

—

Put a small plate or saucer into the freezer to
chill. Make a sugar syrup: weigh the fruit and
use the same quantity of sugar as the fruit.
Heat the sugar with ½ cup (3½ fl oz/100 ml)
water per 5 cups (2¼ lb/1 kg) sugar, stirring
until the sugar has dissolved, then bring to a
boil and boil rapidly until it reaches the ball
stage, (248°F/120°C): when a small amount of
syrup is dropped into a bowl of cold water, it
forms a soft ball the size of a pea.

—

Carefully lower the rhubarb into the sugar
syrup and cook gently for 20–25 minutes.
Skim with a slotted spoon to remove any scum
floating on the surface. To test for a set, pour
several drops of jam onto the chilled plate and
when you tip the plate the juice should not run.
If it does it's ready, if not heat a little longer and
test again.

—

Pour the jam into sterilized jars (SEE p. 40) and
seal with sterilized lids.

—

Process in a boiling-water canner (SEE p. 53
and follow the manufacturer's instructions) for
5 minutes.

## APPLE AND RHUBARB JAM

Preparation time 40 minutes
Cooking time 1 hour
Canning time 5 minutes
Makes 5 x 1 lb 2 oz (500 g) jars

3 lb (1.4 kg) apples, quartered
2¼ lb (1 kg) rhubarb, leaves cut off and
    discarded, peeled if necessary, and cut into
    ¾-1¼-inch/2-3-cm pieces
sugar
1⅔ cups (14 fl oz/400 ml) apple juice

Put the apples into a large preserving
pan with just enough cold water to cover.
Bring to a simmer and cook for 10 minutes
until tender. Strain to collect the juice and
measure it. Set aside.

—

Place the rhubarb into a large pan and pour
in enough cold water to cover. Bring to a boil
and cook for 5–8 minutes, then drain and set
aside.

—

Put a small plate or saucer into the freezer
to chill. Make a sugar syrup. Heat the same
weight of sugar as the fruit weight and the
apple juice gently in a pan, stirring until the
sugar has dissolved, then bring to a boil and
boil rapidly until it reaches the ball stage,
(248°F/120°C): when a small amount of
syrup is dropped into a bowl of cold water,
it forms a soft ball the size of a pea.

—

Carefully lower the rhubarb into the sugar
syrup and cook gently for 20–25 minutes.
Skim with a slotted spoon to remove any
scum floating on the surface. Test for a set,
by pouring several drops of jam onto the
chilled plate and when you tip the plate the
juice should not run. If it does it's ready, if
not heat a little longer and test again.

Pour the jam into sterilized jars (SEE p. 40)
and seal with sterilized lids.

—

Process in a boiling-water canner (SEE p. 53
and follow the manufacturer's instructions)
for 5 minutes.

# MIXED FRUITS

## FOUR-FRUIT JAM

**Preparation time 30 minutes**
**Steeping time 12 hours**
**Cooking time about 1 hour**
**Canning time 5 minutes**
**Makes 8 x 1 lb 2 oz (500 g) jars**

4½ lb (2 kg) sour cherries, pitted
4½ lb (2 kg) strawberries, hulled
15 cups (6½ lb/3 kg) sugar

**For the red currant and raspberry jelly**
7 oz (200 g) red currants, washed
7 oz (200 g) white currants, washed
7 oz (200 g) raspberries, stalks removed
sugar

Using equal quantities of sour cherries and strawberries, weigh three quarters of the combined weight of these fruit in sugar, then mix the fruit and sugar in a large preserving pan, cover with a lid, and steep for 12 hours.

—

To make the red currant and raspberry jelly, place the currants, still in clusters, and the raspberries, in a large preserving pan with a little water (¼ cup/2 fl oz/60 ml water per 4½ lb/2 kg fruit) and heat for 5 minutes, or until the fruit splits. Bring to a boil and boil for 8 minutes, stirring constantly.

—

Strain the mixture through a strainer to collect the juice. Do not push or squeeze the fruit or the jelly will be cloudy.

—

Put a small plate or saucer into the freezer to chill. Measure the juice and pour it into a clean pan and add with the same weight of sugar. Heat over low heat, stirring constantly for 5 minutes, or until the sugar dissolves. Bring to a boil and just as it is boiling stop stirring. Boil for exactly 3 minutes. This is the time it takes the pectin in the red currants to set into a jelly. To test for a set, pour several drops of jam onto the chilled plate and when you tip the plate the juice should not run. Pour the jelly into sterilized jars (SEE p. 40) and seal with sterilized lids.

—

The next day, put a small plate or saucer into the freezer to chill. Cook the cherry and strawberry mixture over low heat for 25–30 minutes. Skim with a slotted spoon to remove any scum floating on the surface. Add the red currant and raspberry jelly and boil for 1 minute. To test for a set, pour several drops of jam onto the chilled plate and when you tip the plate the juice should not run. If it does it's ready, if not heat a little longer and test again.

—

Pour the jam into sterilized jars (SEE p. 40) and seal with sterilized lids.

—

Process in a boiling-water canner (SEE p. 53 and follow the manufacturer's instructions) for 5 minutes.

## FOUR-FRUIT JELLY

Preparation time 30 minutes
Cooking time 15 minutes
Canning time 5 minutes
Makes 8 x 1 lb 2 oz (500 g) jars

2¼ lb (1 kg) sour cherries, pitted
2¼ lb (1 kg) strawberries, hulled
2¼ lb (1 kg) raspberries
2¼ lb (1 kg) red currants, stripped from stalks
20 cups (8¾ lb/4 kg) sugar

Place the fruit and sugar in a large preserving pan and cook over high heat for 15 minutes, or until the sugar has dissolved and the fruit has split open to release all the juice.

—

Push the mixture through a fine strainer to collect the juice, making sure you extract all of it as the last drops have a high pectin content. Pour into sterilized jars (SEE p. 40) and seal with sterilized lids.

—

Process in a boiling-water canner (SEE p. 53 and follow the manufacturer's instructions) for 5 minutes. The jelly will set after a few days.

—

NOTE: The fruit residue can be served as a compote. It is sweet and excellent.

## SUMMER FRUIT JAM

Preparation time 30 minutes
Steeping time 12 hours
Cooking time 35 minutes
Canning time 5 minutes
Makes 10 x 1 lb 2 oz (500 g) jars

2¼ lb (1 kg) apricots, halved and pitted
2¼ lb (1 kg) plums, halved and pitted
1 lb 2 oz (500 g) strawberries, hulled
1 lb 2 oz (500 g) cherries, pitted
1 lb 2 oz (500 g) red currants, stripped from stalks
sugar

Combine the fruit with 3¾ cups (1 lb 10 oz/750 g) sugar per 2¼ lb (1 kg) fruit in a large preserving pan, cover with a lid, and steep for 12 hours.

—

The next day, put a small plate or saucer into the freezer to chill. Bring the mixture to a boil over low heat and cook for 30 minutes. Skim with a slotted spoon to remove any scum floating on the surface. To test for a set, pour several drops of jam onto the chilled plate and when you tip the plate the juice should not run. If it does run, heat a little longer and test again.

—

Pour the jam into sterilized jars (SEE p. 40) and seal with sterilized lids.

—

Process in a boiling-water canner (SEE p. 53 and follow the manufacturer's instructions) for 5 minutes.

## FALL FRUIT JAM

Preparation time 30 minutes
Steeping time 12 hours
Cooking time 50 minutes
Canning time 5 minutes
Makes 8 x 1 lb 2 oz (500 g) jars

2¼ lb (1 kg) fall (autumn) plums, halved and
    pitted
2¼ lb (1 kg) pears, peeled, cored, and
    quartered
2¼ lb (1 kg) apples, peeled, cored, and
    quartered
20 cups (8¾ lb/4 kg) sugar

Combine the fruit with 3¾ cups (1 lb 10 oz/
750 g) sugar per 2¼ lb (1 kg) fruit in a large
preserving pan, cover with a lid, and steep for
12 hours.

—

The next day, put a small plate or saucer into
the freezer to chill. Bring the mixture to a
boil over low heat and cook for 45 minutes.
Skim with a slotted spoon to remove any scum
floating on the surface. To test for a set, pour
several drops of jam onto the chilled plate and
when you tip the plate the juice should not run.
If it does run, heat a little longer and test again.

—

Pour the jam into sterilized jars (SEE p. 40) and
seal with sterilized lids.

—

Process in a boiling-water canner (SEE p. 53
and follow the manufacturer's instructions) for
5 minutes.

## FOUR-FRUIT LIQUEUR

Preparation time 40 minutes
Steeping time 2-3 days, plus 1-2 months
Makes 8½ cups (68 fl oz/2 liters)

2¼ lb (1 kg) black cherries
2 cups (9 oz/250 g) raspberries
2¼ cups (9 oz/250 g) red currants
2¼ cups (5 oz/150 g) black currants
sugar
eau-de-vie at 70%

Put the fruit into a fruit press or food mill and
crush to collect the juice. Alternatively, use a
mortar and pestle to crush the fruit, in batches,
placing the crushed fruit into a terrine or large
bowl. Push the fruit through a fine strainer to
remove the pips and skin, and extract the last
of the juice. Alternatively, pit the cherries and
use a juicer.

—

Measure the juice and pour it into a large
ceramic or nonreactive bowl. Add 1½ cups
(11 oz/300 g) sugar per 4¼ cups (34 fl oz/1 liter)
juice and stir to combine. Cover with a lid or
plastic wrap (clingfilm) and keep in a cool place
for 2–3 days to start the fermentation.

—

Make sure the sugar has dissolved completely,
then strain the juice through a strainer into
a large pitcher (jug). Measure it again, and
combine with the same weight in alcohol. The
strength of this alcohol will be halved, for a
finished liqueur at 35°.

—

Pour into sterilized bottles (SEE p. 40), seal,
and steep in a cool, dark place for 1–2 months
before serving.

## FRUIT PIT LIQUEUR

**Preparation time 40 minutes, plus cooling**
**Steeping time 4–5 months**
**Makes 10½ cups (88 fl oz/2.5 liters)**

1.3 oz (050 g) fruit pits
8½ cups (68 fl oz/2 liters) eau-de-vie at 40%
3½ cups (1½ lb/700 g) sugar

This liqueur is made with the pits of fruit, such as cherries, sour cherries, plums, apricots, and peaches. Use only 1 or 2 peach pits per 8½ cups (68 fl oz/2 liters) eau-de-vie as they contain prussic acid.

Crush the pits with a hammer and combine the shells and kernels with the eau-de-vie in a large sterilized jar (SEE p. 40). Seal with a sterilized lid and steep in a cool, dark place for at least 4–5 months.

Strain the alcohol to remove all pit fragments, and measure the amount. Set aside in a large pitcher (jug) or bowl.

Make a sugar syrup. Bring 1⅔ cups (11⅔ oz/ 330 g) sugar per 1½ cups (12 fl oz/350 ml) water per 4¼ cups (34 fl oz/1 liter) eau-de-vie to a boil in a pan. Boil for 2–3 seconds then remove from the heat and cool.

Pour the cold sugar syrup into the alcohol and stir well. Strain again through a strainer and pour into sterilized bottles before sealing, and store in a cool, dark place.

# CHARCUTERIE

If you live in the countryside, you may consider keeping pigs: provided the animals are fed well, looked after, and kept in clean conditions, they provide an extremely high yield of meat.

While usable meat might make up 60–65 percent of the weight of beef, a pig provides up to 75 percent. Given the space, time, and inclination, it is worth taking the trouble to raise a pig to benefit from this very real material profit.

Some of the meat from the pig can be eaten fresh, and there are of course many and varied recipes for preparing it. The rest can be preserved in a number of different ways, including smoking and salt curing, and some of these relatively simple preparation techniques can also be done successfully at home.

This work will not be for nothing, and will give you some useful supplies during the winter. If you are not in a position to keep a pig yourself, you may be able to get hold of a piece of pork that is large enough to use in some of the preserving techniques in this chapter.

### RAISING A PIG IN THE COUNTRY

This part requires more extensive learning than the scope of this book permits, but we will mention the key points to which particular attention should be paid.

### CHOOSING A BREED

Depending on where you live, different breeds of pork will be available to you, which can generally be told apart by the color and pattern of their coat, the shape of their ears and snouts.

It is important to select a breed that is fully adapted to your climate, and is suitable for keeping domestically. It should be fertile, easy to fatten, and give high-quality, not-too-fatty meat.

Generally, these are animals with a long body, graceful limbs, and a squat neck.

HYGIENE

Your pigsty should provide more than just shelter from the cold: it should be a clean and well-ventilated home for the animals. Arrange it so the ground is slightly raised at the opposite side from the door and made of concrete slabs or cement, so the feces will run down toward the door: cleaning will then be easier. You should put in new bedding straw as often as required, without letting it get too damp.

The floor should be disinfected from time to time with water to which a little bleach has been added, and the walls should be whitewashed once a year.

Allow 27 ft$^2$ (2.5 m$^2$) per animal, but the animals need to be able to move about, so you should allow ready access to a yard where they can get some fresh air and exercise.

### FEEDING

Pigs are omnivores but don't make the mistake of giving them any old food, especially spoiled foods, the taste of which would be detectable in the meat. Their basic feed should revolve around potatoes, various roots, dairy by-products (such as whey), chestnuts, and acorns. For especially tasty meat, feed them green fodder, dairy, and tubers.

It is a good idea to add salt to their food, about ¾–1 oz (20–25 g) per day. Naturally, making sure the pig eats enough is important for fattening them up.

When the pig is around four or five months, a well-fed pig should be putting on about 1 lb 2 oz (500 g) a day. By seven or eight months, it should have got up to 187 or 220 lb (85 or 100 kg). The animal will give a good yield if slaughtered at a weight of around 220 lb (100 kg).

Pigs are susceptible to catching certain diseases, some of which are dangerous for humans, so no meat should be used for consumption without the animal having been examined by a vet.

### SLAUGHTERING AND BUTCHERING

In 1948 when this book was originally published, it was common practice in rural France for people to raise, slaughter and butcher their own animals. These days, you need to get a professional to slaughter your animals for you, taking your animals to a local slaughterhouse for killing. The following text explains how a pig would have been butchered in rural France in 1948.

### BUTCHERING

Cutting up the carcass requires three instruments:

- A chopper with a 7-inch/18-cm blade
- A thin meat cleaver with a 12-inch/30-cm blade
- A bone saw with a blade 14–20 inches/35–50 cm long

The animal must be cut in half, starting from the crotch, before butchering each half. The technique used for this will differ based on region and personal preference. As a general rule, having cut off the front and rear legs, separate the loin from the belly and then divide each of these parts into various cuts.

Figures 12 and 13 (SEE pp. 248–9) show the cuts that can be drawn from a half-pig.

- Carve out the ham, trying to give it a circular shape at the top without cutting into the thigh bone. Cut off the hock and the trotter from this piece.
- Separate the belly from the loin. The loin is covered by a layer of back fat. This is generally removed and set aside. The rest of the meat is cut into pieces that will be used fresh: shoulder, rack with seven chops, hind loin with two chops, and the chomp end.
- Separate the blade, which can be smoked, or rolled and brined.
- The lean belly (without the spare ribs attached to the sternum) can be salted, smoked, or ground (minced).
- The leaf lard surrounding the kidneys is removed from the abdominal region.
- The neck meat, consisting of the lower part of the neck and part of the front leg, are reserved for ground (minced) meat.
- The front hock is separated from the trotter.

Part of the offal must be used the same day you slaughter your pig and will be turned into cooked dishes (brain, kidneys, heart) while other parts can be preserved (tongue, ears, pigs' feet/trotters, tail).

The head will be turned into head cheese, also known as brawn.

As you work, take care to group together those pieces that are destined to be used in the same way:

- All the cuts that will be eaten fresh;
- The hams, shoulders, and hocks;
- The bacon and leaf lard;
- The cuts to be salted;
- The head.

**AVERAGE YIELD FROM A 220-LB (100-KG) PIG**

**(WEIGHED AFTER SLAUGHTERING)**

| | |
|---|---|
| Hams | 26½ lb (12 kg) |
| Belly | 33 lb (15 kg) |
| Hind loin | 37½ lb (17 kg) |
| Shoulder | 13¼ lb (6 kg) |
| Blades | 9 lb (4 kg) |
| Belly and neck meat | 41 lb (18.75 kg) |
| Head | 15 lb (7 kg) |
| Pigs' feet (trotters) | 5½ lb (2.5 kg) |
| Hocks | 10 lb (4.5 kg) |
| Back fat | 30 lb (13.75 kg) |
| Leaf lard | 6½–7¾ lb (3–3.5 kg) |
| Blood | 4¼–5¼ quarts (7–8¾ UK pints/4–5 liters) |
| Variety meats (Offal) | 13¼–15 lb (6–7 kg) |

### PURCHASING MEAT

If you decide to purchase pork meat rather than raise it, make sure it is high quality: it should be whitish pink in color, slightly darker around the bone, and with a firm, tight grain.

There should be plenty of fat marbling. The outer fat should not be too thick (about 1¼ inches/3 cm) and should be firm but creamy to the touch, white with a pink hue.

Avoid meat with soft fat, and do not buy if it displays blemishes or blotches, or if the bacon is moist or bloodshot.

The following table shows typical uses of different cuts, either preserved (charcuterie) or fresh (cooking).

| CUT | CHARCUTERIE | COOKING |
|---|---|---|
| Rack (7 ribs) | | Broiled (grilled) <br> Roasted |
| Shoulder (5 ribs) | Salted <br> Smoked | Roasted <br> Stewed <br> Boiled |
| Hind loin (2 ribs) | Salted <br> Smoked | Roasted <br> Braised <br> Broiled (grilled) <br> Sliced thinly and <br> cooked briefly |
| Ham | Salted <br> Smoked <br> Ground (minced) | Boiled <br> Braised |
| Chump end | | Roasted |
| Shoulder | Ground (minced) <br> for sausages and rillettes Salted <br> Smoked | Roasted <br> Stewed <br> Boiled |
| Belly | Ground (minced) for rillettes <br> Salted | Boiled |
| Neck meat | Ground (minced) for sausages <br> Salted | Used for stuffing <br> Boiled |
| Hock | Salted and smoked | Boiled |
| Back fat | Lard and bacon strips | Used as a fat in cooking and to <br> lard roasts |
| Leaf lard | Lard | Used as fat in cooking |
| Pigs' feet (trotters) | | Stuffed <br> Broiled (grilled) |
| Tails | Salted | Boiled <br> Braised <br> Broiled (grilled) |

ESSENTIAL EQUIPMENT

For charcuterie making, you will need the following tools:

FOR CHARCUTERIE-MAKING

- A manual or electric grinder (mincer). An electric grinder (mincer) is very practical but it should not cut the meat too quickly or it will bruise it
- A sausage-maker, with funnels of different sizes
- An oven and broiler (grill)
- A cutting board for meat
- Cooking pots
- Casserole dishes, a large bowl
- A saw, a slicing knife, a cleaver
- Funnels in different sizes for blood sausage (black pudding) and sausages
- Earthenware dishes in various sizes
- Metal or ceramic pâté and terrine dishes, which can sometimes be decorated
- Boards and string for pigs' feet (trotters)
- A salting tub. This is a wooden cask that is narrower at the top than the bottom. It has a round wooden lid that fits through the opening, and on which a large stone is placed. You can also use earthenware jars of various shapes, either with straight or rounded sides with wooden or earthenware lids that fit the jars perfectly. It is better to use a number of smaller salting tubs than one large one.
- A smoker (see p. 305). This is a cabinet with brick walls, located above or beside the stove, and through which the smoke from a low fire can be directed. You can burn specially selected woods such as beech, bay, juniper, elm, hornbeam, or birch. It has poles and hooks inside from which the meat to be smoked is suspended from. These days, you can buy a food smoker from specialist catering stores.

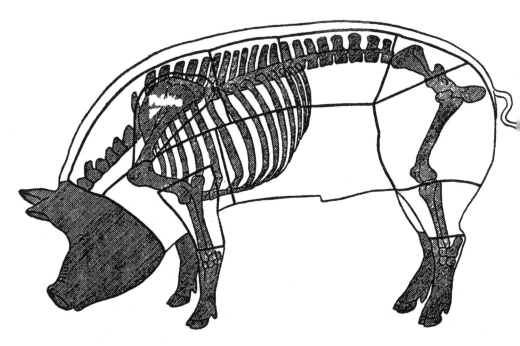

Figs. 12 and 13 showing the traditional butchering divisions
of a pig (SEE p. 245)

Paris-style cuts of pork
by M. Martel (1936)
(From *Meat – Classes and Categories*)
(Lajeunesse Editions, 24 Rue Brunel, Paris)

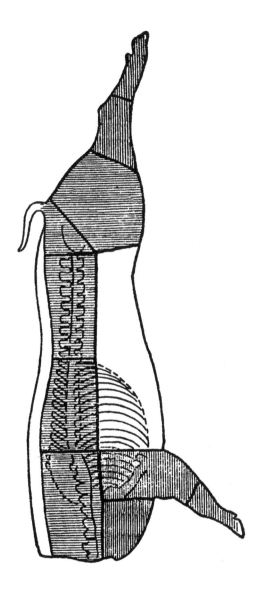

Fig. 13

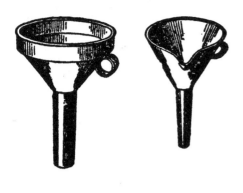
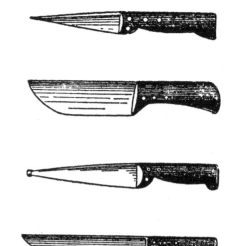
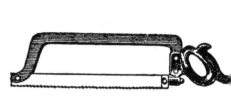

Fig. 14 Traditional butchering equipment

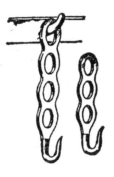

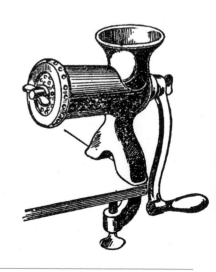

The French word 'charcuterie' comes from *chair cuite*, or 'cooked meat'. The profession of charcutier, which consists of processing, cooking, and working with pork meat to give a range of different products, has existed since 1475, when the Provost-Marshal of Paris granted the foundation of a guild.

The term 'charcuterie' has come to encompass products other than pork: veal, beef, rabbit, and pheasant, and a range of doughs used with meats such as pasta dough, puff pastry, and basic pie dough (shortcrust pastry).

Charcuterie-making requires precision and accuracy, as well as speed and dexterity. While it is difficult to excel in preserving meat the way a specialist would, if you live in the countryside you may have the opportunity to make certain kinds of food that will serve you well all the year round.

Charcuterie-making is a highly skilled craft, but you will soon develop a feel for it, and will get to know when to add seasoning, when to taste, and when something is ready.

It is a true delight to serve well-made dishes, succulent pâtés, or perfect sausages that you have made to your family and guests! This section features a variety of methods for preserving pork (for a longer or shorter period) using different techniques, together with suggestions for making use of the different conserves.

### CLEANLINESS AND HYGIENE

To be certain of the quality and freshness of your home charcuterie, you should only use meat of the finest quality and when it is very fresh. As with all preserved foods, you should take all precautions to ensure food safety.

You should maintain the highest standards of hygiene yourself, wear appropriate clothing (coat, apron, and headwear) and keep your hands perfectly clean by washing them frequently as you work.

The room in which you process your meat should be cleaned with plenty of water and diluted bleach, and your equipment should be washed after each use.

### SEASONINGS

When making charcuterie, the following range of seasonings and condiments will contribute to the flavor of the finished product. Some of them act as antiseptics (such as salt, for example) that slow down microbial action.

### SALT

It is extremely important that the salt be as dry as possible, so it is useful to have some set aside, kept as dry as possible, and well away from any potential damp.

### GARLIC

Remove the papery outer skin from garlic bulbs and break into individual cloves. Peel the cloves, removing any shoots, and chop very finely. Select garlic bulbs that feel firm, heavy for their size, and with their outer skin intact. Once the outer skin dries and cracks, the cloves become dry and you run the risk of starting fermentation that will damage the preserved dish.

### SHALLOT

This is used especially in making *andouilles* and *andouillettes*, and to heighten the taste of the meat in sausages. It is always used finely chopped.

### ONION

This is used both cooked and raw, but always ground (minced), in cold cuts. It is used in great quantities in blood sausage (black pudding), for which it is always cooked until just softened or browned, and in sausage meat. Sliced into circles (rounds), onion is also used to lift the flavor of marinades.

### ANISE

The seeds of the anise plant are used in the same way as cumin or fennel in seasoning. The dried seeds can also be ground into a powder and added to mixed spices.

### STAR ANISE, CHINESE STAR ANISE

Same use as aniseed.

### CINNAMON STICK

It is best to use Sri Lankan cinnamon, purchased in curled, tan-colored sticks. These pieces should be ground to a powder and mixed with other spices.

### CORIANDER SEED

These strongly flavored seeds are dried, ground, and mixed with other spices such as aniseed or cumin.

### CUMIN SEED

These tiny brown seeds are used to flavor some sausages.

### CARAWAY SEED

Also known as "meadow cumin," these aromatic seeds are used in the same way as cumin.

### SPICE MIXES

When making sausages and saucissons, you will often use seasoning mixtures that have a number of different ingredients and which have been made in advance. All the spices used should be carefully ground to a powder, together if possible, so they are perfectly mixed.

Here are two recipes for mixed ground spices (SEE also Sausage meat on p. 258 and Veal and Pork Stuffing on p. 259).

### SPICE MIX I

| | |
|---|---|
| Anise | 2 teaspoons (10 g) |
| Cinnamon | 1½ teaspoons (8 g) |
| Ginger | 11/2 tablespoons (40 g) |
| Marjoram | 11/4 teaspoons (6 g) |
| Nutmeg | 1 teaspoon (5 g) |
| Mint | 1 teaspoon (5 g) |
| Jamaica pepper | 1 teaspoon (5 g) |
| Savory | 1 teaspoon (5 g) |
| Sage | 1 tablespoon (16 g) |
| | 31/2 oz (100 g) |

### SPICE MIX II

| | |
|---|---|
| Anise | 11/2 teaspoons (8 g) |
| Cumin | 1/2 teaspoon (2 g) |
| Coriander | 2 tablespoons (30 g) |
| Fennel | 1 teaspoon (6 g) |
| Bay leaf | 2 tablespoons (32 g) |
| Savory | 2 teaspoons (10 g) |
| Sage | 11/2 teaspoons (8 g) |
| Jamaica pepper | ¼ teaspoon (1 g) |
| Cayenne pepper | 3/4 teaspoon (3 g) |
| | 31/2 oz (100 g) |

### TARRAGON

An aromatic plant containing a strongly scented essential oil, it is usually used raw, but is used cooked in some sauces, such as Béarnaise.

### FENNEL SEED

The seeds of this plant are used in the same way as caraway and cumin.

### JUNIPER

Juniper berries have a bitter and slightly resinous flavor; they are dried and used some time after picking in later Fall (autumn)/early Winter. They are used in sauerkraut, and the smoke produced when they are burned over a low fire gives pork a particular flavor that is widely appreciated. It also gives gin its distinctive flavor.

### GINGER

The root of a tropical plant, it has a warm, sweet aroma and a very strong flavor.

### CLOVES

The cloves used in cooking and charcuterie are the flower buds of an evergreen tree. Cloves should be brown in color and give off a strong scent when crushed.

### CURRY POWDER

This is an Indian-style spice mix, mustard yellow in color, made up of several ground spices including pepper, chili powder, cloves, turmeric, and ginger.

### BAY LEAVES

Bay leaves have a very strong scent when fresh. They are usually used dried and whole in bouquet garni, or ground to a powder in spice mixes.

### NUTMEG

This is the kernel of a large seed. It is gray-brown, covered in grooves, and contains a scented oil that lends a pleasant scent to dishes. The nut should be purchased whole, and grated when you wish to use it.

### MACE

This is the thick membrane that surrounds the nutmeg seed. It is red when fresh, and dries to a grayish yellow. Mace has an extremely pleasant aroma and is used in ground form in spice mixes.

### MARJORAM

The dried leaves are ground to a powder and used in some spice mixes.

### FOUR-SPICE BLEND

This is a mixture of the following ground spices: cinnamon, cloves, nutmeg, and black pepper.

### PAPRIKA

The Hungarian name for a mild type of chile; the version you will find in the stores is a bright, red powder. You can get mild, hot, and smoked varieties.

### PARSLEY

An aromatic plant whose leaves and stems are used to garnish dishes, as seasoning in bouquet garni, or finely chopped, such as in stuffing. It is also commonly used in charcuterie products. There are both flat-leaf and curly-leaf varieties.

### CAYENNE PEPPER

This is very hot and should be used sparingly.

### JAMAICA PEPPER (ALSO CALLED ALLSPICE)

These pea-size, dark brown berries are very aromatic. They are used ground, like pepper, but in small quantities and mixed with other spices.

### PEPPER

Black pepper is the dried, fleshy fruit of the pepper plant. White pepper is the seed that is inside the fruit; it is milder than black pepper. Pepper is used in a powdered form, ground in a special mill.

There are also green and pink varieties commonly used in charcuterie. Never buy ground pepper as it is often stale.

### ROSEMARY

The leaves of this plant can be used fresh or dried and finely chopped after removal from the coarse stalk. They are used on their own or mixed with other spices and herbs.

### SAFFRON

The orange-colored stigmas of the saffron plant. It is better to buy saffron as filaments than to buy it ground as it may be fake. It is the world's most highly prized spice and pound-for-pound is more expensive than gold. Saffron is sold wrapped in dark orange cellophane to protect it from the light.

### SAVORY

Used in the same way as rosemary.

### SAGE

Used in the same way as rosemary.

### THYME

An aromatic plant used in bunches for bouquet garni. The leaves can also be ground.

### TRUFFLES

These can be used fresh in stuffings, galantines, and pâtés. The truffle should be firm and the black flesh should be covered with tiny whitish veins. Truffles are incredibly expensive and the areas where they can be found are not just protected, but guarded with high security.

# SOME CHARCUTERIE BASICS

## SAUSAGE MEAT

Preparation time 30 minutes
Makes 2¼ lb (1 kg)

1 lb 2 oz (500 g) neck meat
1 lb 2 oz (500 g) pork shoulder and green
   (unsmoked) fatback bacon (½ meat,
   ½ bacon)
1½ teaspoons spice mix (SEE p. 254)
1½ teaspoons salt

This is used for sausages and pâtés.

—

Use the meat and bacon straight from the
refrigerator. Trim all the sinews and veins from
the lean meat and cut the bacon and meat into
small, even-size pieces.

—

Season with the salt and spice mix.

—

Process the meat through the meat grinder
three times, changing the disks from coarse
to fine so that by the third pass you have
extremely finely ground meat.

## FINE SAUSAGE MEAT

Preparation time 30 minutes
Makes 2¼ lb (1 kg)

1 lb 2 oz (500 g) neck meat
1 lb 2 oz (500 g) pork shoulder and green
   (unsmoked) fatback bacon (½ meat,
   ½ bacon)
1½ teaspoons spice mix (SEE p. 254)
2 eggs
scant ½ cup (3½ fl oz/100 ml) cognac
1½ teaspoons salt

Use the meat and bacon straight from the
refrigerator. Trim all the sinews and veins from
the lean meat and cut the bacon and meat into
small even-size pieces.

—

Season with the spice mix , salt, eggs and
cognac.

—

Process the meat through the meat grinder
three times, changing the disks from coarse
to fine so that by the third pass you have
extremely finely ground meat.

## VEAL AND PORK STUFFING

Preparation time 40 minutes
Makes 2½ lb (1.2 kg)

just under 2 lb (875 g) lean veal meat
4 oz (125 g) green (unsmoked) fatback bacon
4 oz (125 g) lean pork meat
2 teaspoons salt
1 tablespoon spice mix (SEE p. 254)
scant ½ cup (3½ fl oz/100 ml) milk or cream

___

This is a very rich stuffing so would be well-suited to game or duck.

___

Use the meat and bacon straight from the refrigerator.

___

Cut the meat into pieces and process through the meat grinder, changing the disk each time from coarse to medium to fine. Season with the salt and spice mix.

___

Transfer the mixture to a large bowl and work in the milk or cream with a spoon or a fork until evenly combined.

## TRUFFLE STUFFING

Preparation time 40 minutes
Makes 3 lb (1.4 kg)

just under 2 lb (875 g) lean veal meat
4 oz (125 g) green (unsmoked) fatback bacon
4 oz (125 g) lean pork meat
2 teaspoons salt
2½ teaspoons spice mix (SEE p. 254)
5 oz (150 g) truffle shavings, very finely
    chopped
scant ½ cup (3½ fl oz/100 ml) milk or cream

Obviously, in this day, this stuffing would be very expensive to make because of the truffle shavings. Perhaps it is best saved for a very special occasion. To achieve the truffle flavor without the expense, you could use truffle oil very sparingly. The flavor is very intense. Use this stuffing for poultry, especially chicken and turkey.

___

Use the meat and bacon straight from the refrigerator.

___

Cut the meat into pieces and process through the meat grinder, changing the disk each time from coarse to medium to fine. Season with the salt and spice mix, then add the very finely chopped truffle.

___

Place the mixture in a mortar, and work in the milk or cream with a pestle.

## STUFFING MIXTURE FOR PÂTÉS

Preparation time 30 minutes
Makes 3¼ lb (1.5 kg)

13 oz (375 g) boned and skinned poultry meat
1 lb 2 oz (500 g) lean veal meat
1 lb 2 oz (500 g) fatback
4 teaspoons salt
1 teaspoon freshly ground black pepper
3½ oz (100 g) truffle shavings (optional)
scant ½ cup (3½ fl oz/100 ml) cognac (optional)

Use the meat and fatback straight from the refrigerator. Cut the meat and fatback into pieces and process through the meat grinder, changing the disk each time from coarse to medium to fine.

—

Season with the salt and pepper, and add the truffle shavings and cognac, if desired.

—

This can be used as a stuffing or baked in a ceramic dish, covered with foil in a roasting tin half-filled with hot water. Cook in a preheated oven at 325°F/160°C/Gas Mark 3 for about 1½–2 hours.

## STUFFING MIXTURE FOR GAME (TERRINES, PÂTÉS)

Preparation time 20 minutes
Makes 1¾ lb (800 g)

9 oz (250 g) game meat
2¼–3½ oz (60–100 g) game liver
1 lb 2 oz (500 g) pork neck meat
1 tablespoon salt
1½ teaspoons freshly ground black pepper
1½ teaspoons spice mix (SEE p. 254)

Use the meat straight from the refrigerator. Cut the meat into pieces and process through the meat grinder, changing the disk each time from coarse to medium to fine.

—

Season with the salt, pepper, and spice mix.

—

This can be used as a stuffing or baked in a ceramic dish, covered with foil in a roasting tin half-filled with hot water. Cook in a preheated oven at 325°F/160°C/Gas Mark 3 for about 1½–2 hours.

## ASPIC

**Preparation time 1 hour, plus cooling**
**Cooking time about 7–8 hours**
**Makes 5¼ quarts (8¾ UK pints/5 liters)**

2¼ lb (1 kg) beef shin
2¼ lb (1 kg) veal bones
3¼ lb (1.5 kg) veal shank
2 carrots, sliced
3 small onions, sliced
2 oz (50 g) leeks, sliced
3 calves' feet, deboned and blanched
7 oz (200 g) uncured pork rinds, blanched and
    tied together
1 bouquet garni (SEE p. 273)
4 teaspoons salt

This jelly must be made the day before using.

—

To make the aspic, preheat the oven to
350°F/180°C/Gas Mark 4.

—

Place the bones with the beef and veal shank in
an ovenproof dish and roast in the oven for
30 minutes.

—

Place the carrots, onions, and leeks in a stock
pot or very large, heavy-bottomed pan and
cover with the calves' feet, pork rinds, browned
bones and meat, and the bouquet garni. Cover
and cook over medium heat for 10 minutes.

—

Add scant ½ cup (3½ fl oz/100 ml) water and
cook for another 10 minutes. Pour in 8⅓ quarts
(14 UK pints/7.9 liters) water and add the salt,
then bring to a boil. Skim, reduce the heat to
low, and simmer for 6–7 hours. Strain through
a clean cloth and cool.

—

Skim off the fat that has formed at the surface.
When the jelly is completely cooled, any
impurities remaining will have sunk to the
bottom. For a clear jelly, pour slowly when
using, taking care to leave the impurities
behind.

—

NOTE: If the aspic is not as firm as you need it,
you can add gelatin: ⅓ teaspoon/1.5 g gelatin
per 4¼ cups (34 fl oz/1 liter) of jelly, softened
in cold water for 5 minutes and squeezed with
your hands to remove excess water. After
skimming the jelly of fat, return to the clean
pot, add the drained gelatin, and bring just to
a simmer, stirring frequently. You can flavor
the jelly with Madeira, which will also give it a
good color.

## POULTRY JELLY

Preparation time 1 hour
Soaking time overnight
Cooking time 6 hours 10 minutes–7 hours
    10 minutes
Makes 8½ cups (60 fl oz/2 liters)

2 tablespoons vinegar
3 pigs' feet (trotters)
3½ oz (100 g) fresh pork rinds
12 oz (350 g) pork bones, scrubbed
1 large carrot, sliced
1 large onion, sliced
1 leek, sliced
salt

Fill a large bowl with water and add the
vinegar. Add the pigs' feet (trotters) and soak
overnight.
—
Tie the fresh pork rinds together and place
them in a large pan with the bones and pigs'
feet (trotters). Cover with water, measuring the
amount, and bring to a boil over medium heat.
—
When it comes to a boil, skim to remove scum
and add the sliced carrots, onion, and leek.
Add ½ teaspoon salt per 4¼ cups (34 fl oz/1
liter) water and bring back to a boil. As soon as
it is boiling, reduce the heat to low and simmer
for 6–7 hours.
—
Remove from the heat and cool, removing
the fat from the surface. When the jelly is cold,
any impurities remaining will have sunk to
the bottom. For a clear jelly, pour slowly when
using, taking care to leave the impurities
behind.

## MEAT GLAZE

Preparation time 5 minutes
Cooking time about 7 hours
Makes 4½ cups (39 fl oz/1.1 liters)

12¾ cups (105 fl oz/3 liters) beef stock with the
    fat skimmed off
3¼ lb (1.5 kg) brisket, cubed
1 veal shank
2 carrots, sliced
3½ oz (100 g) leeks, sliced
1 small onion, sliced
½ teaspoon salt
3½ oz (100 g) lard

In a large pan, bring the stock, beef, and
veal shank to a boil, skimming the surface to
remove any scum. Add the vegetables and salt,
then reduce the heat and cook over low, steady
heat for 6–7 hours until the beef is very soft.
—
Strain the cooking liquid and remove the fat.
Return the liquid to the clean pan and stir as it
is brought to a simmer. Simmer for 10 minutes,
or until it coats a spoon and just sticks to it.
—
Pour the meat glaze into small sterilized jars
(SEE p. 40). Let cool completely and set. Melt
the lard in a pan over low heat, then pour a
thin layer of melted lard on top of the jars. Seal
with a tight-fitting sterilized lid. Store in the
refrigerator and use within a few weeks.

## QUENELLE DOUGH

**Preparation time 50 minutes**
**Cooking time 25 minutes**
**Makes 1¾ lb (800 g)**

7 oz (200 g) pork meat (loin)
14 oz (400 g) veal suet
3½ oz (100 g) flour panade (SEE below)
2 eggs
¼ teaspoon freshly grated nutmeg
salt and freshly ground black pepper

**For the flour panade**
2½ cups (11 oz/300 g) all-purpose (plain) flour
scant ¼ cup (2 oz/50 g) butter, diced

For the panade, in a bowl, mix the flour with just enough cold water from 2¼ cups (17 fl oz/500 ml) water to form a paste. Bring the rest of the water to a boil in a pan.

—

Add the flour paste to the boiling water and stir well over medium heat until the dough pulls away from the sides of the pan. Stir in the butter and salt and set aside.

—

Use the meat and suet straight from the refrigerator. Cut the meat and suet into small pieces and process through the fine disk of a meat grinder to make a smooth paste. Add the panade mixture and eggs, and season with salt, pepper, and the nutmeg.

—

To shape the quenelles, use a pair of dessertspoons. Dip one spoon into a bowl of hot water and scoop up some of the mixture, then dip the second spoon into the hot water and scoop the mixture from the first spoon, smoothing it. Repeat, keeping the spoons hot to make a smooth, elongated oval shape. Alternatively, put the mixture into a pastry (piping) bag and pipe the mixture onto a lightly floured counter (work surface).

—

Bring a large pan of lightly salted water to a boil, then reduce the heat and make sure it's simmering before carefully lowering the quenelles into the water. Poach for several minutes until cooked through, then drain carefully and use immediately, or cool in the cooking liquid and store in the refrigerator.

## POACHED PORK QUENELLES

**Preparation time 1 hour**
**Cooking time 25 minutes**
**Makes 1¾ lb (800 g), serves 6**

1 lb 5 oz (600 g) pork loin
2 eggs
scant ½ cup (3½ oz/100 g) butter
¼ teaspoon freshly grated nutmeg
salt and freshly ground black pepper

**For the flour panade**
2½ cups (11 oz/300 g) all-purpose (plain) flour
scant ¼ cup (2 oz/50 g) butter, diced

For the panade, in a bowl, mix the flour with just enough cold water from 2¼ cups (17 fl oz/500 ml) water to form a paste. Bring the rest of the water to a boil in a pan.

—

Add the flour paste to the boiling water and stir well over medium heat until the dough pulls away from the sides of the pan. Stir in the butter and set aside.

—

Make sure the meat is used straight from the fridge. Cut the meat into small pieces and process through the fine disk of a meat grinder. Put it through the grinder again to make sure it is a fine paste.

—

Put the meat paste in a mortar and, using the pestle, pound in the eggs, panade, and butter, adding them in small amounts. Season with salt, pepper, and the nutmeg.

—

To shape the quenelles, use a pair of dessertspoons. Dip one spoon into a bowl of hot water and scoop up some of the mixture, then dip the second spoon into the hot water and scoop the mixture from the first spoon,

smoothing it. Repeat, keeping the spoons hot to make a smooth, elongated oval shape. Alternatively, put the mixture into a pastry (piping) bag and pipe the mixture onto a lightly floured counter (work surface).

—

Bring a large pan of lightly salted water to a boil, then reduce the heat and make sure it's simmering before carefully lowering the quenelles into the water. Poach for several minutes until cooked through, then drain carefully and use immediately, or cool in the cooking liquid and store in the refrigerator.

## JUS

**Preparation time 30 minutes**
**Cooking time about 6 hours 10 minutes**
**Makes 8½ cups (68 fl oz/2 liters)**

generous ¾ cup (5 oz/150 g) lard
1 onion, sliced
4 carrots, sliced
1 head of garlic, thinly sliced
5 oz (150 g) leeks, sliced
9 lb (4 kg) veal bones, split
9 lb (4 kg) pork and beef bones, split
½ cinnamon stick
1 tablespoon coriander seeds
6 allspice berries
blade of mace
1 tablespoon black peppercorns
1 bouquet garni (SEE p. 254)
salt

This jus can be used when making terrines and pâtés.

Heat the lard in a very large pan or stock pot over medium heat. Add the onion, carrots, garlic, leeks, bones, and spices and cook for about 8–10 minutes, or until everything is browned. Drain off the fat, then add 6⅓ quarts (10½ UK pints/6 liters) water and the bouquet garni. Reduce the heat to low and cook for at least 6 hours.

—

Strain the jus through a cheesecloth- (muslin-) covered strainer into a large pitcher (jug) or bowl. Season with salt if necessary.

—

NOTE: If you substitute stock or jelly for the water, your jus will be even tastier.

# MARINADES

Marinades are used either to preserve meat for a few days, or to improve its taste and to tenderize it.

## CLASSIC MARINADE

**Preparation time 5 minutes**
**Marinating time 1–2 days**
**Makes 6¼ cups (53 fl oz/1.5 liters)**

4 sprigs thyme
3 bay leaves
1 shallot, chopped
1 medium onion, chopped
3 cloves garlic, chopped
1–2 carrots, sliced
1 tablespoon coriander seeds
2 teaspoons black peppercorns
6 juniper berries
2¼ cups (17 fl oz/500 ml) wine vinegar
4¼ cups (34 fl oz/1 liter) white or red wine
    (depending if the meat is white or red)
salt and freshly ground black pepper

Arrange the raw meat that is going to be marinated in a terrine or large nonreactive dish and cover it with the herbs, vegetables, spices, and salt and pepper. Pour in 1 part vinegar to 2 parts wine until the meat is covered and put on the lid or cover with plastic wrap (clingfilm).

—

Marinate in the refrigerator for 1–2 days, flipping it twice daily.

## PORK MARINADE

Preparation time 5 minutes
Marinating time 1–2 days
Makes sufficient marinade for a 3¼ lb (1.5 kg)
    roast

1 small onion, cut into slices
3 cloves garlic, chopped
scant ½ cup (3½ fl oz/100 ml) oil
scant ½ cup (3½ fl oz/100 ml) vinegar
juniper berries
1–2 teaspoons walnut liqueur (or brandy, port or
    Madeira) (optional)
salt and freshly ground black pepper

Using the walnut liqueur gives the meat the
dark color of game.

—

Place the joint to be marinated in a large
ceramic or nonreactive bowl. Mix all the
ingredients together with 2 tablespoons cold
water and pour over the pork. Cover the bowl
with plastic wrap (clingfilm) and marinate in
the refrigerator for 1–2 days, turning the joint
twice daily.

# PANADE MIXTURES
# FOR STUFFINGS

When making meat stuffings, panade is the
ingredient that holds all the others together.

## FLOUR PANADE

Preparation time 10 minutes
Cooking time 8–10 minutes
Makes sufficient for 1 lb 5 oz (600 g) meat

2½ cups (11 oz/300 g) all-purpose (plain) flour
scant ¼ cup (2 oz/50 g) butter, diced

For the panade, in a bowl, mix the flour with
just enough cold water from 2¼ cups (18 fl oz/
500 ml) water to form a paste. Bring the rest of
the water to a boil in a pan.

—

Add the flour paste to the boiling water and
stir well over medium heat until the dough
pulls away from the sides of the pan. Stir in the
butter and set aside.

## RICE PANADE

Preparation time 10 minutes
Cooking time 55 minutes
Makes 2 cups (13 oz/370 g)

1¼ cups (9 oz/250 g) rice
scant ¼ cup (2 oz/50 g) butter
salt and freshly ground black pepper

Preheat the oven to 400°F/200°C/Gas Mark 6.

—

Bring 2¼ cups (17 fl oz/500 ml) water to a boil
in a large ovenproof Dutch oven (casserole
dish) with a lid. Add the rice and cook for 2–3
minutes. Add the butter, cover with the lid, and
cook in the oven for about 45 minutes until the
rice is tender.

—

Season the cooked rice, then process in a food
processor or blender until it is very smooth.

—

Put the paste back into the Dutch oven
(casserole) and cook for a few more minutes,
stirring well with a spatula until the panade
comes together.

# PASTRY DOUGHS
# FOR PÂTÉS

## BASIC PIE DOUGH
## (SHORTCRUST PASTRY/PÂTE À FONCER)

Preparation time 10 minutes
Chilling time 24 hours
Makes 1 lb 10 oz (750 g)

scant 4¼ cups (1 lb 2 oz/500 g) all-purpose
    (plain) flour
2 teaspoons salt
1 egg
generous 1 cup (9 oz/250 g) cold butter, diced

Make the dough the day before you need it as it
will be easier to roll out and will have a crisper
texture.

—

Place the flour in a large bowl, make a well
in the center, and add the salt, egg, and diced
butter. Working with your fingertips, rub the
butter into the flour. Add just enough chilled
water for the dough to become soft, not sticky.
Alternatively, place all the ingredients together
in a food processor and pulse until the dough
reaches the desired consistency.

—

Turn the dough out onto a counter (work
surface) dusted with flour and knead lightly
until smooth. Cover the dough in plastic wrap
(clingfilm) and chill in the refrigerator for 24
hours before using.

—

NOTE: For a sweet shortcrust, stir 2 oz (50 g)
confectioners' (icing) sugar into the flour.

## LARD PASTRY DOUGH
### (PÂTE À FONCER AU SAINDOUX)

Preparation time 10 minutes
Chilling time 24 hours
Makes 1½ lb (700 g)

scant 4¼ cups (1 lb 2 oz/500 g) all-purpose
    (plain) flour
2 teaspoons salt
1 egg
scant 1¼ cups (7 oz/200 g) lard, at room
    temperature

Make the dough the day before you need it.

—

Place the flour in a bowl, make a well in the center, and add the salt, egg and lard. Using your fingertips, rub the ingredients together, adding just enough water from scant ½ cup (3½ fl oz/100 ml) to make a smooth and pliable dough.

—

Turn the dough out onto a counter (work surface) and knead just twice. Cover the dough with plastic wrap (clingfilm) and chill in the refrigerator for 24 hours before using.

## PASTRY DOUGH FOR SAVORY PIES AND MEAT
### PIES (PÂTE A CROUSTADES ET PÂTÉS CHAUDS)

Preparation time 10 minutes
Chilling time 3 hours
Makes 1¾ lb (800 g)

scant 4¼ cups (1 lb 2 oz/500 g) all-purpose
    (plain) flour
2½ teaspoons salt
3 egg yolks
generous 1 cup (9 oz/250 g) soft, diced butter

Make this dough 3 hours in advance.

—

Place the flour in a bowl, make a well in the center, add the salt and egg yolks, and stir with a spatula until combined. Add the butter and, using your fingertips, rub it into the flour. Stir in just enough chilled water, about 2 tablespoons, to mix to a soft dough.

—

Turn the dough out onto a counter (work surface) dusted with flour and knead lightly until smooth. Cover the dough with plastic wrap (clingfilm) and chill in the refrigerator for 3 hours before using.

—

NOTE: The egg yolks help prevent this dough from cracking when cooked.

## PIE DOUGH (PÂTE BRISÉE)

**Preparation time 10 minutes**
**Chilling time 24 hours**
**Makes 13 oz (375 g)**

2 cups (9 oz/250 g) all-purpose (plain) flour,
    plus extra for sprinkling
1 teaspoon salt
¼ cup (2¼ oz/60 g) butter, diced
⅓ cup (2¼ oz/60 g) lard, diced, or use ½ cup (4
    oz/120 g) butter in total

This dough can be used to make small pies filled with ground (minced) meat or coarse pâté. Make the dough the day before you need it.

—

Put the flour on a pastry board and make a well in the center. Add the salt, butter, and lard and, using your fingertips, rub them in gently. Incorporate just enough water from ¼ cup (2 fl oz/60 ml) to make a supple dough that is not too moist. Knead just twice.

—

Sprinkle with a little flour, cover the dough with plastic wrap (clingfilm), and chill in the refrigerator for 24 hours before using.

## PUFF PASTRY (PÂTE FEUILLETÉE)

Preparation time 2 hours
Chilling time 1 hour 45 minutes
Makes 1¾ lb (800 g)

scant 4¼ cups (1 lb 2 oz/500 g) all-purpose
(plain) flour, plus extra for dusting
2 teaspoons salt
1⅓ cups (11 oz/300 g) soft butter, lard, or a mix
of both, diced

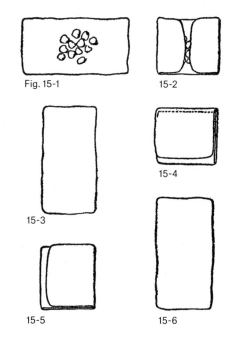

Fig. 15-1          15-2

15-3          15-4

15-5          15-6

Puff pastry can be made with varying amounts of fat: some use the same weight as the flour, others as little as a third of it. The quantity you use should not go over or below these proportions, but any amount within them will work.

—

Puff pastry must be made in a cool atmosphere but both the fat and dough should be quite soft. If either are too cold and too firm, when you wrap the dough around the fat and begin to roll it out, the fat wil break through the dough. If this happens, the pastry will not rise properly when it bakes and many of the crisp, flaky layers will be lost.

—

Place the flour on a pastry board and make a well in the center. Add the salt and generous ¾ cup (7 fl oz/200 ml) water and, using your hands or a spatula, mix them in gently, adding more water as needed to make a soft dough that is not sticky. Knead gently just a few times.

—

Dust the board with flour and roll out the dough to a thickness of ½ inch/1 cm, giving it the shape shown in fig. 15-1.

—

Arrange the fats in the center of the dough (FIG. 15-1).

—

Fold the two smaller edges of the dough so they will meet snugly in the center, covering the fat entirely (FIG. 15-2).

—

Roll this out carefully without letting the fat escape, until you get a new rectangular strip of pastry, ½ inch/1 cm thick (FIG. 15-3). Fold in three like a letter (FIG. 15-4).

—

Cover the dough with plastic wrap (clingfilm) and chill in the refrigerator for 15 minutes.

—

Remove the dough from the refrigerator and give the dough a quarter of a turn (FIG. 15-5) then roll it out into a new rectangle (FIG. 15-6). Cover again and chill for 10–15 minutes. This step is called a turn.

—

Repeat five more times; the dough is ready for use after the sixth turn.

## SEALING DOUGH (PÂTE À LUTER)

**Preparation time 10 minutes**
**Makes 7 oz (200 g)**

1⅔ cups (7 oz/200 g) all-purpose (plain) flour

This dough provides an airtight seal between a terrine or casserole dish and its lid that prevents any liquid or other juices evaporating during cooking.

—

Mix the flour and about scant ½ cup (3½ fl oz/ 100 ml) cold water together in a bowl, until it is a soft consistency, a little sticky but not too wet. Roll the dough into a rough log and press onto the rim of the terrine, making sure it is covered all around. Place the lid on the terrine and press to seal.

## BREAD CRUMBS

**Preparation time 10 minutes**
**Drying time 20 minutes**

bread, sliced

Bread crumbs are used a lot in charcuterie—both dried and fresh.

—

Preheat the over to 250°F/120°C/Gas Mark ½.

—

To make fresh bread crumbs, cut or tear the bread into chunks and whizz in a food processor. Alternatively, rub the bread through a fine wire strainer (sieve) set over a bowl.

—

If you are making dry bread crumbs—they are a good way to use up stale bread—spread out the slices in a single layer on baking sheets and dry in the oven for about 20 minutes until the slices are dry enough to crumble with your fingers but not toasted.

—

Put the slices in a polythene bag and hit with a rolling pin, or put the pieces in a food processor and pulse.

—

If the bread slices are quite thick, they might not dry all the way through in the oven so once you have made the bread crumbs, you may need to spread them out on a baking sheet and dry out completely in the preheated oven for 10 minutes. If you store the bread crumbs before they are completely dry, they may go moldy.

—

Store dried bread crumbs in an airtight jar. Store fresh bread crumbs in the freezer.

# TRUFFLES

The truffle is a fungus that lives as a parasite on the roots of hazel, sweet chestnut, and oak trees. Truffles can vary from the size of a walnut to a small orange and the variety that is most often harvested in France is the black truffle, or *Tuber melanosporum*

The scent and flavor of a truffle are extremely fine and delicate. It can be sliced or shaved as a garnish for terrines or pâtés. Chopped truffle can be used in some stuffings, and it is also an ingredient in some sausages, pigs' feet (trotter) dishes, and other charcuterie preparations.

In France, the most highly prized black truffles come from Périgord in the southwest and are harvested during the late fall (autumn) and winter. They are rooted out by specially trained pigs.

Black truffles are also found in other parts of the world, including North America and Australia.

## STORING

A fresh truffle will keep for a week in the refrigerator, neither washed nor brushed, but placed in an airtight container with a folded paper towel to absorb excess moisture.

Truffles can be frozen for up to two weeks in a freezer-proof glass jar.

Truffles can also be stored in a flavorless oil for up to two weeks, leaving a truffle-flavored oil for use in salads and cooking.

## CLEANING

Brush carefully under cold running water, taking care to remove any trace of dirt lodged in any small cavities. Wipe dry before use.

## SHAVING

For best results, use a special truffle slicer and add the freshly shaved truffle directly to a dish.

## BOUQUET GARNI

**Preparation time 5 minutes**
**Makes 1 bouquet**

3 sprigs rosemary
3 sprigs thyme
1 bay leaf
4 parsley stalks
3-inch (7.5-cm) piece of leek, green part only

Lay the piece of leek on a board and place the rosemary, thyme, bay leaf and parsley stalks in the center. Wrap the leek around the herbs and tie together firmly in a bundle with thin kitchen twine (string).

—

Add the bouquet garni to stews, stocks, sauces, and soups, and remove the bundle at the end of the cooking time.

## WHITE ROUX

**Preparation time 10 minutes**
**Cooking time 5 minutes**

1½ oz (40 g) butter, lard, or cooking fat
1½ oz (40 g) all-purpose (plain) flour

for a thick sauce, add 1¼ cups (10 fl oz/300 ml) milk, or half milk, half broth (stock)

for a medium sauce, add scant 2 cups (16 fl oz/450 ml) milk, or half milk, half broth (stock)

for a thin sauce, add 2½ cups (20 fl oz/600 ml) milk, or half milk, half broth (stock)

Melt the fat in a pan over low-medium heat without allowing it to color.

—

Remove the pan from the heat and add the flour. Stir well with a whisk, then return to medium heat and cook for 2–3 minutes, stirring frequently, until the roux has thickened slightly, but not colored.

—

Add the liquid component slowly, stirring continuously until the desired consistency is reached.

—

NOTE: A roux is used as the base for making a white sauce. The quantities of fat and flour remain the same, but depending on how thick you want the sauce, the amount of liquid varies.

# CHARCUTERIE

This text, from the original 1948 edition, shows the process of charcuterie making followed at that time.

—

Once the pig has been slaughtered and jointed into its various cuts, the charcuterie-making can begin, following the established chronological order.

—

For these tasks you will need two people to help, ensuring everything is ready when you need it. If you will be making sausages, dry-cured sausages, and blood sausage (black pudding), keep a range of casings of different sizes to hand; it won't be practical to make them on the same day you are making the sausages themselves.

—

Your work can be divided into the following steps:
Butcher the meat and set aside the cuts intended to be cooked and eaten fresh: shoulder, rack with 7 ribs, hind loin with 2 ribs, and chump end.

—

Remove the belly fat and trim it into little pieces (lardons) that will be rendered to obtain lard and rillons (small pieces of belly meat) for blood sausage (black pudding). The rendering will take some time; while it is in progress, make sausage meat and head cheese (brawn), and prepare the onions you will need for blood sausage (black pudding).

—

While the head is cooking for head cheese (brawn), about 4–5 hours, you will have time to make pâtés, terrines, sausages, and dry-cured sausages.

—

Blood sausage (black pudding) can be made as soon as the rillons (small pieces of belly meat) are ready, when they are still white but tender.

—

Finally, you will put the pieces you have reserved for dry-cured meat (petit salé) in the salting tub.

—

NOTE: Weather conditions and temperature are very important when making charcuterie. If it is hot or humid, you will have to work much faster to ensure the meat remains fresh. Watch out for flies in particular: if a single one gets to a ham while it is on the table, the whole piece of meat can be spoiled, and neither salting nor smoking will stop the eggs growing.

---

It is just as important to decide beforehand what you want to do with the meat, as one pig isn't enough to make every kind of pâté, sausage, and dry-cured sausage. Here is one possible plan:
With the sausage meat, make sausage patties (crépinettes) and long sausages, dry-cured sausages, and meat pâté (choose just one recipe).

—

With some of the meat and the intestines, make andouille or andouillette.

—

Leaf lard is the top grade of lard from the soft fat around the kidneys and loin of a pig. It doesn't have any real flavor of its own, but it is excellent for cooking because it can be heated to high temperatures. With the leaf lard, make lard and rillons.

—

With the blood and rillons, make blood sausage (black pudding).

—

With the liver and sausage meat, make liver pâté (choose just one recipe).

—

With the head, make head cheese (brawn).

—

With the remaining meat, make salt pork, rillettes, and hams for smoking.

## SAUSAGE PATTIES (CRÉPINETTES)

Preparation time 30 minutes
Cooking time 15-20 minutes
Makes 12 patties

1 lb 2 oz (500 g) lean pork meat from neck or
  shoulder
1 lb 2 oz (500 g) green (unsmoked) fatback
  bacon
12 pieces of caul (also known as the
  peritoneum), 4¾ x 4¾ inches/12 x 12 cm
2 oz (50 g) pork fat
12 oz (350 g) white bread crumbs
scant ½ cup (3½ fl oz/100 ml) white wine
  (optional)
salt and freshly ground black pepper

To prepare the sausage meat, make sure the meat and bacon are used straight from the refrigerator. Trim all the sinews and veins from the lean meat and cut the bacon and meat into pieces.

Season with 4 teaspoons salt and 1 heaping teaspoon black pepper per 2¼ lb (1 kg) meat.

Process the meat and bacon through the meat grinder three times, changing the disks from coarse to fine so that by the third pass you have extremely finely ground meat.

Lay the caul pieces out on a counter (work surface) and place a rounded spoonful of the sausage meat in the center of each. Wrap the sides of the caul around the filling to form small packages and flatten with your hand.

To cook the crépinettes in a skillet or frying pan, melt the fat gently in a pan and spread the bread crumbs out on a plate. Using a pastry brush, brush the patties with the melted fat, then roll them in the bread crumbs until coated.

Heat a little more fat in a skillet or frying pan over medium heat and fry the patties for 15 minutes until browned on both sides and cooked through.

To roast the crépinettes, preheat the oven to 400°F/200°C/Gas Mark 6. Place the patties in a greased, ovenproof dish, pour over a little white wine, and roast in the oven for 15–20 minutes, basting with the cooking juices, until cooked through. Eat hot or cold.

## VEAL AND PORK SAUSAGE PATTIES
## (CRÉPINETTES DE PARIS)

Preparation time 30 minutes
Cooking time 15-20 minutes
Makes 8 small patties

4 oz (125 g) veal meat
13 oz (375 g) pork meat
4 oz (125 g) fatback
12 oz (350 g) white bread crumbs
1 egg
1½ tablespoons finely chopped parsley
¼ teaspoon freshly grated nutmeg
8 pieces of caul (also known as the
    peritoneum), 4¾ x 4¾ inches/12 x 12 cm
1½ oz (40 g) fat
⅓ cup (3 fl oz/75 ml) white wine (optional)
salt and freshly ground black pepper

Make sure the meat and fatback are used straight from the refrigerator. Remove any sinew or veins from the veal and pork meat. Process with the fatback through a meat grinder fitted with the medium disk.

—

Sprinkle 2 oz (50 g) bread crumbs with a little water and mix this with the meat, together with the egg and parsley. Season with salt, pepper, and the grated nutmeg and stir well to combine.

—

Lay the caul pieces out on a counter (work surface) and place a rounded spoonful of the sausage meat in the center of each. Wrap the sides of the caul around the filling to form small packages and flatten with your hand.

—

To cook the crépinettes in a skillet or frying pan, melt the fat gently in a pan and spread the bread crumbs out on a plate. Using a pastry brush, brush the patties with the melted fat, then roll in the remaining bread crumbs until coated.

—

Heat a little more fat in a skillet or frying pan over medium heat and fry the patties for 15 minutes until browned on both sides and cooked through.

—

To roast the crépinettes, preheat the oven to 400°F/200°C/Gas Mark 6. Place the patties in a greased, ovenproof dish, pour over a little white wine, and roast in the oven for 15–20 minutes, basting with the cooking juices.

—

Heat a little fat in a skillet or frying pan over medium heat and fry the patties for 15 minutes until browned on both sides.

—

To roast the crépinettes, preheat the oven to 400°F/200°C/Gas Mark 6. Place the patties in a greased, ovenproof dish, pour over a little white wine, and roast in the oven for 15–20 minutes, basting with the cooking juices, until cooked through. Eat hot or cold.

## CHIPOLATAS

Preparation time 1 hour
Cooking time 8 minutes
Makes 1 string of sausages weighing about
2¼ lb (1 kg)

1 lb 2 oz (500 g) pork neck meat
9 oz (250 g) each pork shoulder and green
(unsmoked) fatback bacon
sheep casings
2 oz (50 g) fat
salt and freshly ground black pepper

To make the sausage meat, make sure the meat and bacon are used straight from the refrigerator. Trim all the sinews and veins from the lean meat and cut the bacon and meat into pieces.

—

Season with 4 teaspoons salt and 1 heaping teaspoon black pepper per 2¼ lb (1 kg) meat.

—

Process the meat through the meat grinder three times, changing the disks from coarse to fine so that by the third pass you have extremely finely ground meat.

—

Pipe the sausage meat into sheep casings, making sure you don't pack it in too tightly so you can twist the casing on itself twice every 1½–2 inches/4–5 cm. This will give you a string of small sausages that can be used as a garnish to other meats such as roast chicken or pork, or on their own as part of a main meal, accompanied by mashed potatoes and other vegetables.

—

To cook the chipolatas, prick each sausage a few times with a skewer or fork.

—

Melt the fat in a frying pan or skillet over high heat and fry the sausages for 8 minutes, or until browned all over and cooked through.

## TRUFFLED SAUSAGES

Preparation time 1 hour
Chilling time 24 hours
Cooking time 8 minutes
Makes about 8 sausages

1 lb 2 oz (500 g) pork neck meat
9 oz (250 g) each pork shoulder and green
(unsmoked) fatback bacon
¾ oz (20 g) salt
1 teaspoon four-spice mix made of the
following ground spices: ½ teaspoon
cinnamon, ¼ teaspoon black pepper, and a
pinch each of cloves and nutmeg
3½ oz (100 g) finely chopped truffle shavings
sheep casings

Make sure the meat and bacon are used straight from the refrigerator. Trim all the sinews and veins from the lean meat and cut the bacon and meat into pieces.

—

Season with the salt and spice mix and add finely chopped truffle shavings.

—

Process the meat through the meat grinder three times, changing the disks from coarse to fine so that by the third pass you have extremely finely ground meat.

—

Cover the sausage meat with plastic wrap (clingfilm) and chill in the refrigerator for 24 hours so the truffle flavor permeates the sausage stuffing.

—

Place the sausage meat into a pastry (piping) bag and pipe into the sheep casings.

—

Cook as in the previous recipe.

## TOULOUSE SAUSAGE

Preparation time 1 hour
Cooking time 8-10 minutes
Makes 16 sausages

3¼ lb (1.5 kg) lean pork meat, deveined
1 lb 2 oz (500 g) fatback
1¼ tablespoons confectioners'(icing) sugar
2¼ tablespoons salt
1¼ tablespoons freshly ground black pepper
pork casings (small intestine)

Make sure the meat and fatback are used straight from the refrigerator. Cut the lean meat and fatback into pieces and process through the meat grinder using the coarse disk. Put the meat into a large bowl, add the sugar, salt, and pepper, and mix well.

—

Place the sausage meat into a pastry (piping) bag and pipe into pork casings, tying it off every 4 inches/10 cm.

—

To cook the sausages, preheat the broiler (grill) to high. Prick the sausages a few times with a thin skewer or fork. Put the sausages on the broiler (grill) rack and broil (grill) for 8–10 minutes, or until browned and cooked through.

## SAUSAGES IN WHITE WINE

Preparation time 15 minutes
Cooking time 25-30 minutes
Serves 2-3 depending on the size of your
    sausages

6 sausages of your choice
1-1½ oz (25-40 g) fat
1 large onion, chopped
2 tablespoons (1 oz/30 g) all-purpose (plain)
    flour
scant ½ cup (3½ fl oz/100 ml) dry white wine
salt and freshly ground black pepper

Preheat the oven to 212°F/100°C/Gas Mark ¼.

—

Prick the sausages a few times with a thin skewer or fork.

—

Melt some fat in a skillet or frying pan over medium heat, add the sausages and fry for 8–10 minutes, or until browned and cooked through. Remove from the pan, keeping all the cooking juices, and keep warm in the oven.

—

Cook the chopped onion in the cooking juices over low heat for about 8 minutes, or until translucent. Dust the onions with the flour and stir well until they are coated. Pour in the white wine and stir to scrape up all the bits from the bottom of the pan. Season to taste with salt and pepper and cook for another 10 minutes. Pour the sauce over the cooked sausages.

## COUNTRY PÂTÉ

**Preparation time 20 minutes**
**Cooking time 3 hours**
**Serves 12**

2¼ lb (1 kg) pork meat
12 oz (340 g) veal meat
11 oz (300 g) leaf lard (very high-quality lard)
4 eggs
scant ¼ cup (1¾ fl oz/50 ml) brandy (Calvados or cognac)
1 onion, finely chopped
1 teaspoon four-spice mix made of the following ground spices: ½ teaspoon cinnamon, ¼ teaspoon black pepper, and a pinch each of cloves and nutmeg
2 tablespoons chopped parsley
3½ teaspoons salt
¾ teaspoon freshly ground black pepper
12 oz (350 g) fatback slices (or bacon)
1⅔ cups (7 oz/200 g) all-purpose (plain) flour

Make sure the meat and leaf lard are used straight from the refrigerator.

Preheat the oven to 325°F/160°C/Gas Mark 3.

Process the pork meat, veal, and leaf lard through the meat grinder. Put the meat in a large bowl, add the eggs, brandy, onion, spices, parsley, salt, and pepper, and mix thoroughly with a spatula.

Line one large or several small terrine dishes with slices of fatback and fill with the mixture. Level the surface and make a lattice pattern across the top using slices of fatback about ¾ inch/1.5 cm wide.

For the sealing dough, mix the flour and about scant ½ cup (3½ fl oz/100 ml) cold water together in a bowl, until it is a soft consistency, a little sticky but not too wet. Roll the dough into a rough log and press onto the rim of the terrine, making sure it is covered all around. Place the lid on the terrine and press to seal.

Put the terrine dish in a roasting tin half-filled with hot water and cook in the oven for 3 hours. (The inside temperature of the meat should reach 158°F/70°C.)

## LIVER PÂTÉ

**Preparation time 1 hour**
**Cooking time 2-3 hours**
**Resting time 3 days**
**Serves 8-10**

**For the sausage meat**
1 lb 2 oz (500 g) pork neck meat
9 oz (250 g) each pork shoulder and green
    (unsmoked) fatback bacon
2 teaspoons salt
½ teaspoon spice mix (SEE p. 254)

**For the pâté**
1 lb 2 oz (500 g) sausage meat
1 lb 2 oz (500 g) pork liver, trimmed, deveined,
    and outer membranes removed
1 lb 2 oz (500 g) bread, with the crusts removed,
    finely crumbled
2 fl oz (50 ml) milk
3 eggs
1 onion, chopped
scant ¼ cup (1¾ fl oz/50 ml) brandy (cognac or
    Calvados)
1 teaspoon four-spice mix made of the
    following ground spices: ½ teaspoon
    cinnamon, ¼ teaspoon black pepper, and a
    pinch each of cloves and nutmeg
1 cup (2¼ oz/60 g) chopped parsley
2 teaspoons salt
12 oz (350 g) fatback slices
1 sprig thyme
1 bay leaf
3 cloves
caul, dependent on the size and number
    of dishes
1⅔ cups (7 oz/200 g) all-purpose (plain) flour

If using more than one terrine, you will need to add more thyme, bay leaves, and cloves to the top of the pâté before cooking.

—

To make the sausage meat, make sure the meat and bacon are used straight from the refrigerator. Trim all the sinews and veins from the lean meat and cut the bacon and meat into pieces. Season with the salt and spices.

—

Process the meat through the meat grinder

three times, changing the disks from coarse to fine so that by the third pass you have extremely finely ground meat. Cover with plastic wrap (clingfilm) and chill.

—

Preheat the oven to 325°F/160°C/Gas Mark 3.

—

Make sure the sausage meat and liver are used straight from the refrigerator. Process the liver through a meat grinder using the fine disk. Place in a large bowl and set aside.

—

Put the bread crumbs into a large bowl, add the milk and eggs and mix until combined. Add the mixture to the liver, then mix in the sausage meat and onion. Add the brandy, four-spice mix, parsley, and salt and mix to combine.

—

Line one large or several small terrine dishes with the fatback slices and add the mixture. Level the surface and place a thyme sprig, a bay leaf, and 3 cloves on top. Arrange a few thin slices of fatback in a lattice and cover with some caul cut to the size of the terrine.

—

For the sealing dough, mix the flour and about scant ½ cup (3½ fl oz/100 ml) cold water together in a bowl, until it is a soft consistency, a little sticky but not too wet. Roll the dough into a rough log and press onto the rim of the terrine, making sure it is covered all around. Place the lid on the terrine and press to seal.

—

Put the terrine dish in a roasting tin half-filled with hot water and cook in the oven for 3 hours until cooked through. (The inside temperature of the meat should reach 158°F/70°C.)

—

Remove the lid and cool. Place a small board to fit the inside of the terrine and press it down with a 2¼–6½-lb (1–3-kg) weight, depending on the size of the terrine. Rest for three days in the refrigerator before serving.

## HEAD CHEESE (BRAWN)

Preparation time 2 hours
Soaking time 2–3 hours
Cooking time 5 hours
Chilling time 24 hours
Serves 8–10

1 pig's head
1 lb 2 oz (500 g) pork rinds
4 large carrots, sliced
1 large onion, sliced
2 bay leaves
1 tablespoon four-spice mix of the following
    ground spices: 1½ teaspoons cinnamon,
    1 teaspoon black pepper, and ½ teaspoon
    each of cloves and nutmeg
1 sprig thyme
4¼ cups (34 fl oz/1 liter) white wine or hard
    (dry) cider
coarse salt and freshly ground black pepper

First, wash the pig's head very thoroughly, shaving off any bristles with a disposable razor, then soak in a large bowl of salted water for at least 2 hours. Drain, then pour boiling water over the head.

—

Divide the head into pieces: remove the tongue, saw the snout open, and saw the head into 6 pieces, so the brain can be removed without damaging it. Wash the snout and ears again if necessary.

—

Put all the pieces into a pan large enough to accommodate them. Add the carrots and onion, bay leaves, spice mix, thyme, salt, pepper and the wine or cider, then pour in enough water to cover.

—

Cover with a lid and cook over low heat for about 5 hours. The meat should come away from the bones easily and should fall apart. When it is ready, remove the meat from the cooking liquid, cut all the pieces into strips and transfer to one or more serving bowls, depending on how large the head is. Check the seasoning and adjust if necessary, keeping in mind that the flavor will be less strong when chilled.

If you wish, you can leave a few pieces of onion or carrot in with the head cheese (brawn); add a little of the cooking liquid, just to make the meat wet.

—

Cover with a plate and place a weight of 4½–6½ lb (2–3 kg) on top to press down the mixture, and chill in the refrigerator until the next day.

—

Head cheese (brawn) will keep for a week in the refrigerator. You can keep it for a little longer if you top the surface with a layer of good-quality melted lard.

## SAUSAGE FRIANDS

**Preparation time 45 minutes**
**Cooking time 20 minutes**
**Makes 12**

1 egg yolk
1 lb 2 oz (500 g) puff pastry (SEE p. 270)

**For the sausage meat**
1 lb 2 oz (500 g) lean pork neck meat
9 oz (250 g) each pork shoulder and green
    (unsmoked) fatback bacon
2 teaspoons salt
½ teaspoon spice mix (SEE p. 254)

To make the sausage meat, make sure the meat and bacon are used straight from the refrigerator. Trim all the sinews and veins from the lean meat and cut into small pieces, along with the bacon. Season with the salt and spices.

—

Process the meat through the meat grinder three times, changing the disks from coarse to fine so that by the third pass you have extremely finely ground meat. You only need 11 oz (300 g) sausage meat for this recipe.

—

Preheat the oven to 350°F/180°C/Gas Mark 4.

—

Beat the egg yolk with 1 tablespoon water in a bowl. Set aside.

—

Roll out the pastry on a lightly floured board to a thickness of ⅝ inch/1.5 cm.

—

Use a cookie cutter to cut out circles of dough about 2½ inches/6 cm in diameter, gathering up the trimmings and stacking them on top of each other so they can be re-rolled to cut out more rounds. Don't press the trimmings together in a ball or you will lose the layers of

fat in the dough and the pastry won't rise when it is baked. Place half the dough rounds on a baking sheet and scoop some sausage meat into the center of each one.

Dampen the dough with a brush dipped in cold water and place a second disk of dough on top. Repeat with the remaining dough rounds and sausage meat. Brush with the egg wash and bake in the oven for 20 minutes until cooked through. Serve warm.

—

NOTE: You can also cut the dough into rectangles of 4 x 5 inches/10 x 12 cm. Place some sausage meat in a sausage shape down the middle of the dough and roll up the dough, sealing the open ends. Use a knife to make a pattern on the top, then brush with egg wash and cook as described in the recipe.

## HAM PÂTÉ (PÂTÉ EN CROÛTE)

**Preparation time 2 hours 30 minutes**
**Chilling time 24 hours**
**Cooking time 8½-9½ hours**
**Serves 8-10**

7 oz (200 g) lean veal meat
9 oz (250 g) lean ham, diced
2 eggs, plus 1 egg yolk
brandy (optional)
2 oz (50 g) truffle shavings (optional)
5 oz (150 g) slices fatback
salt and freshly ground black pepper

For the aspic
2¼ lb (1 kg) veal bones
2¼ lb (1 kg) beef shin
3¼ lb (1.5 kg) veal shank
2 carrots, sliced
3 small onions, sliced
2 oz (50 g) leeks, sliced
3 calves' feet, deboned and blanched
7 oz (200 g) uncured pork rinds, blanched and
    tied together
1 bouquet garni (SEE p. 273)
4 teaspoons salt

For the basic pie dough (shortcrust pastry)
4½ cups (1 lb 2 oz/500 g) all-purpose (plain)
flour, plus extra for dusting
2 teaspoons salt
1 egg
generous 1 cup (9 oz/250 g) cold butter, diced,
    plus extra for greasing

For the sausage meat
1 lb 2 oz (500 g) lean pork neck meat (FIG. 21)
9 oz (250 g) each pork shoulder and green
    (unsmoked) fatback bacon
½ teaspoon spice mix (SEE p. 254)
2 teaspoons salt

Make the dough and the aspic the day before
you need them.

—

To make the aspic, preheat the oven to
350°F/180°C/Gas Mark 4.

—

Place the bones with the beef and veal shank in
an ovenproof dish and roast for 30 minutes.

Place the carrots, onions, and leeks in a large
stock pot or other heavy-bottomed pan and
cover with the calves' feet, pork rinds, browned
bones and meat, and the bouquet garni. Cover
and cook over medium heat for 10 minutes.

—

Add scant ½ cup (3½ fl oz/100 ml) water and
cook for another 10 minutes. Pour in 7 quarts
(14 UK pints/7.9 liters) water, and add the salt,
then bring to a boil. Skim, reduce the heat to
low, and simmer for 6–7 hours. Strain through
a clean cloth.

—

Skim off the fat that has formed at the surface
after cooling. When the jelly is completely
cooled, any impurities remaining will have
sunk to the bottom. For a clear jelly, pour
slowly, taking care to leave the impurities
behind.

—

To make the pie dough (shortcrust pastry), place
the flour in a large bowl, make a well in the
center, and add the salt, egg, and diced butter.
Working with your fingertips, rub the butter
into the flour. Add just enough chilled water to
the dough to make it soft, but not sticky.

—

Turn the dough out onto a counter (work
surface) and knead lightly until smooth. Cover
the dough in plastic wrap (clingfilm) and chill
in the refrigerator for 24 hours before using.

—

To make the sausage meat, make sure the
meat and bacon are used straight from the
refrigerator. Trim all the sinews and veins from
the lean meat and cut the bacon and meat into
pieces. Season with the salt and spices.

—

Process the meat through the meat grinder
three times, changing the disks from coarse
to fine so that by the third pass you have
extremely finely ground meat. You only need
1 lb 2 oz (500 g) sausage meat for this recipe.

Process the veal meat through the meat grinder using the fine disk to make a smooth fine paste. Combine with the sausage meat and ham. Mix in the whole eggs, season with salt and pepper, adding a splash of brandy and truffle shavings, if liked.

—

Preheat the oven to 425°F/220°C/Gas Mark 7.

—

If you are using a springform pâté mold, on a lightly floured counter (work surface), roll out the dough to a thickness of ½ inch/1 cm. Line the mold with the dough, setting aside a piece to cover the top.

—

Arrange the slices of fatback across the bottom, then fill the pie with the prepared mixture. Place several strips of fatback across the top. Roll out the reserved dough to a round large enough to cover the pie. Dampen the pastry edges and press on the top of the filling, trimming the pastry with a sharp knife to fit.

—

If you are making a free-form pâté on a baking sheet, on a lightly floured counter (work surface), roll out the pastry dough to ½ inch/1 cm in thickness and cut out a rectangle, about 5½–11 inches/14 x 28 cm. Set aside the rest of the dough. Lift the rolled-out dough onto a greased baking sheet. Arrange a few strips of fatback in the center of the dough, and pile the stuffing mixture on top, shaping it into a neat load. Fold up the edges of the dough to enclose the sides of the stuffing completely.

—

Roll out the rest of the dough and cut it into a rectangle slightly larger than the top of the stuffing to make a lid. Dampen the pastry edges, lift the lid over the stuffing and press the pastry edges together. Crimp the edges to give a tight seal.

Glaze with some brushed egg yolk mixed with water.

—

In both pâtés, pierce two or three small holes in the dough for the steam to escape, and insert little cones made out of stiff paper to keep them open.

—

Create some decorations, such as flowers or leaves, using scraps of the dough; you will bake these at the same time as the pâté and use them to hide the vent holes once the pâté is cooked.

—

Bake in the oven for 15 minutes, then lower the temperature to 350°F/180°C/Gas Mark 4 and cook for a further 1¼ hours, until cooked through, covering the top of the pie with foil when it is sufficiently brown.

—

Heat the aspic in a pan over low heat until melted, then pour it into the crust through the vent holes; this will fill any gaps that may have been created during cooking and will firm up as the pâté cools.

—

Let the pâté cool completely before slicing and serving.

—

NOTE: If the aspic is not as firm as you need it, you can add gelatin, ⅓ teaspoon/1.5 g gelatin per 4¼ cups (34 fl oz/1 liter) of jelly, softened in cold water for 30 minutes. After skimming the jelly of fat, return to the clean pot, add the drained gelatin, and bring just to a simmer, stirring frequently. You can flavor the jelly with Madeira, which will also give it a good color.

# DRY-CURED SAUSAGES

Let's first draw our attention to the pitfalls of sausage-making, so we can avoid those mistakes.

—

Curing of meat should be done in a cool, dry, and dark environment at a temperature between 35.6 and 41°F/2 and 5°C.

—

Always use perfectly fresh meat; if it is on the turn, the sausage itself will go off or go moldy. As dry curing sausages is done over an extended period of time, curing salts are necessary to ensure the meat remains safe as the sausages may be eaten raw. Traditionally salt peter was used to dry cure meat but as it's no longer possible to buy this, nowadays packs of ready-prepared curing salts can be purchased from specialist suppliers. More than one type of curing salt is available but for the recipes in this book it is important to buy curing salt # 2 which is made up of salt (89.25%), sodium nitrate (4%) and sodium nitrite (6.25%). Manufacturers often tint the mix to make it easier to distinguish from ordinary salt. The salts work by the sodium nitrate first breaking down over time into sodium nitrite which then breaks down to nitric oxide, keeping the meat safe to eat during the curing process and beyond. As sodium nitrate and sodium nitrite are toxic it is imperative that you read the instructions on the packet carefully before using and not to exceed the quantity of curing salts given in the recipes. To ensure you use the exact quantity required and no more, measure the curing salts with digital scales – ½ teaspoon curing salts weighs 2.5 g.

—

You should take great care in drying your sausages:

If dried for too long, sausage meat goes greasy and the casing starts to glisten;

—

If it dries too quickly in air that is too dry, it will become hollow inside;

—

If it dries too quickly with too many changes in temperature, the sausage meat will form a crust on the outside and the pores in the casing will become blocked. This will prevent the inside moisture from evaporating, and you risk the development of harmful microorganisms.

—

Before your sausage is ready to eat, it must undergo the proper maturation process; this occurs through the action of yeasts, which give the meat its particular taste and smooth texture.

—

Professionals use special ferments that guarantee the same quality and the same flavor each time. When making sausage meat at home, you will not always achieve the same results each time, but this is part of the charm of making food at home for your family.

You should allow the sausage meat to ripen for 3–4 weeks. It should lose about 40 percent of its weight during this period, which gives you a way to gauge whether it is ready: if the sausage meat weighs 14 oz (400 g) when first made, it will be "ripe" for eating when it weighs about 9 oz (250 g).

—

NOTE: The casings used for dry-cured sausages are either pork (bung and pig middles) or beef middles.

## HOMEMADE SAUCISSON
## (DRY-CURED SAUSAGE)

Preparation time 1 hour
Chilling time 1 hour
Drying time 3-4 weeks
Makes 2 lb (900 g)

1 lb 2 oz (500 g) pork neck meat
1 lb 2 oz (500 g) pork shoulder and green
   (unsmoked) fatback bacon (2 parts meat to
   1 part bacon)
1½ tablespoons salt per 2¼ lb (1 kg) meat
2.5 g curing salt #2 (SEE page 285)
1 teaspoon four-spice mix made with the
   following ground spices: ½ teaspoon
   cinnamon, ¼ teaspoon black pepper, and a
   pinch each of cloves and nutmeg
casings, about 12-14 inches/30-35 cm long

Make sure the meat and bacon are used
straight from the refrigerator. Trim all the
sinews and veins from the pork meats and cut
into pieces with the bacon. Season with the
salts and spice mix.

—

Process through the meat grinder three times,
changing the disks from coarse to fine so that
by the third pass you have extremely finely
ground meat.

—

Chill in the refrigerator for 1 hour.

—

Prepare some casings about 12–14 inches/
30–35 cm in length, and check them carefully
to make sure that there is not even the
smallest hole.

—

Tie off the end of each casing and fill it,
packing the meat in well to remove any air
pockets. Tie off the other end.

—

Hang the sausages up in pairs over a wooden
beam for 3–4 weeks.

The traditional storing method was to bury
the sausages in a crate containing wood ash
or sand, but nowadays it is recommended that
they are wrapped in parchment paper and
stored in the refrigerator.

## HOMEMADE GARLIC SAUCISSON

Preparation time 1 hour
Chilling time 1 hour
Drying time 3-4 weeks
Makes 2 lb (900 g)

1 lb 2 oz (500 g) pork neck meat
1 lb 2 oz (500 g) pork shoulder and green
    (unsmoked) fatback bacon (2 parts meat to
    1 part bacon)
2 cloves garlic, peeled
1½ tablespoons salt per 2¼ lb (1 kg) meat
2.5 g curing salts #2 (SEE page 285)
1 teaspoon four-spice mix made with the
    following ground spices: ½ teaspoon
    cinnamon, ¼ teaspoon black pepper, and a
    pinch each of cloves and nutmeg
casings, about 12-14 inches/30-35 cm long

Make sure the meat and bacon are used straight from the refrigerator. Trim all the sinews and veins from the pork meats and cut into pieces with the bacon. Season with the salts and spice mix.

Process through the meat grinder three times, changing the disks from coarse to fine so that by the third pass you have extremely finely ground meat.

Chill in the refrigerator for 1 hour.

Prepare some casings about 12–14 inches/30–35 cm in length, and check them carefully to make sure that there is not even the smallest hole.

Tie off the end of each casing and fill it, packing the meat in well to remove any air pockets. Tie off the other end.

Hang the sausages up in pairs over a wooden beam for 3–4 weeks.

## SMOKED SAUSAGES (GENDARMES)

Preparation time 1 hour, plus chilling
Smoking time 2 days
Drying time 3-4 weeksh
Makes 2¼ lb (1 kg)

11 oz (300 g) lean pork meat
11 oz (300 g) lean beef
14 oz (400 g) lean (streaky) bacon
1¾ tablespoons salt
2.5 g curing salts #2 (SEE page 285)
1½ teaspoons freshly ground black pepper
2 teaspoons chili powder
casings, 12 inches/30 cm long

Make sure the meat and bacon are used straight from the refrigerator. Cut the meat and bacon into pieces and season with the salts and spices.
—
Process the meat through a meat grinder three times, changing the disks from coarse to fine so that by the third pass you have extremely finely ground meat.
—
Prepare some casings about 12 inches/30 cm in length, and check them carefully to make sure there is not even the smallest hole. Tie off the end of each casing and fill it, packing the meat in well to remove any air pockets. Tie off the other end.
—
Arrange the sausages on a board, top with another board, and place a weight on it. Refrigerate until the sausages are flattened to about ½ inch/1 cm thick.
—
Prepare a smoker as per the manufacturer's instructions, and then leave the sausages in the smoker for 2 days until they have taken on the brown color typical of smoked meat. Hang the sausages up in pairs over a wooden beam for 3–4 weeks.
—
Eat the sausages raw when they have gone crunchy, or prick with a thin skewer and simmer over low heat for 45–50 minutes.

## ANDOUILLETTES (TRIPE SAUSAGES)

Preparation time 1 hour
Soaking time overnight
Chilling time 2 days
Cooking time 4-5 hours
Makes 2¼ lb (1 kg)

3 large intestines
vinegar, for washing
3½ teaspoons salt
1½ teaspoons freshly ground black pepper
1 teaspoon four-spice mix made from the
    following ground spices: ½ teaspoon
    cinnamon, ¼ teaspoon cloves, and a pinch
    each of nutmeg and black pepper
8 strips of fatback
2 carrots, sliced
2 onions, finely chopped
1 bouquet garni (SEE p. 285)
3 cloves
¼ teaspoon freshly grated nutmeg
17 cups (140 fl oz/4 liters) broth (stock)

Preparing the casings. The day before you wish to use them, empty the large intestines, turn them inside out with a thin rod and let them soak in a large bowl of cold water overnight, changing the water every 4 hours. Drain and cut 1 intestine into lengths of 10 inches/25 cm to serve as casings for the andouillettes.
—
Fill a large bowl with hot water and add a little vinegar. Wash the casings first in warm water, then in the vinegared hot water, and then in cold water again. Refrigerate until ready to use. You will now use the remainder of the intestines to make up the contents of the andouillettes.
—
To prepare the filling for the andouillettes, fill a large bowl with hot water and a little vinegar and another bowl with boiling water. Wash the

remaining intestines as you did the casings in warm water, then in hot vinegared water, and then cold water again. Carefully plunge them into the boiling water for 1 minute and drain thoroughly.

—

Split the intestines open lengthwise and scrape with a blunt knife to remove the fat and any impurities.

—

Using scissors or a sharp knife, cut the intestines into strips about ½–¾ inch/1–2 cm wide and double the length of the casings (20 inches/50 cm). Season with the salt, pepper, and ¼ teaspoon four-spice mix per 2¼ lb (1 kg) intestines. Place in a dish and chill in the refrigerator for two days.

—

For each andouillette, cut a strip of fatback about ¾ inch/2 cm wide and the same length as the casings. Gather the strips of intestines into bundles, fold the bundle in half, and place a strip of fatback in the center of each. The folded bundle should be just the thickness that the casing can hold.

—

To stuff the casings can be a tricky task at first, but with a bit of practice you will soon get the hang of it. Turn the andouillette casings inside out, so the smooth side is on the inside.

—

Lay a bundle of strips with the folded side facing the opening of the first casing. Tie a piece of string around the folded end of the bundle and thread it through the casing.

—

Hold the string in your left hand, and use your right hand to unroll the casing over the bundle of strips so the smooth side of the casing ends up on the outside.

Cut off the string, and tuck the excess casing inward on both open ends, making sure the filling is fully enclosed. Repeat with the remaining casings and bundles.

—

To cook the andouillettes, add the sliced carrots, finely chopped onions, bouquet garni, cloves and grated nutmeg to a pot of broth (stock) and bring to a low simmer.

—

Prick the andouillettes with a sharp skewer, lower into the water, and cook for 4–5 hours just under a simmer. Remove the pan from the heat and let them cool in the stock, then drain completely. Store in a refrigerator.

—

Andouillettes can be broiled (grilled) or pan-fried, browning each side for 5 minutes, and served with mustard.

## BOUDIN NOIR (FRENCH BLOOD SAUSAGE/ BLACK PUDDING)

There are several important aspects to consider when making blood sausage (black pudding).

### THE BLOOD

This is collected in a container when the animal's throat is cut. One person should be assigned to stir it constantly to stop it coagulating.

—

If you wish to use the blood immediately, when it is still warm, you should have prepared some casings and fatback in advance, which of course won't be taken from the animal you have just slaughtered since it needs to cool completely before it can be butchered.

—

If you prefer to make blood sausage (black pudding) with both the blood and the fat of the animal you have just slaughtered, you should cover the container of well-stirred blood and chill it until you can start the work.

—

An average pig weighing about 243 lb (110 kg) should yield 5¼–6⅓ quarts (8¾–10½ UK pints/5–6 liters) of blood.

### THE CASINGS

Check the casings for holes and cut off any area that is damaged.

—

Tie a knot carefully in the end of each casing you have checked. Place in a dish of water to soak, but leave the unknotted ends resting on the lip of the container so you can get hold of them easily when it is time to fill them.

### THE FAT

In some regions of France, it is the raw fat around the kidneys (leaf lard) that is used, cut into small pieces. Fatback is sometimes cooked for 30 minutes in salted water before being cut into small cubes. However, the more common procedure is to cut the leaf lard into small pieces, melting it and removing the little pieces of meat (rillons) while they are still white and tender. This will leave you with lard.

—

You will need 1 lb 2 oz (500 g) leaf lard for each 4¼ cups (34 fl oz/1 liter) blood.

### THE FLAVORINGS

The onions should be peeled, finely chopped, and cooked over low heat in a little lard to reduce and soften without browning. The pieces of onion should stay springy and soft. To make standard blood sausage (black pudding), use equal amounts of onions and leaf lard.

—

Although it's difficult to make boudin without onions, in some regions of France they substitute cooked spinach or endives. In Alsace, they complement the onions with finely chopped apples cooked in lard like the onions.

—

The different recipes for blood sausage (black pudding) vary in their choice of seasoning and condiments: for example, you might add crème fraîche, parsley, chives, tarragon, chervil, various spices, chili powder, sugar, eggs, or milk, etc.

## MAKING BOUDIN NOIR

Cut the leaf lard (1 lb 2 oz/500 g per 4¼ cups/34 fl oz/liter blood) into small cubes and set aside uncooked, or melt in a pan over low heat.

—

Measure the same weight of onions as leaf lard, peel, and finely chop. Reduce them in a small amount of lard over very low heat.

—

Mix the onions and the cubes of lard or rillons. The mixture should be lukewarm. Now add the blood, stirring constantly so it does not coagulate. Season with 1¾ teaspoons salt per 4¼ cups (34 fl oz/1 liter) blood, and any other seasoning you wish to use.

—

Place the end of the blood sausage (black pudding) funnel in the unknotted end of the first casing.

—

Pour the mixture into the casing. Do not overfill it, otherwise the casing will split when cooked; simply allow the casing to arrange itself in circles on the counter (work surface) as it fills.

—

Tie off the other end of the casing securely.

## COOKING THE BOUDIN NOIR

Fill a large pan two-thirds full of water and bring it to low simmer. The cooking water should not go above 176°F/80°C or the casing may split. Carefully place the sausages into the water and poach for about 1 hour. The sausage is cooked when no more blood comes out if you prick it with a fine skewer.

Remove the pieces of boudin noir carefully with a slotted spoon, rinse by running cold water over them, and place on a rack to drain. You should take particular care when removing the pieces of sausage from the pan to avoid bursting the sausages. It is a good idea to make the links small or cook the sausage in a large colander immersed in the cooking liquid.

—

Buff the sausages with some pork rind or a little lard to give them a nice shine. Store in the refrigerator.

—

Boudin noir can be broiled (grilled) or pan-fried, browning for 12–15 minutes and turning several times. Serve with mashed root vegetables and mustard.

## CLASSIC BOUDIN

**Preparation time 1 hour, plus cooling**
**Cooking time 2–2½ hours**
**Makes 9 lb (4 kg)**

6¾ lb (3 kg) onions, finely chopped
6⅔ lb (3 kg) leaf lard
6¼ cups (53 fl oz/1.5 liters) pouring cream with
    a fat content of around 20%
6⅓ quarts (10½ UK pints/6 liters) blood
scant ¼ cup (2¼ oz/60 g) salt
2 teaspoons confectioners' (icing) sugar
2 teaspoons mixed spices eg. cinnamon,
    ginger, Jamaica pepper (allspice)
casings
pork rind or lard, for rubbing
freshly ground black pepper

In a large pan, cook the onions in 1 lb 2 oz
(500 g) of the leaf lard over very low heat
for 1–1½ hours without browning. Cut the
remaining leaf lard into small pieces and warm
in another pan over low heat.

—

When the onions are cooked, add the warmed
leaf lard. Remove the pan from the heat.
Set the onions and lard aside until they are
lukewarm. Mix in the cream and the pepper.
Now add the blood, stirring constantly so it
does not coagulate. Season with 1¾ teaspoons
salt per 4¼ cups (34 fl oz/1 liter) blood, and any
other seasoning you wish to use.

—

Place the end of the blood sausage (black
pudding) funnel in the unknotted end of the
first casing.

—

Pour the mixture into the casing. Do not
overfill it, otherwise the casing will split when
cooked; simply allow the casing to arrange
itself in circles on the counter (work surface) as it

fills. Tie off the other end of the casing securely.

—

To cook, fill a large pan two thirds full of water
and bring it to low simmer. The cooking water
should not go above 176°F/80°C or the casing
may split. Carefully place the sausages into the
water and poach for about 1 hour. The sausage
is cooked when no more blood comes out if you
prick it with a pin.

—

Remove the pieces of boudin noir carefully
with a slotted spoon, rinse in cold water, and
place on a rack to drain. You should take
particular care when removing the pieces of
sausage from the pan to avoid bursting the
sausages. It is a good idea to make the links
small or cook the sausage in a large colander
immersed in the cooking liquid.

—

Buff the sausages with some pork rind or a
little lard to give them a nice shine. Store in
the refrigerator.

## ALSATIAN BOUDIN

Preparation time 1 hour
Cooking time 2 hours 25 minutes
Makes 5½ lb (2.5 kg)

4½ lb (2 kg) onions, finely chopped
3¼ lb (1.5 kg) leaf lard
3¼ lb (1.5 kg) apples, peeled, cored, and diced
4¼ cups (34 fl oz/1 liter) pouring cream with a
    fat content of around 20%
6⅓ quarts (10½ UK pints/6 liters) blood
scant ¼ cup (2¼ oz/60 g) salt
2 teaspoons four-spice mix made from the
    following ground spices: 1 teaspoon
    cinnamon, ½ teaspoon cloves, ¼ teaspoon
    nutmeg, and 2 teaspoons black pepper
casings
Pork rind or lard, for rubbing

In a large pan, cook the onions in 1 lb 2 oz
(500 g) of the leaf lard over very low heat for 1
hour until soft but not brown. Add the apples to
the pan with the onions and cook for another 25
minutes. Remove from the heat and cool.

—

Cut the remaining leaf lard into small pieces
and warm in another pan over low heat.
Remove the lard from the heat and cool. Mix
in the cream. Now add the blood, stirring
constantly so it does not coagulate. Season with
1¾ teaspoons salt per 4¼ cups (34 fl oz/1 liter)
blood, and any other seasoning you wish to use.

—

Place the end of the blood sausage (black
pudding) funnel in the unknotted end of the
first casing.

—

Pour the mixture into the casing. Do not
overfill it, otherwise the casing will split when
cooked; simply allow the casing to arrange
itself in circles on the counter (work surface) as it
fills. Tie off the other end of the casing securely.
To cook, heat a large amount of water in a large
pan and bring it to low simmer. The cooking
water should not go above 176°F/80°C or the
casing may split. Carefully place the sausages
into the water and poach for about 1 hour. The
sausage is cooked when no more blood comes
out if you prick it with a pin.

—

Remove the pieces of boudin carefully with a
slotted spoon, rinse in cold water, and place on
a rack to drain. You should take particular care
when removing the pieces of sausage from the
pan to avoid bursting the sausages. It is a good
idea to make the links small or cook the sausage
in a large colander immersed in the cooking
liquid.

—

Buff the sausages with some pork rind or a
little lard to give them a nice shine. Store in the
refrigerator.

## BOUDIN DE NANCY

Preparation time 1 hour
Cooking time 2 hours 10 minutes
Makes 5½ lb (2.5 kg)

3¼ lb (1.5 kg) onions, finely chopped
scant 3½ cups (1 lb 5 oz/600 g) lard
½ cup (1¼ oz/30 g) chopped fresh parsley
9 oz (250 g) fatback, cut into cubes
6 eggs, beaten
6⅓ quarts (10½ UK pints/6 liters) blood
scant ¼ cup (2¼ oz/60 g) salt
2 teaspoons mixed spices eg. cinnamon,
    Jamaica pepper (allspice) and ginger
6½ lb (3 kg) leaf lard
1¼ cups (10 fl oz/300 ml) brandy
casings
pork rind or lard, for rubbing
salt and freshly ground black pepper

In a large pan, cook the onions in the lard, with the lid on, over very low heat, for 1 hour, or until soft and not brown. Add the chopped parsley.

Add the fatback to the onions and warm it through over low heat. Remove the pan from the heat and add the eggs, the blood, seasonings, leaf lard, and brandy.

Place the end of the blood sausage (black pudding) funnel in the unknotted end of the first casing.

Pour the mixture into the casing. Do not overfill it, otherwise the casing will split when cooked; simply allow the casing to arrange itself in circles on the counter (work surface) as it fills. Tie off the other end of the casing securely every 7–8 inches/18–20 cm as you fill it.

To cook, heat two thirds of a large pan full of water and bring it to low simmer. The cooking water should not go above 176°F/80°C or the casing may split. Carefully place the sausages into the water and poach for about 1 hour. The sausage is cooked when no more blood comes out if you prick it with a thin skewer.

—

Remove the pieces of boudin carefully with a slotted spoon, rinse in cold water, and place on a rack to drain. You should take particular care when removing the pieces of sausage from the pan to avoid bursting the sausages. It is a good idea to make the links small or cook the sausage in a large colander immersed in the cooking liquid.

—

Buff the sausages with some pork rind or a little lard to give them a nice shine.

## BOUDIN BLANC
## (WHITE BLOOD SAUSAGE/WHITE PUDDING)

Preparation time 1 hour
Cooking time 40–45 minutes
Makes 5½ lb (2.5 kg)

2¼ cups (17 fl oz/500 ml) milk
12 oz (350 g) sandwich bread, crusts removed
1 lb 2 oz (500 g) pork (hind loin)
11 oz (300 g) leaf lard
11 oz (300 g) poultry meat
6 eggs, beaten
2 teaspoons four-spice mix made from the
    following ground spices: 1 teaspoon
    cinnamon, ½ teaspoon Jamaica pepper
    (allspice), and ½ teaspoon nutmeg
1 tablespoon salt
1¼ teaspoons freshly ground black pepper
white blood sausage (white pudding) casings
butter, for cooking

Heat the milk in a pan over low heat until
warm, then remove from the heat and add the
bread and soak.

—

Meanwhile, make sure the meat and lard are
used straight from the refrigerator. Process
the pork meat, lard, and poultry meat through
a meat grinder three times, changing the disks
from coarse to fine so that by the third pass
you have extremely finely ground meat.

—

Squeeze the bread well so it is soft but not too
moist. Add to the stuffing mixture together
with the eggs and stir the mixture with
a spatula well, adding the spice mix and
seasoning gradually.

—

Use the mixture to fill white blood sausage
(white pudding) casings, making lengths of
about 6 inches/15 cm that are tied securely at
both ends.

To poach, heat a large amount of water in a large
pan and bring it to low simmer. The cooking
water should not go above 176°F/80°C or the
casing may split. Carefully place the sausages
into the water and poach for 20–25 minutes.

—

Drain, cover with a thick, clean cloth, and cool;
this will keep the boudin blanc nice and white.

—

To fry, prick the boudin with a thin skewer so
they don't burst. Heat a little butter in a pan
over low-medium heat, add the boudin, and fry
gently for 20 minutes until browned all over.

## COUNTRY RILLETTES

Preparation time 30 minutes
Cooking time 4 hours 10 minutes
Makes 4 jars, 1 lb 2 oz (500 g)

3¼ lb (1.5 kg) lean pork meat
3¼ lb (1.5 kg) fatback
2 oz (50 g) onions, roughly chopped
4 sprigs thyme
2 bay leaves
scant ¼ cup (2¼ oz/60 g) salt
2 oz (50 g) lard
freshly ground black pepper

Cut the meat and fatback into small pieces and place them in a heavy-bottomed pan with the onions, thyme, and bay leaves. Season with the salt and pepper and cook over low heat for about 4 hours, or until the rillettes are a reddish color and the meat separates into strands.

—

Pour out and set aside some of the fat that floats on top.

—

Process the meat through the meat grinder, then pound it in a bowl, adding the fat you have reserved. Adjust the seasoning, reheat the meat for a few minutes in a pan, and pour into sterilized jars (SEE p. 40), making sure there are no air pockets.

—

Melt the lard gently in a pan over low heat, then use to top off the jars with a good layer. Seal tightly with sterilized lids. They will keep for a few weeks in the refrigerator.

## RILLETTES FROM TOURS

Preparation time 30 minutes
Cooking time 4 hours 5 minutes
Makes 4 jars, 1 lb 2 oz (500 g)

2¼ lb (1 kg) lean pork meat
3¼ lb (1.5 kg) leaf lard
2½ teaspoons four-spice mix of the following
    ground spices: 1 teaspoon cinnamon, ¼
    teaspoon cloves, ¼ teaspoon nutmeg, and 1
    teaspoon black pepper
2¾ tablespoons salt
2 oz (50 g) lard
freshly ground black pepper

Rillettes de Tours are made with finely pounded meat.

—

Cut the meat and leaf lard into very small pieces and season with the spices, salt, and pepper. Place the meat in a heavy-bottomed cooking pan and cook over low heat for about 4 hours. When the meat is reddish brown, transfer it to a large mortar or bowl and pound it carefully with the pestle or a rolling pin to make a fine puree. Adjust the seasoning.

—

Transfer the mixture to sterilized jars (SEE p. 40), packing it in well to make sure there are no air pockets.

—

Melt the lard gently in a pan over low heat, then use to top off the jars with a good layer. Seal tightly with sterilized lids. They will keep for a few weeks in the refrigerator.

## RILLETTES FROM LE MANS

Preparation time 30 minutes
Cooking time 4 hours 5 minutes
Makes 4 jars, 1 lb 2 oz (500 g)

2¼ lb (1 kg) lean pork meat
3¼ lb (1.5 kg) leaf lard
2½ teaspoons four-spice mix of the following
    ground spices: 1 teaspoon cinnamon, ¼
    teaspoon cloves, ¼ teaspoon nutmeg, and 1
    teaspoon black pepper
2¾ tablespoons salt
2 oz (50 g) lard
freshly ground black pepper

Rillettes du Mans are not chopped, so the consistency is like strands of pork coated with pork fat.

—

Cut the meat and fat into very small pieces and season with the spice mix and salt. Place the meat in a heavy-bottomed pan and cook over low heat for about 4 hours, or until the meat is well cooked and is beginning to separate into strands, but don't let the meat brown.

—

Transfer the mixture to sterilized jars (SEE p. 40), packing it in well to make sure there are no air pockets.

—

Melt the lard gently in a pan over low heat, then use to top off the jars with a good layer. Seal tightly with sterilized lids. They will keep for a few weeks in the refrigerator.

## PIGS' FEET (TROTTERS)

Preparation time 40 minutes
Cooking time 4 hours 10 minutes
Serves 6

6 pigs' feet (trotters)
3½ oz (100 g) carrots
2¼ oz (60 g) onions
1 cup (9fl oz/250 ml) white wine or cider
3½ oz (100 g) pork rinds
1 bouquet garni (SEE p. 254)
3 cloves
salt and freshly ground black pepper

Clean the pigs' feet (trotters) thoroughly, scalding them and scraping them with a knife to remove all the bristles. Cut them in half, wrap in cheesecloth (muslin), and tie with string.

—

Transfer the pigs' feet (trotters) to a large pan, pour in enough cold water (about 4¼ quarts (7 UK pints/4 liters) to cover, and add the carrots, onions, white wine or cider, pork rinds, bouquet garni, salt, pepper, and cloves.

—

Bring to a simmer over low heat, skim with a slotted spoon to remove any scum that floats to the top, and cook for 4 hours.

## PIGS' FEET (TROTTERS) À LA SAINTE-MENEHOULD

**Preparation time 1 hour, plus cooling**
**Cooking time 4 hours 30 minutes**
**Serves 6**

6 pigs' feet (trotters)
3½ oz (100 g) carrots
2¼ oz (60 g) onions
1 cup (9fl oz/250 ml) white wine or cider
3½ oz (100 g) pork rinds
1 bouquet garni (SEE p. 254)
3 cloves
8 oz (225 g) bread crumbs
3 oz (75 g) butter
1 egg
salt and freshly ground black pepper

Clean the pigs' feet (trotters) carefully, scalding them and scraping them with a knife to remove all the bristles. Cut them in half, wrap in cheesecloth (muslin), and tie with string.

Transfer the pigs' feet (trotters) to a large pan, pour in enough cold water (about 4¼ quarts (7 UK pints/4 liters) to cover, and add the carrots, onions, white wine or cider, pork rinds, bouquet garni, salt, pepper, and cloves.

Bring to a simmer over low heat, skim with a slotted spoon to remove any scum that floats to the top, and cook for 4 hours. Remove the pigs' feet (trotters) from the cooking liquid with a slotted spoon and drain. Cool and untie them, then remove all the small bones, leaving just the largest bone.

Preheat the oven to 350°F/180°C/Gas Mark 4.

Spread the bread crumbs out on a large plate. Melt the butter in a pan over low heat, then remove from the heat. In a shallow bowl, beat the egg with the melted butter and salt. Brush the pigs' feet (trotters) with the melted butter mixture, then roll in the bread crumbs, and dip in the beaten egg mixture, then roll in the bread crumbs again until coated.

Place on a baking sheet and bake in the oven for 20 minutes, or until golden. Serve hot.

## PIGS' FEET (TROTTERS) IN VINAIGRETTE

Preparation time 1 hour
Cooking time 1 hour 10 minutes
Serves 6

6 pigs' feet (trotters)
3½ oz (100 g) carrots
2¼ oz (60 g) onions
1 cup (9 fl oz/250 ml) white wine or cider
3½ oz (100 g) pork rinds
1 bouquet garni (SEE p. 254)
3 cloves
1 tablespoon chopped parsley
1 tablespoon chopped chervil
1 tablespoon snipped chives
2 shallots, chopped
⅔ cup (5 fl oz/150 ml) olive oil
2 tablespoons white wine vinegar
salt and freshly ground black pepper

Clean the pigs' feet (trotters) thoroughly, scalding them and scraping them with a knife to remove all the bristles. Cut them in half, wrap in cheesecloth (muslin), and tie with string.

Transfer the pigs' feet (trotters) to a large pan, pour in enough cold water (about 4¼ quarts (7 UK pints/4 liters) to cover, and add the carrots, onions, white wine or cider, pork rinds, bouquet garni, salt, pepper, and cloves.

Bring to a simmer over low heat, skim with a slotted spoon to remove any scum that floats to the top, and cook for 4 hours. Remove the pigs' feet (trotters) from the cooking liquid with a slotted spoon and drain. Cool and untie them, then remove all the small bones, leaving just the largest bone.

Place the pigs' feet (trotters) on a serving plate.

In a bowl or pitcher (jug), mix together the remaining ingredients to make a vinaigrette, then drizzle it over the pigs' feet (trotters). Serve as hors-d'oeuvres.

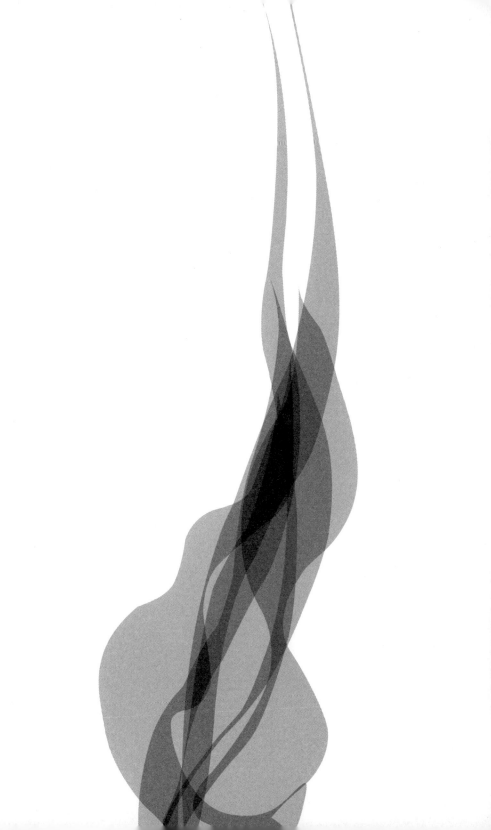

# CURING AND SMOKING

### SALTING

Pork is salted to make it easier to preserve. Salting is used either on its own (such as for dry-cured pork), or to start a process that will continue with smoking (such as for smoked ham).

Salt is an antiseptic and its action helps to preserve meat. It is hydrophilic (i.e. it has an affinity for water), so it draws out water contained in the outer parts of the meat and replaces it. These outer parts will in turn draw out the water contained at the center.

During salting there is a slow and constant exchange between the water contained within the meat and the salt. After about six weeks, the meat will have lost a quarter of the water it contained and the liquid in which it is immersed will be an unfavorable environment for microbial growth, as long as the meat has been kept in a dry and cool place, at a temperature between 35.6–41°F/2–5°C.

As always, make sure you work methodically, with the utmost care toward the cleanliness of your equipment and work environment.

### CHOOSING YOUR MEAT

Pork meat for salting should have a nice grain and not be too tough or too dry. If the animal is old, its salted meat will be leathery and the skin will go hard. Bear in mind that cuts containing bones are more difficult to preserve and require particular attention when you are salting them. Wherever possible, remove the bones.

The meat pieces for salting should ideally be 5–7 oz (150–200 g).

### CHOOSING YOUR CUTS

The belly, shoulder, and hocks (knuckles of pork) are typically salted. You can also salt the ears and the tail if you are not going to use them in any other dishes or recipes. You should also brine the cuts that are going to be smoked later, such as hams and shoulders.

### CONTAINERS

You will need salting tubs: these are jar-shaped stoneware containers with openings that are generally a little narrower than the body of the jar, with a lid on top.

It is best to use several salting tubs; this will allow you to sort your cuts by category and when you want to take out the cut you need, you will be able to find it easily.

As a general rule, you should place the dry-cured pork and any meat pieces left over after making sausage meat in one salting tub. Into the second, place larger cuts, such as hams and the cuts containing bones. Set aside a third salting tub for any fatback you intend to preserve. Attach labels to the tubs to identify.

Meat placed in a salting tub should always be covered with a wooden disk wrapped in a clean dish (tea) towel and pressed down with a heavy weight.

Salting tubs should be stored in a cool, dry place, at a temperature between 35.6–41°F/2–5°C.

Never take meat out of a salting tub with your hands: use clean forks or tongs. Never return a piece to the salting tub once it has been removed; you would risk contaminating the brine.

### PREPARING THE SALTING TUBS

The tubs should be cleaned very carefully the day before you slaughter your pig. Wash them with a brush and water in which you have dissolved sodium carbonate crystals. Rinse and dry.

Prepare a mixture with 4¼cups (1¾ pints/1 liter) vinegar, 3½ cups (2¼ lb/1 kg salt), 3 tablespoons (¾ oz/20 g) black pepper, and 1 oz (30 g) curing salt #2 (containing 4% sodium nitrate and 6.25% sodium nitrite). Pour it into the tubs, making sure you have run it down all the sides. Leave overnight. The next day, discard the mixture and turn the tubs upside down to drain.

### SMOKING

Smoking imparts a characteristic color, smell and flavor. The process exposes meat to hot air charged with smoke particles produced by the slow burning of certain types of woods. This kills some bacteria, slows the growth of others, prevents the fat from turning rancid, and helps extend the preservation time of the meat. Nowadays, domestic hot or cold smokers are common but, when this book was written, smoking in a chimney above a fire was the usual method, as described below.

### ARRANGING THE CUTS OF MEAT FOR SMOKING

Fix a bar to both sides of the chimney. The meat to be smoked will hang from this on S-shaped hooks.

Placed the meat a good distance from the fire, about 118–157 in (3–4 m) so there is no danger of the heat cooking it. Aim for an average temperature of 77°F/25°C, in other words, the smoke should already almost have cooled. Always provide an exit for the smoke; it should pass over the meats but not envelop them.

### CHOOSING YOUR WOOD

Avoid using resinous wood such as pine or fir, as it will leave a bitter taste. The best woods to use are hard, like oak, hornbeam, elm, and birch. Beech chips are very popular. All the scented shrubs, such as bay, heather, juniper, or thyme are also good to use, but always use dry wood; green wood produces acrid smoke.

### SMOKING TIMES

For typical home smoking, you should allow 2–3 weeks; by this time, the meat should have lost 25 percent of its weight.

### PRESERVING SMOKED MEATS

After smoking, place the meat in cloth bags and hang them up in a dark, dry place at a temperature between 35.6–41°F/2–5°C. This smoked meat will typically keep for up to a year.

# CURED AND SMOKED DISHES

## HAMS

Preparation time 1 hour
Hanging time 2-3 days
Salting time 3-8 weeks
Drying time 2 weeks
Smoking time 2-3 weeks

2 hams
3⅓ cups (2¼ lb/1 kg) aromatic salt (SEE Brine
    Bouquet p. 308) (optional)
salt

Hams are the last cuts on which to focus
when butchering a whole pig. Ham requires
meticulous attention and, whichever method
you choose to prepare it, you will first have to
dress it. This procedure must be started on
the day of butchering.

—

Check that the pieces of meat that were cut
off at the joints have been removed evenly with
a rounded shape. Remove the hip bones.

—

Beat the hams vigorously on the skin using a
wooden stick. This will force out any blood that
could spoil the ham if left inside. It also flattens
the skin, which will have contracted as it cooled
and formed folds that need to be removed.

—

Tie a piece of strong string around the shank
and hang the hams up to dry upside down in
a dark, dry place at a temperature between
35.6 and 41°F/2 and 5°C for 2-3 days, so that
any liquid remaining in the hams can run out.
Wipe with a clean cloth at least twice a day.

### SALTING THE HAMS

Rub the hams with salt or the aromatic salt,
if using, making sure it is rubbed in thoroughly
around the bone.

Arrange a good layer of very dry, clean salt at
the bottom of the salting tub. Place the first
ham inside the prepared tub with the skin
against the side, then place the other one on
top, with the meat side against the meat of the
first ham, skin side up and facing the top of
the tub. Cover with a wooden disk wrapped
in a cloth. Tamp down by placing flat, heavy
stones on top (you will need a weight of about
55 lb/ 25 kg). Depending on the weight and size
of the hams, leave them in the salting tub for
3-4 weeks if they are going to be cooked and
two months if the hams are to be eaten raw.

—

Once the hams are properly salted, remove
and wash them in fresh water. Hang them up
in a cool, dry place at a temperature between
35.6 and 41°F/2 and 5°C, and let them air-dry
for at least two weeks; the salt will continue to
penetrate into the insides of the meat.

### SMOKING THE HAMS

Hang the hams up on an S-shaped hook in the
chimney or the smoking room, and let them
smoke for 2-3 weeks. After they have finished
smoking, place the hams in coarse linen bags
and hang them up in a cool, dry place at a
temperature between 35.6 and 41°F/2 and 5°C.

—

These hams can be eaten raw or cooked.

## COOKED HAM

Preparation time 40 minutes, plus cooling
Soaking time 24 hours
Cooking time 5–8 hours
Serves 20

1 ham about 8 lb (3.6 kg)
1 carrot, sliced
1 onion, sliced
1 bouquet garni (SEE p. 273)
2 garlic cloves
10 black peppercorns

If the ham has been stored for some time, trim it before cooking. Use a knife to remove the bits of skin and any outer bits that have turned black. These may have gone rancid and would give an unpleasant taste to the cooking water (court-bouillon).

Soak the ham in fresh water for 24 hours to remove excess salt.

Prepare a stock. Put the sliced carrot, onion, bouquet garni, garlic, and black peppercorns in a very large pan.

Wrap the ham in a clean cloth, tie it up well with string, add to the pan, and pour in enough water to cover. Bring to a boil, then reduce the heat to low and cook for 5–8 hours, depending on the size of the ham, until tender. Prick the meat with a larding needle; if it still offers some resistance, carry on cooking. Check and top off with water during cooking.

Remove the ham from the pan, drain, and cool overnight.

The next day, remove the cloth from the ham, slice, and serve cold.

## PARIS HAM (JAMBON DE PARIS)

Preparation time 2 hours, plus cooling
overnight
Salting time 10 days
Cooking time 3–4 hours
Resting time 24 hours
Serves 12

1 ham, deboned, boned weight
about 8 lb (3.6 kg)
3⅓ cups (2¼ lb/1 kg) aromatic salt (SEE Brine
Bouquet p. 308) (optional)
1 carrot, sliced
1 onion, sliced
1 bouquet garni (SEE p. 245)
2 garlic cloves
10 black peppercorns
3½ oz (100 g) pork rinds and bones (optional)

Rub the ham with salt or the aromatic salt.

Arrange a good layer of very dry, clean salt at the bottom of the salting tub. Place the ham inside the prepared tub with the skin against the side. Cover with a wooden disk wrapped in a clean dishtowel (tea towel) and place a large stone on top to weigh it down. Leave in the salting tub for 10 days.

To give the ham a rounded shape, tie it with string and then wrap it in a clean cloth, and tie the cloth up well with string.

Prepare a stock. Put the sliced carrot, onion, bouquet garni, garlic, and black peppercorns in a very large pan. Add the ham to the pan with some pork rinds and bones, if available, then pour in enough water to cover. Bring to a boil, then reduce the heat to low and cook for 3–4 hours.

Remove the pan from the heat and let the ham cool in the cooking liquid overnight. The next day, drain the ham and place on a board. Place another board on top and weight down with a large weight for around 24 hours.

## ROLLED SHOULDER

Preparation time 1 hour
Salting time 12–14 days
Drying time 1 week
Smoking time 2 weeks

4½ lb (2 kg) pork shoulder joint
3⅓ cups (2¼ lb/1 kg) aromatic salt (SEE Brine
    Bouquet SEE below) (optional)
salt

Remove the bone from the shoulder and fill
the gap with meat taken from the outer parts
of the shoulder. Roll and tie with string to
make a nice regular shape.

—

Rub the pork with salt or the aromatic salt,
if using.

—

Arrange a good layer of very dry, clean salt at
the bottom of the salting tub. Place the pork
inside the prepared tub with the skin against
the side. Cover with a wooden disk wrapped
in a clean dishtowels (tea towels) and place a
large stone on top to weigh it down. Leave in
the salting tub for 12 days–2 weeks.

—

Remove the meat from the tub, rinse in fresh
water and hang for one week to dry.

—

Hang the pork up on an S-shaped hook in
the chimney or the smoking room, and let
it smoke for two weeks. After it has finished
smoking, place the pork in a coarse linen
bag and hang it up in a cool, dry place at a
temperature between 35.6 and 41°F/2 and 5°C.

## BRAISED HAM

Preparation time 30 minutes
Cooking time 5 hours
Serves 8

¼ whole boneless ham, weighing about
    3 lb (1.4 kg)
3½ oz (100 g) bacon rinds
7 oz (200 g) smoked bacon, diced
7 tablespoons (3½ oz/100 g) lard
1 bouquet garni (SEE p. 254)
1 carrot, sliced
1 onion, sliced
10 black peppercorns
4 cloves
2¼ cups (18 fl oz/500 ml) white wine
scant ½ cup (3½ fl oz/100 ml) Madeira
salt

Put the ham with the rinds, smoked bacon,
and lard in a large pan and place over low
heat. Add the bouquet garni, carrot, onion,
pepper, cloves, season with salt, and 1 cup
(9 fl oz/250 ml) water, and cover with the lid
and bring to a simmer.

—

Cook for 2½ hours, checking the water levels
from time to time and topping off if necessary.
Add the white wine and Madeira and cook for
another 2½ hours. Serve the ham hot, carved
into slices with vegetables of your choice and
parsley sauce.

## BRINE BOUQUET

Preparation time 5 minutes
Makes 2¼ lb (1 kg) salt

½ teaspoon black peppercorns
1 oz (25 g) juniper berries
½ teaspoon thyme leaves
1 clove
2 bay leaves
2¼ lb (1 kg) salt

Mix together with the salt or put the spices in a
cheesecloth (muslin) bag.

## D–d

## E–e

# F–f

# G–g

# P–p

Phaidon Press Limited
Regent's Wharf
All Saints Street
London N1 9PA

Phaidon Press Inc.
65 Bleecker Street
New York, NY 10012

www.phaidon.com

*Preserving* originates from:
*Je sais faire les conserves* by Ginette Mathiot,
first published in 1948 © Éditions Albin Michel.

A CIP catalogue record for this book is available
from the Library of Congress.

Commissioning Editor: Emilia Terragni
Project Editor: Ellie Smith
Production Controller: Leonie Kellman
Design and coloured illustrations: CCRZ
Translated by JMS Books, LLP

Amendments and updates to the original text
provided in association with Clotilde Dusoulier.

Revised quantities in recipes provided in
association with Wendy Sweetser.

Printed in China

The publishers would like to thank Kathy Steer,
Jo Murray, Clare Churly, Jacky Ching, and Hans
Stofregen for their contributions to the book.

## RECIPE NOTES

Butter should always be unsalted.

Unless othewise stated, all herbs are fresh and
parsley is flat-leaf parsley.

Pepper is always freshly ground black pepper,
unless otherwise specified.

Eggs, vegetables and fruits are assumed to be
medium size, unless otherwise specified.

Milk is always whole, unless otherwise specified.

Garlic cloves are assumed to be large; use two
if yours are small.

Ham means cooked ham, unless otherwise
specified.

Cooking and preparation times are for guidance
only, as individual ovens vary. If using a fan oven,
follow the manufacturer's instructions concerning
oven temperatures.

To test whether your deep-frying oil is hot
enough, add a cube of stale bread. If it browns
in thirty seconds, the temperature is 180–190°C/
350–375°F, about right for most frying. Exercise
caution when deep frying: add the food carefully
to avoid splashing, wear long sleeves, and never
leave the pan unattended.

All spoon measurements are level.
1 teaspoon = 5 ml
1 tablespoon = 15ml.
Australian standard tablespoons are 20 ml,
so Australian readers are advised to use
3 teaspoons in place of 1 tablespoon when
measuring small quantities.

58001792R00272